THE BAREFOOT EMPEROR

By the same author

THE BAREFOOT EMPEROR

An Ethiopian Tragedy

PHILIP MARSDEN

HarperPress

An Imprint of HarperCollins*Publishers*

HarperCollins*Publishers*
77–85 Fulham Palace Road,
Hammersmith, London W6 8JB
www.harpercollins.co.uk

Published by HarperCollins*Publishers* 2007

Maps © HarperCollins*Publishers*, designed by Two Dot Media

1

A catalogue record for this book is
available from the British Library

ISBN 978-0-00-717345-7

Set in PostScript Granjon by
Rowland Phototypesetting Ltd, Bury St Edmunds, Suffolk

Printed and bound in Great Britain by Clays Ltd, St Ives plc

To Clio

CONTENTS

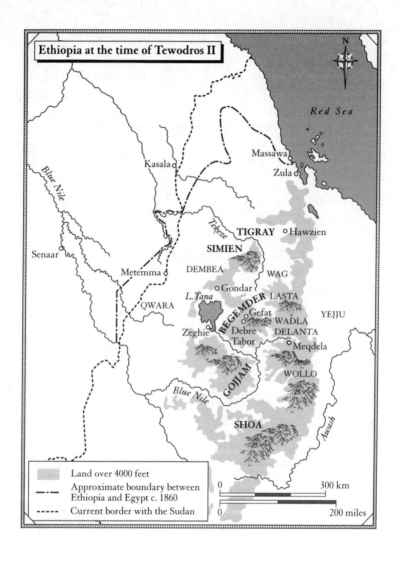

Ethiopia at the time of Tewodros II

Red Sea

Kasala

Massawa
Zula

Blue Nile

Senaar

Metemma

TIGRAY   Hawzien

SIMIEN

DEMBEA   WAG

Gondar

L. Tana   LASTA

Gefat

BEGEMDER   WADLA   YEJJU

Zeghie   DELANTA

Debre
Tabor   Meqdela

WOLLO

Blue Nile

GOJJAM

Awash

SHOA

☐ Land over 4000 feet

—··— Approximate boundary between
        Ethiopia and Egypt c. 1860

------ Current border with the Sudan

0   300 km

0   200 miles

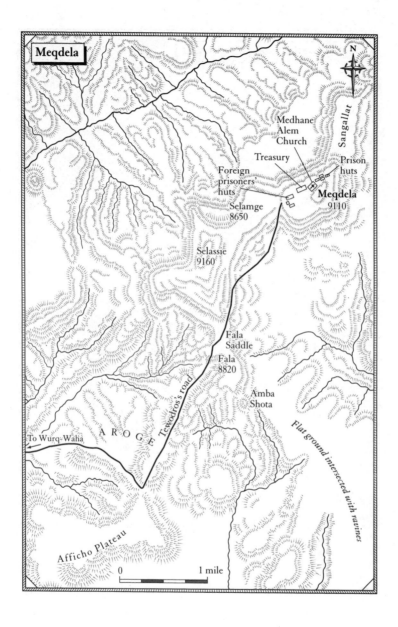

Meqdela

N

Sangallat

Medhane
Alem
Church

Treasury

Prison
huts

Foreign
prisoners'
huts

Meqdela
9110

Selamge
8650

Selassie
9160

Fala
Saddle

Fala
8820

Amba
Shota

A R O G E

Tewodros's road

To Wurq-Waha

Flat ground intersected with ravines

Afficho Plateau

0   1 mile

AUTHOR'S NOTE

For the purposes of the story, the names 'Ethiopia' and 'Abyssinia' can be seen as interchangeable. I have used Ethiopia in the text, but have not changed Abyssinia where it appears in quoted material. A degree of revisionist spelling has been necessary to rid Ethiopian places and people of their Eurocentric tarnish – thus Magdala becomes Meqdela, Theodore, Tewodros (pronounced with a silent 'w' – *Te-odros*).

Over the years, many hundreds of people have contributed to my own understanding of Ethiopia, its people and its past – monks and farmers, scholars and patriots, politicians and painters, all too numerous to mention. But for the Tewodros story particular thanks are due to: Professor Richard Pankhurst, for his encouragement, for digging out references and notes; the historian Shiferaw Bekele of Addis Ababa University, for his time and his clear-sighted view of Tewodros and his legacy; Dr Mandefro Belayneh for his enthusiasm; Hiluf Berhe, as always a tireless walker and perfect companion, for his help in Bahir Dar, Debre Tabor, Meqdela, and for translating the *Chronicles* of Zeneb; Kidame of the town of Kon, who came with us to Meqdela with his donkeys, for his fighting off of the hyenas that night in the valley of Wurq-Waha; Tony Hickey, for equipment; Sandy Holt-Wilson, an eye surgeon who has gathered together an archive of Tewodros's son, Alemayehu Tewodros, and lectures about him to raise money for an eye unit at Gondar University (www.GondarEyeSite. com); Jean Southon, great-niece of Captain Speedy, who allowed me to see family papers; Colonel Damtew Kassa and his cousins, direct descendants of Tewodros; HE Bob Dewar, British Ambassador to Ethiopia; the Scholarship Committee of the Harold Hyam Wingate Foundation; Susi Rech for translation of the German of Flad and Waldmeier; Will Hobson for his multilingual skills; Roland Chambers for help with Ransome references; Dr Iain Robertson Smith, Colin Thubron, Gillon Aitken, Mike Fishwick, Richard Johnson and Robert Lacey for their support; and Charlotte, whose judgements have greatly improved what follows and whose tireless enthusiasm made producing it so enjoyable.

GLOSSARY

abet – a greeting call, used to attract attention, or to acknowledge such a call

abun, abune – the head of the Ethiopian Orthodox Church, at this time always a Copt

adarash – meeting hall

afe-negus – literally 'mouth of the king', royal spokesman

aleqa – chief or head

alga – bed, wooden-framed and sprung with a lattice of leather straps; also means throne

amba – a flat-topped mountain peak, often surrounded by cliffs, a natural fortress or isolated site for a monastic community

ato – Mister

Ayzore! – 'Be strong!' Comradely call of encouragement in battle, travel or labour

azmari – minstrel, composer and singer of witty verses, accompanied by *masenqo*, single-stringed fiddle

balderada – a chaperon and translator appointed to assist foreign visitors at the Ethiopian court

basha – from the Turkish 'pasha', used for high officials, and with irony in the case of Captain Speedy ('Basha Felika')

belg – the 'small' rains, usually occurring between late January and early March

bitwedded – 'favourite', court title, used often as qualifier to other titles like *ras*

debtera – a non-ordained rank of the Ethiopian Church, responsible for singing and dancing, and often possessed of peripheral religious powers, as herbalist and spell-maker

dejazmach – literally 'commander of the gate', a military and noble rank just below *ras doomfata* – the recital of heroic deeds

falasha – an Ethiopian Jew

farenj – foreigner (adjectival form – *farenji*)

Fekkare Iyesus – *The Interpretation of Jesus*, Ethiopian sacred text

Fetha Negest – 'laws of the kings', the book of Ethiopian law

fitawrari – 'commander of the front' or 'vanguard'

Galla – former name of the Oromo people, originally pastoralists from the southern and eastern highlands

giraf – hippo-hide whip

godjo – stone-built hut typical of Tigray and the north of Ethiopia

grazmach – literally 'leader of the left', military and noble rank below *dejazmach*

gugs – a game of mock combat, involving two teams of horsemen charging each other: beautiful to watch, hazardous to play

Habesh – the name Ethiopians often use for themselves, from the Arabic 'mixed', and the basis of the name 'Abyssinia'

hakim – doctor

hudaddie – Lenten fast, fifty-six days long

ichege – head monk of Ethiopia, and being native often more powerful than the Coptic *abun*

ika-bet – 'thing house', repository of church treasures

injera – flat bread

isshi – ubiquitous Amharic expression, meaning OK/of course/very well

itege – empress or queen

Jan Hoi – Your Majesty

kebbero – large church drum

Kebre Negest – 'the glory of the kings', Ethiopia's mythical charter dating to about the thirteenth century, drawing together many myths including the story of Solomon, Sheba and Menelik their son, and the Ethiopian inheritance of Mosaic law and the Ark of the Covenant

kegnazmach – literally 'leader of the right', military and noble rank below *dejazmach*

kentiba – mayor

ķiddus – saint or holy man

ķinķob – ceremonial robe

ķoso – a purgative against intestinal worms, used regularly by Ethiopian highlanders

lemd – cape or tunic

lij – 'son' or 'child', used as title for young noble males

liqemekwas – high court official

margaf – cotton scarf or small shawl

mekdes – the sanctuary of a church, the section in which is housed the *tabot*

mesob – free-standing flat-topped basket, on which is spread *injera*

naib – a Turkish name for the local rulers of the coastal region around Massawa

negarit – war drum, used to call men to arms, as well as acting as a symbol of authority

negus – king

shamma – large cotton shawl

shifta – bandit

shum – regional ruler, military chief

tabot – the sacred object at the heart of each Ethiopian church, never seen by laymen, representing both the Ark of the Covenant and the church's given saint

tankwa – boat of lashed-together papyrus, used on Lake Tana

teff – indigenous Ethiopian wheat used to make *injera*

tej – mead

tella bet – beer house

thaler – the Maria Theresa thaler, common currency of the highlands, minted without alloy, and equivalent to about six shillings at this time

Tigrigna – the language of Tigray, northern Ethiopia, derived as Amharic from Ge'ez and the Semitic family of languages

timtim – white turban worn by priests

wat – sauce

weyzero – Mrs

PROLOGUE

I

'*Yetewodros menged.*' The monk's finger pushed out from the folds of his shawl, far out into the morning, to a shadowy line on the opposite slope. 'Tewodros's road.'

After the easy undulations of the plateau, the main road here drops to a place they call the 'natural bridge'. It's one of those sudden sights in the Ethiopian highlands that pull you up short, as if the earth's skin has been ripped aside to expose the skeletal frame of chasms beneath. At the natural bridge itself, beyond the clifftop monastery, the road runs the length of a ridge of rock so narrow that on each side you look down to a shingle bed some 3,000 feet below. To the north is the Tekeze basin, to the south the Abbai, the Blue Nile. The two rivers do not merge until seven hundred miles to the north-west, in the yellow heat of the Sahara desert.

After the bridge is a new cutting. Within the last few years, as part of the government's ambitious transport programme, it has been bulldozed and blasted through the hill. To one side, forgotten and unused, is an old grassy track – *Tewodros's road*.

In Addis Ababa, no one could tell me what remained of the road. No account exists of it later than its building. I asked scholars at the university, and they were vague – those who had reached Tewodros's mountaintop fortress of Meqdela had walked in from the south-east. At Bahir Dar University too they knew nothing, nor did a local historian at the school in the emperor's old capital of Debre Tabor – a school named Tewodros II Secondary School, with the emperor's spear-carrying image daubed on its classroom wall.

I stepped onto the old road. My boots crunched in its basalt dust. It wasn't much to look at – a little wider than the mule paths and market routes that criss-cross the highlands. Sumach bushes dotted its course. The inner edge was sliced back well into the rock. A century and a half of rains had rounded its outer edges, washing loose soil and stones down gullies that plunged far into the gorge below.

Yet of all the moments of his extraordinary reign, Tewodros's building of this road stands out as the most heroic and the most tragic. In October 1867, he burnt his capital at Debre Tabor and with 50,000 people left for the mountain at Meqdela. Week after week, led by the emperor himself, his half-starved army hacked at the ground with their spears, with mattocks, with their bare hands. They felled trees, banked up slopes, rubble-filled streams and smoothed off the rocks with soil. It was a journey of about 150 miles; a good messenger could do it in a few days. It would take Tewodros six months.

Little remained to him at that point, no territory and no support beyond his slow-moving camp. Untouchable on high cliffs, and from the shadows of thick forest, rebels followed his progress. They picked off water-carriers, the sick and the slow, the stragglers. They didn't dare mount an attack. In part, Tewodros was protected by the strange air of invincibility that had surrounded him throughout his reign. But with him, on wooden wagons, was something more solid – dozens of pieces of artillery, and one in particular, the largest of all, cast in his own foundry a few months earlier, a seven-ton monster he had named Sevastopol. He was building the road for his guns.

Tewodros had another enemy. Years earlier he had chained up the British consul and the man was still in chains, with a number of other Europeans, high on the flat summit of Meqdela. Diplomacy had run its course. Now the British, irritated and affronted, had landed their forces on the Red Sea coast to try to release the hostages. Every week a few thousand more arrived. They were building a port in the desert, landing supplies in vast quantities. They were installing condensers to provide water, building a railway to the mountains. Soon they would be ready to march to Meqdela. All his life, the emperor had dreamed of bringing European technology to his people. Now it was coming.

So Tewodros was hurrying. He was desperate to reach Meqdela before the British, to line the clifftops with Sevastopol and his other big guns, to face the enemy. Hour by hour, his men flattened the ground so that the timber gun-carriages could creak forward over the rocks. If they managed two miles or more, it was a good day.

Here at the natural bridge, they paused for weeks in order to hack out the section across the broken ground, then up the slope towards Zebit. When it was ready, hundreds of men bent to the leather straps that fanned forward from the wagon of Sevastopol, and inch by inch hauled the gun up the slope. Many fell as they did so. From the cliffs the rebels hurled down rocks and spears.

Up on the high plateau again, the going was easier. Like some slow parade of votive statues, Sevastopol and the other guns slid across the plains towards Meqdela. Sometimes at day's end, with the sun dropping over the short section of new road behind them, and as his men rested in the sudden chill of dusk, Tewodros would climb up and stretch his arms over Sevastopol's great girth, as if its bulk might correct the fragility of his position. For years his followers had seen him as the incarnation of divine prophecy, a champion of their own Christian and Judaic inheritance. Now they gazed up at him on the gun-carriage and began to whisper of '*yetewodros amlak*' – 'the idol of Tewodros'.

At Bet Hor, on the edge of the Jidda gorge, British forces reached Tewodros's road shortly after he had passed. They were amazed. Travelling with them was the geographer Clements Markham, and he stood at the cliff-edge and conceded the determination of the enemy: 'A most remarkable work – a monument of dogged and unconquerable resolution.

Rocks were blasted, trees sawn down, revetment walls of loose stone mixed with earth and branches built up, and everywhere a strengthening hedge of branches at the outer sides, to prevent the earthwork from slipping.'

Later Markham gathered more information about how Tewodros had transported Sevastopol from Debre Tabor, and became convinced that the story 'entitles his march to rank as one of the most remarkable in history'. Dr Blanc, at the time a prisoner on Meqdela, and no friend of Tewodros, echoed Markham's words. It was, he wrote in his own account, 'a march unequalled in the annals of history'.

From Bet Hor, the route to Meqdela drops several thousand feet to the Jidda gorge, up onto the Delanta plateau and down again to the Beshilo river. Tewodros's road is still visible in places, chiselled into the side of cliffs, scored around the bulge of steep-sided bluffs, zigzagging up dusty slopes. It took him and his followers months to build this section. I walked it in a few days. At eleven o'clock one morning, five o'clock Ethiopian time,* I reached the Fala saddle and saw the peak of Meqdela ahead, half-hidden by scarves of cloud. As I crossed Selamge, the cloud blew away to reveal a shadowy row of cliffs. It was a grim sight. The mountain's flat peak was edged on all sides by a sheer drop of black basalt.

At the northern end of the massif, below the peak of Selassie, the entire scene was spread out below. I looked back at the way I had come. In the haze was the far-off horizon of Delanta, the descent to the Beshilo, the snaking valley of Wurq-Waha – 'golden water' – and the final ascent. When Tewodros began to haul Sevastopol across this section, the advance guard of the British were just twenty or thirty miles behind him.

A short way along the clifftop was a small settlement. Thatched huts stood beneath the silvery-leaved eucalyptus;

---

* Ethiopian time is measured from dawn: thus seven o'clock is one o'clock, midday and midnight are six o'clock.

stockades were ringed by pickets of giant euphorbia. A young boy was following a slow herd of cattle back towards the huts. To one side stood a crude canopy of corrugated iron. Lying beneath it, looking somewhat like a fallen bell, still lay the bronze mass of Sevastopol.

II

I first heard about Ethiopia and Tewodros at the same time. My grandmother had a companion known simply as 'Pillio', who had tutored my uncle and father as boys and, so the story went, was the daughter of an Ethiopian princess from the days of 'mad King Theodore'. From that time on, her high-necked beauty, her mysterious silence and this mad King Theodore took up lodgings together in some quiet suburb of my mind.

Much later, in the early 1980s, I went to Ethiopia for the first time. One evening, after curfew, I read Alan Moorehead's sketch of Tewodros and the Meqdela campaign in *The Blue Nile*: 'It has always been accepted that the Emperor Theodore was a mad dog let loose, a sort of black reincarnation of Ivan the Terrible.' Clements Markham likened him to Peter the Great. During the bloody days of the Derg regime, with its random killings and its merciless war in Tigray and Eritrea, I saw parallels much closer to hand – with Colonel Mengistu and his 'Red Terror'.

When I next visited Ethiopia some fifteen years later, Mengistu had gone. The paralysing fear had disappeared, replaced by a lurching and chaotic openness. Self-expression was no longer a subversive act. The iconography of globalised culture had shunted aside Soviet agitprop. On T-shirts and posters were stencilled the images of Leonardo DiCaprio, Tupac Shakur, Madonna and David Beckham. Emperor Haile Selassie's regal figure had reappeared both in its local form and in the much-travelled Rastafarian version. In internet cafés, the most commonly consulted website was for US immigration and the Green Card Lottery.

I was surprised to find Tewodros among all this. But he was everywhere – on the walls of bars and on locally-printed T-shirts. I watched a teenager idly chalk his image on a rock. Market stalls sold Tewodros badges and Tewodros cotton tunics. In a government office, I spotted his fierce glare above an anti-corruption slogan: 'Governing Self Behaviour is Best Skill of All'. At political rallies, I was told, a mention of his name was guaranteed to win the crowd. Everyone had an opinion of him, from taxi-drivers to suited businessmen, and it was universally positive. 'Tewodros was our greatest patriot, a hero.'

'But he was a monster!' I spluttered.

'So much Tewodros loved his country – I'm sorry, only to think of him makes me cry.'

I went to see an old friend. Teshome and I had travelled together years earlier, in the dark days of Colonel Mengistu. Teshome had always been a convincing and witty sceptic – sceptical about Mengistu and his Soviet backers, sceptical about Emperor Haile Selassie before them. Several years at an American law school had only made his suspicion of all power more articulate. The current regime was just as bad. But when it came to Tewodros, the scepticism vanished. 'Tewodros?' He paused, steepling his fingers in a courtroom gesture of reasoned thought. 'What you have to understand, Philip, is that without him there would be no modern Ethiopia. Period.'

At the Institute of Ethiopian Studies, I thumbed through the library's card index. It was all there – the Tewodros dramas, the Tewodros novels, the poems and the doctoral theses. One or two voices spoke out against him, but the predominant tone was hagiographic. Tsegaye Gabre-Medhin, who wrote a play called *Tewodros* in 1962, said that the 'heroification' of the emperor was necessary in part because foreign authors had so tarnished his image. He in turn accused the critical Ethiopian scholars of '*meqegna*', jealousy, or needless iconoclasm.

Somewhere between the cult of Tewodros and its bloodless deconstruction lay the story itself. Only by reading the accounts of contemporary witnesses do the raw impressions of the time emerge. The European hostages left between them a mass of memoirs and letters. The Ethiopian side is less well represented, but there are a good number of contemporary Amharic letters, including those from Tewodros himself. Several Amharic chronicles too survive. Scholars have dismissed these for their eccentric chronology and distortions, but like the letters their viewpoint and language (even in translation) are wonderfully evocative. With the European accounts they conjure up a remarkable moment in history.

Until the middle of the nineteenth century, the world was an archipelago of loosely connected peoples. All over Africa and Asia, a pushy Europe was coming face to face with long-isolated nations. It is a process that has, in little more than a century, accelerated into a global frenzy of connectivity – skies criss-crossed by vapour trails, overhead cables pulsing with hypertext. In few instances were the initial meetings so bright and hopeful, or so swiftly shadowed, as they were in the 1850s and 1860s in Ethiopia.

For the ancient empire, tracing its roots to the reign of King Solomon nearly 3,000 years earlier, the episode was a bracing and too-sudden encounter with the modern age. For the British, reaching the height of imperial power, what began as an irksome diversion required in the end one of the most bizarre and elaborate military campaigns ever undertaken.

Yet for all its historical interest, the story belongs to the individuals – the European envoys, the adventurers and missionaries drawn into Tewodros's thrilling and perilous world; the Ethiopians who followed him with such passion; and the emperor himself with his messianic appeal, his capricious brutality.

Few images survive of Tewodros and many of those that do are fanciful. The one that is pinned to my wall as I write this comes from the frontispiece of Hormuzd Rassam's two-volume *Narrative of the British Mission to Theodore, King of Abyssinia* (1869). Said to have been a fair likeness, the lithograph shows him on a high rock on the edge of the Blue Nile. He is dressed simply, in cotton *shamma* and loose cotton trousers. His feet are bare. Gripped in his right hand is a slender seven-foot spear; his left wrist rests on the stock of one of two pistols thrust into his belt. He is looking to one side, at a group of his followers struggling to follow him up the slope. In his stance and expression is a tense ambiguity, between impatience and concern, compassion and anger.

In Addis Ababa, just before I returned in 2003, the cult of Tewodros had found physical expression on one of the most prominent roundabouts in the city. Squatting on a high stony plinth, on the back of a vast wooden wagon, was a reproduction of Sevastopol. The installation had been encouraged by the country's president, Girma Welde Giyorgis – a fan of Tewodros – and instigated by the mayor of Addis Ababa and Professor Richard Pankhurst. I'd known Richard for over twenty years, and when I went to see him and his wife Rita in their leafy villa, he told me the story in his own dry and ironic way. But he too recognised Tewodros's stature.

'We flew up in an old Soviet helicopter, landed on Meqdela. We were back in Addis by teatime.' They took measurements of the gun where it lay. On the roundabout halfway down Churchill Avenue, looking at the dimensions and the traffic island, Richard began to have doubts. In Tewodros's day, on its wagon, Sevastopol may have been an impressive sight, but now, on a busy interchange, dwarfed by Isuzu trucks and Toyota Land Cruisers, the seven-ton mortar would look tiny.

'What did you have in mind?' the mayor asked Richard.

'Something bigger, about the size of a Volkswagen.'

So the mayor brought a small crane and they hoisted a VW Beetle on the back of a minibus, and they all agreed that that was much more like it. They multiplied the measurements and commissioned a metal-worker to forge it. A ramp was built, and the gun placed at the sort of angle at which it had rolled up to Zebit, or from the Jidda and Beshilo rivers, or for the final ascent of Meqdela itself.

The metal-worker also made a smaller model. Richard reached out and took it down from his mantelpiece. He handed it to me. I held it in my palm, a mini-Sevastopol to match the exaggerated one on Churchill Avenue. I marvelled once again at Tewodros's gargantuan will, and at the strange distortions of scale that he had undergone since his death.

III

In 1863, Emperor Tewodros wrote in a letter to the French vice-consul: 'Having heard reports from the time I was born until I reached maturity, being told over and over again that, by the power of God, there are in Europe, in the countries of the Europeans, those whose governments do not fall, who lack nothing in terms of law and order, in whom there is no deceit, by the power of God, I was very happy.'

From the start, contacts between Ethiopia and Europe were characterised by impossible expectations. Europeans came to the country with their own lofty ideas. They thought the emperor was an all-conquering Christian potentate (Prester John and his seventy vassal kings), or they wanted to locate the source of the Nile (a certain bog to the south of Lake Tana), or they came to hunt wild beasts, collect exotic flowers or correct the religious delusions of the country's Christians. The Ethiopian emperors had their own hopes of the visitors. They wanted Christian solidarity, support in their wars, and technology – in short, they wanted guns.

The very first official visit from Europe set the pattern. One night in 1520 a small band of Portuguese arrived at the hedge outside the camp of Emperor Lebne Dengel with a letter of friendship for 'Prester John'. The emperor refused to admit them. In frustration, a couple of the Portuguese raised their guns to the stars, and fired.

At once a messenger appeared: 'His Majesty asks, how many guns do you have for him?'

'We have three or four muskets and those for our own use.' The emperor still refused to see them.

A few years earlier, the Ottoman Turks, under Sultan Selim the Grim, had conquered Egypt, received the keys of Mecca and with money and weapons spread their influence on down the Red Sea. They encouraged the emirates of the coast to annex Christian Ethiopia. Having no port, the Ethiopians found it hard to obtain arms to defend themselves. Now these Christian foreigners had come to see the emperor, and all they brought him was a useless letter.

In the end, Lebne Dengel did consent to see them and at once asked them 'Do the Turks have good bombards?'

'As good as ours,' replied the ambassador. 'We are not afraid of the Turks. We are valiant in the name of Jesus Christ.'

'Who taught the Turks to make bombards?'

'The Turks are men. They have skills and knowledge.'

And so it went on. The Portuguese ambassador wanted only to read out his letter from King Manuel I, and return home. But now he had admitted them, the emperor wouldn't let them go (thereby establishing another pattern of the Ethiopian court – the detention of foreign visitors).

'You have only just arrived,' the emperor said. 'You have seen only a fraction of my kingdom. Play your spinet for me. *Dance*.' The ambassador danced.

A few days later Lebne Dengel asked for a musket demonstration. There were more requests, and as the days became weeks, the Portuguese grew uneasy. In the end it was six years before they were allowed to return to the coast. During that time the emperor gained from them just two swivel guns.

Three decades later in, 1557, the Turks finally occupied

Massawa. Their plans to add Ethiopia to the Ottoman Empire were checked less by military means than by the Christians' own natural defence, the highlands. For the next three hundred years, until the time of Tewodros, the Red Sea port of Massawa – Ethiopia's gateway to the outside world – was governed by Muslims.

Meanwhile Spanish and Portuguese Jesuits had remained in Ethiopia, and early in the seventeenth century managed to persuade Emperor Susenyos to abandon fifteen hundred years of religious teaching, forsake the Christology of Alexandria and come over to Rome. Susenyos had underestimated the convictions of his subjects. The country collapsed into civil war. 'How long,' cried his people, 'shall we thrust our swords into our own bowels?' Susenyos abdicated and the Jesuits were expelled. There was great rejoicing: 'At length the sheep of Ethiopia freed from the bad lions of the West!' Disgust for Europeans was so intense that it drove the Ethiopians to arrange a treaty with the hated Muslims of Massawa: they agreed to prevent any European Christians from reaching the highlands. When the Ethiopian emperor received from the coast the stuffed heads of some French and Italian Capuchins, he knew he had found a reliable ally. Secure from both Turks and proselytising Christians, the Ethiopians remained isolated in the fortress of their mountains, free to pursue their own internal squabbles.

In 1798, Napoleon's occupation of Egypt brought a new era of European power to the Middle East and introduced to Egypt the restless spirit of the Enlightenment. Twenty years later the Egyptian ruler, Muhammad Ali, pushed southwards down the Nile. For decades, pressing at the lowlands around Ethiopia, Egyptian forces made periodic forays into the mountains. Conquest by Egypt was the most persistent outside threat to Ethiopia during the nineteenth century.

The young Tewodros never forgot the encounter he had on the edge of the Sahara desert. In March 1848, as a warlord, he and his thousands of followers moved against the under-manned garrison at Dabarki. They were destroyed. The Egyptians had been well-drilled and well-armed. They also had two cannon. The guns turned Tewodros's forces more effectively than 20,000 men and established in him a lifelong yearning for artillery.

At the same time, on the coast, France and Britain had shipped their perennial rivalry to the Red Sea. As Ottoman power declined and the port of Massawa grew sleepier, so the two European states found a new cause to fight over — access to India and the Far East. The existence of Christian Ethiopia just inland lured a new generation of European envoys and adventurers.

Two hundred years after the expulsion of the Jesuits, a young Englishman reached the highlands and conceived the idea of Anglo–Ethiopian contacts. It was the tentative start of a relationship that would stumble on through years of inertia, calamity and ignorance, grow stronger through expediency and expressions of mutual love, stumble again through bereavement, suspicion, muddle and imprisonment before entering the arena of its bloody dénouement, some twenty years later, amidst the dark basalt cliffs of Meqdela.

Tewodros's Order of the Cross and Solomon's Seal. From Hormuzd Rassam, *Narrative of the British Mission to Theodore, King of Abyssinia* (1869)

1

Walter Plowden lay on deck. It was April 1847. A warm wind filled the great lateen sail above his head; beneath him the dhow pitched to the short swells of the Red Sea. Far astern, to the south, he could see the distant rise of the Ethiopian highlands. Four years he'd spent there among its mountains, its roving courts, shifting from fief to fief, from battle to battle. He drew on his pipe, leaned back against the *alga*, and was filled with the reckless joy of parting.

'Once more on the free waves,' he wrote, 'my heart beat lightly.'

Plowden was on a mission. He had persuaded Ethiopia's ruler, Ras Ali, that there was one thing a modern state could not be without, and that was a trade treaty with Britain. Ras Ali himself couldn't see the point. How would a trade treaty keep Dejazmach Wube to heel? Or the peoples of Wag and Lasta? What use was it against Biru Goshu, who had made off with his wife and who every year slaughtered the governors he appointed in Gojjam?

But all right, *isshi*, he would send an envoy with the young Englishman.

And here he was, the envoy, a poor highlander who had never before laid eyes on the sea, squatting in wide-eyed terror in Plowden's cabin. With him were the gifts Ras Ali had selected for Queen Victoria – some rusting lances, a few bolts of homespun cotton and three very rare gazelle calves. The gazelles were also strangers to the sea. Plowden had bought them a nanny-goat for milk, and whenever they heard her bleating they would tug at their halters, squeak and whinny, and the deck would tip-tap with the sound of their delicate little hooves. Such was Ethiopia's first embassy to Britain – a menagerie of the terrified, the untamed and the hopeful, despatched in indifference by a war-weakened ruler.

Plowden passed the days in impatient idleness. He lay on deck. He smoked his pipe. He drank beakers of coffee. Stretching his long limbs over the *alga*, he closed his eyes and felt the desert wind warm on his face.

Four years earlier, in his early twenties, he had been sailing the same waters. Then too he had been heading for England, fleeing India and a death-in-life job at Carr Tagore & Co. of Calcutta. But in Suez he met John Bell, a Scottish sailor as footloose and impulsive as himself. According to his brother, Plowden's 'ardent and ambitious temperament induced him, on the spur of the moment, without preparation and with limited funds, to join that gentleman in an expedition'. To Plowden, Ethiopia was rich with classical and biblical associations, a mountain enclave of Christianity in a Muslim region. Bell's plan also had the whiff of antiquity around it – they would hunt the source of the Nile, whose annual flood had spawned the great civilisation of ancient Egypt.

The two set off overland and entered Ethiopia posing as elephant hunters. Within weeks they had been sucked into the country's dramas. They forgot about the Nile. With each battle, each tented court, each chief who wooed them, they found the outside world receding. John Bell married a local woman and became a general in Ras Ali's army. Neither he nor Plowden ever escaped the strange spell of the upland kingdom.

Plowden in particular found a fascination in Ethiopia's

medieval pageantry, in the 'foppish' self-love of the warrior caste, the 'strain of feudal glamour'. For him Ethiopia's antiquity, isolation and uniqueness were counters to the unsightly spread of modernity: 'there is no parallel to it in this steaming and telegraphing world'. He grew to love the troubadour traditions of the quick-witted *azmari*, the recital of battle deeds in the *doomfata*; he learned to play the battle-polo of *gugs*, a game as deadly as any skirmish. With an ethnographer's eye he began to record his observations, 'Notes on Peculiar Customs' – *'the Galla find the eating of fish disgusting, as do the Shoho . . . On waking, Christians utter a prayer to stop the devil entering their mouth . . . the shadow of a man who has slept with a woman the previous night is considered harmful . . .'* In Tigray he heard a host of proverbs convincing people that 'relatives were of no use till after death'. He noted the prevalence of female circumcision among the peoples of the north.

During those early years he passed through the courts and camps of dozens of minor nobles, warlords and great regional chiefs. He rode with them, was captured by them, campaigned with them. He made many friends, and found himself offered horses, land and gifts. Some offered him their women 'as one might offer the loan of a horse'. One ruler promised him his sister and two provinces. 'For a moment I was tempted, having my full share (and a little more) of youthful folly, loving adventure, not being averse to war.' But he moved on, to other valleys, other forested regions, other noble feuds.

War, he found, drove the ambition and passion of every Ethiopian highlander. War was a way of life, an end in itself. When the big rains finished in September, the month of Meskerem, and the rivers began to recede, the entire country stirred to the sound of the *negarits*, the recruiting drums. In tens of thousands, men then flocked to their *shum*, sitting astride his caparisoned mount in a thigh-length shirt of coloured silk, with a lion's-mane cape over his shoulder.

Plowden's enthusiasm for this world bubbles from every

page of his writing. He was intrigued by its unseen codes and hierarchies. Followers outnumbered the fighting forces by as many as two to one. When Ras Ali moved to war, more than 150,000 people accompanied him. Eighty-eight drummers went before him, under a head drummer who enjoyed a host of enviable privileges because, if captured in battle, his life was never spared.

Apart from the soldiers (each possessing his own rank according to numbers of men killed) there were the keepers of the tent; the 'mouth of the king'; the head of the advance guard; the chief of the night guards; the guard of the women's quarters; the female providers of honey for the *tej*; the hundreds of *tej*-bearers, all women, with their own chief and their own hierarchy; the grass-cutters, wood-cutters, herdsmen, drummers and minstrels, butchers and maidservants. 'So minute are the particulars of all these minor posts,' Plowden wrote, 'that they would fill a volume.' When an ox was slaughtered in camp, he watched the meat being divided into a hundred pieces and distributed, each cut of the carcass corresponding to a different rank.

War was poetic and chivalric. Every year Ras Ali would march his tens of thousands to the province of Gojjam to do battle with its rogue ruler, Biru Goshu, who had taken the *ras*'s wife. Every year Biru would present Ras Ali with a cape to award to the governor the *ras* left behind. As soon as Ras Ali was gone, Biru killed the governor, took the cape and waited for Ras Ali to return again after the following rains. War was also brutal – the 'warrior is bred to consider killing (*geddai*) as the great object of existence'. Musket stocks were hung with 'disgusting trophies', the leathery testicles of slaughtered enemies.

In good Victorian style, the young Plowden was both drawn to the wildness of Ethiopia and motivated by an urge to improve it. As the years passed, his enthusiasm began to veer away from the country's medieval colour towards its worldly prospects. He wrote lovingly of a climate which could bear 'comparison with any in the world', a soil 'fitted for every crop', diversity of flora to amaze botanist and herbalist alike, green slopes for the tea-planter, gold, copper and saltpetre for prospectors. Ethiopia's vineyards could challenge any in Bordeaux. It was India, on a smaller scale, but untouched. The country's problem, Plowden said, was leadership. Calm and conciliatory diplomacy would unite its eternally squabbling chiefs, while those who resisted, who held out on the mountaintops, 'would soon yield to the persuasion of some howitzers, or bombs of larger calibre'.

He puffed at his pipe, sipped his coffee, and shifted his legs on the *alga*'s leather grid. The breeze was good and the sails full. He was impatient to reach England, yet could not forget what he'd left behind. Sometimes during those languid days he thought he could 'hear in fancy, the wild war-cry of the half-naked Galla . . . mingling with the murmur of the restless ocean'.

His mission soon ran into difficulty. The dhow's captain proved to be an idiot. When the goat's milk dried up, the first of the gazelles died. Another was killed leaping from a window in Jeddah, the third when the dhow was wrecked on a coral reef. Plowden alone struggled ashore from the wreck. For days he staggered through the Sinai desert, weakened by thirst, close to death, wondering whether 'it were not better to die at once on my lance'. But after a week or so he reached Suez. There he found that the rest of the embassy had been rescued from the reef. All the presents had been lost or destroyed, and the envoy himself refused ever to go near a boat again. Plowden continued to London on his own.

2

A few weeks later, from a hotel room in Covent Garden, Walter Plowden wrote to the Foreign Office. He laid his plans before them in two detailed, handwritten reports. The Foreign Secretary at the time was Lord Palmerston, and by coincidence he had also been Foreign Secretary some fifteen years earlier when a similar letter was doing the rounds. That earlier letter came through a William Coffin, son of a yeoman farmer from Dorset who had been stuck in Ethiopia for so long he could barely speak English when he emerged. He had brought a letter of friendship from a Tigrayan noble to King George IV. The Foreign Office lost it. Coffin waited three years in London before they gave him the reply.

Plowden had more luck. This time Palmerston was immediately receptive. A foothold on the Red Sea was now of much more relevance, to protect the route to India from the French. He was convinced too of Plowden's optimism about trade. Within a few weeks of landing in England (and after a little quiet investigation into the young man's character), Plowden was appointed HM Consul to Massawa. He was to receive a salary of £500 a year, a gift budget for Ras Ali of £400, a letter signed by Queen Victoria herself and a nineteen-point treaty to lay before the *ras*.

Six months later, Plowden was back in Ethiopia. Thrilled

to be among the mountains again, he took the road to Gondar. As it led higher into the Simiens, the air grew colder, the cliffs steeper, until at a high pass it pushed through a narrow doorway in the rock. With the great inland sea of Lake Tana on his right he entered land ruled by Ras Ali. Striding ahead of his baggage train, he reached the capital of Debre Tabor. There, outside the *ras's* residence, he met his old friend John Bell. Pushing through the crowd, Plowden embraced 'several old acquaintances'. In the semi-darkness of the court he found Ras Ali sitting on a cowhide on the ground, while workmen and courtiers, horses, flies and children milled around him.

'He was much pleased to see me,' wrote Plowden, 'and immediately besieged me with questions as to what I had brought for him.'

After the initial meeting, Plowden retired. Several times that first day, messages arrived from the *ras*. *Let me see the gifts. Have you brought guns?*

Plowden gave no answer.

The next day he again entered the *ras's* court, and read out the letter from Queen Victoria:

'Your Highness will clearly perceive the great advantage to Abyssinia from intimate connection with the Sovereign of the British Empire whose dominions extend from the rising to the setting sun –'

Ras Ali looked up at the long-legged Plowden: Why does the *farenj* stand?

'– and whose fleets are to be met with in every part of the seas which encompass the earth.'

Ras Ali knew nothing of the sea.

Plowden then spread the bulk of the gifts before him. The *afe-negus* – 'mouth of the king' – whispered to Plowden, 'One thing at a time is usually better.'

Plowden waved him away. His queen, he told him, did not mind. He gave a flamboyant bow, left the gifts, and stepped out again into the sunlight. Plowden was no longer the eager

9

young traveller who had left the *ras* two years earlier. He was now Her Britannic Majesty's Consul and he was playing the *ras*. As the days passed Ras Ali began to send requests to Plowden for more gifts.

'It is needless to recall,' boasted the consul, 'all the childish messages with which I was bored every five minutes.' With the *ras* primed, Plowden then subtly introduced the idea of signing the treaty.

But Ras Ali was also playing Plowden. At each meeting, Plowden was forced again to go back to the beginning. What exactly is this treaty? What use is it to me? And each time Plowden had to explain that it offered friendship between sovereigns, and that his own sovereign whose fleets etc. Each time, Plowden had to part with a gift. He began to dig into his own supplies. First the matchlocks brought from Egypt. Then his own private armoury, the guns and pistols kept for his protection. And still Ras Ali put off signing the treaty.

Then Plowden heard a familiar sound. From the tented city, from the plains around Debre Tabor came the beating of the *ras*'s *negarits*. Tens of thousands of souls stirred, packed up their tents, rounded up their sheep and cattle. The chiefs took down their slash-sleeved shirts, men left their homes to join the southbound flood. The *ras* was going to war. He was leaving for his annual fight with Biru Goshu. Plowden had no option but to take his treaty and follow him.

They dropped down into the gorge of the Blue Nile, and crossed into Gojjam, the land of Biru Goshu. In time the campaign reached the stage it always reached. Biru sat safe in his mountain stronghold, Ali was camped below. The rains came, the ground turned to mud. The rains ended and then Ras Ali's hordes began to pack up and leave.

It was at that moment that Ras Ali summoned Consul Plowden. He was ready to sign the treaty.

Ras Ali was on a divan in his tent discussing a horse with

one of his men. The horse stood beside them. His scribe began to read out the Amharic text.

'There shall be a firm, mutually cordial and lasting friendship between the king of Abyssinia and Victoria, the queen of England . . .'

Ras Ali continued talking about the horse.

'Please, master – listen!'

He nodded.

'The king of Abyssinia shall receive and protect the envoys or consuls of the queen of England . . . Likewise the queen of England shall receive and protect the envoys or officials of Abyssinia . . .'

When all nineteen clauses had been heard, everyone looked to the *ras*. The *ras* looked up at the horse, admiring its sleek sides and strong legs.

'I see no harm in this treaty, but it seems useless. The country as it is now is of no use to merchants. No English merchant will be able to reach it for ten years or more.'

But he signed. Plowden prepared to leave for the coast.

Ras Ali would not let him go. He told Plowden to give him his best rifle. Plowden refused. The days passed. His food ran low, his patience thin, and like the Portuguese delegation so many years before, the British envoy had the growing sense that he was a prisoner in these remote highlands. He gave in. He handed the *ras* his best rifle and left for Massawa. There he would wait for peace to spread through the troubled kingdom so that he could attract traders and artisans, and prove Ras Ali wrong.

3

Ethiopia's Christians suffered not only from the endless round of civil war, but from the collective grief of former glory. In their eyes, Ras Ali was a usurper. He was an Oromo, and the Oromo did not share the same blessings as themselves, the high destiny bestowed on them, centuries earlier, by God. The Oromo were a pastoralist people, mainly Muslim, who had pushed up into the central highlands in the eighteenth century. They proved fearless in battle and were used as warriors first by the emperors' rivals against the emperor, then by the emperor himself against his rivals. As the Christian regime weakened, the Oromo grew more powerful. In 1803, Ras Gugsa – grand-father of Ras Ali – became the country's ruler, and converted from Islam to the Christianity of most of his subjects (though they all knew that really a hyena cannot become a goat).

Ras Gugsa ruled for twenty-two years, and according to Zeneb, the Christian chronicler, those men who refused to submit to him had their penises cut off, while women lost their breasts.

In the 1830s, at the age of twelve, Ras Ali became head of the dynasty. During his regency his mother Menen ruled in his stead. Reports describe her variously as capricious, flirtatious, wanton and shameless. She governed from the half-ruined palaces of the city of Gondar. In their rough stone interiors she listened unseen to the affairs of the court, sending judgements and orders through her eunuchs. Outside stood crowds of farmers and soldiers, noblemen and shield-bearers, priests and beggars: 'suppliants', wrote Plowden, 'who cannot obtain admittance, loudly crying their tale of woe ... and perchance some man, once great – whose eyes have been extinguished by the order of her at whose door he is now sitting'.

The traditional rulers of Ethiopia, from the line that had embraced Christianity in the year AD330 but who traced their origins back to the union of King Solomon and the Queen of Sheba, had been in decline for years. King-makers and regional rulers plucked princes from the mountaintop prisons where they were kept from birth. They rarely lasted long on the throne. Soon Gondar was full of toppled emperors, living in penury. Many were crowned and ousted and crowned again – Tekle Giyorgis was enthroned six times. Menen herself took one in 1840 and placed him on the throne as King of Kings Yohannis III. He was sixteen at the time, and she married him in order to become *itege* or empress. He was on and off the throne for years, and grew into a drinker and rarely left his harem. He became known as Yohannis the Fool.

The people of the highlands, the Christian farmers whose land and stores were forever being plundered by shifting hordes of rebels and regional armies, sought solace in the traditions of their faith. The priests reminded them that from the death of Joshua until the rise of King David, the children of Israel suffered a period known as the *Zemene Mesafint*, the Time of Judges, and because there is nothing that happens that has not already happened in the Old Testament, the Christians of Ethiopia realised that they too were living in the *Zemene Mesafint*. Their trials were a punishment for their sins: 'The children of Israel did evil in the sight of the Lord and served Baalim ... And the anger of the Lord was hot against Israel, and he delivered them into the hands of spoilers who spoiled them, and he sold them into the hands of their enemies.'

The Ethiopian chronicles gave voice to the humiliation felt in the heart of every Christian highlander: 'How is it that the kingdom is a laughing stock to the uncircumcised from the very beginning? How is it that the kingdom is the image of a worthless flower that children pluck in the autumn rains?'

Yet just as God had sent the *Mesafint* to punish his errant children, so one day he would end it. It had long been prophesied that in Ethiopia a great ruler would rise and restore the glory of the Christian kingdom. The longer the *Mesafint* went on, the more people remembered the words of the *Fekkare Iyesus*, stating clearly that a ruler would emerge to resurrect Ethiopia, banish her enemies and herald an era of peace, and that this ruler would be called Tewodros. In the 1830s a whisper began to be heard in the highlands. It reached the shores of Lake Tana, the villages of Begemder, and the stony streets of Gondar. *He is come! Tewodros is come!*

Outside a convent on the banks of the River Qaha, the saviour himself raised a horn to his lips:

'I am the king whose name is Tewodros!'

In Gondar, the puppet emperor Sahle Dengel, ruling for the first of his four reigns, heard like Herod of the coming of the new king. He rose and sought him out. Within days, haloed by flies, the severed head of this Tewodros was hanging in the main square of Gondar.

Ras Ali and Menen remained in power. The wars raged on. The *Zemene Mesafint* continued.

4

On the coast, Walter Plowden was living a few miles inland from the unbearable heat of Massawa. In the village of Monculu, only a little less hot, he had built himself a house from palm matting and crude timbers. From his well he dug irrigation channels so that water could flow to the roots of vegetables and fruit bushes. He nurtured shrubs for shade.

Ten years in these regions had drained a little of his old energy. He was often ill. He spent days lying on his *alga*, bored and feverish, while shards of sunlight pierced the fibrous walls. His treaty had yielded nothing – no exports, no imports, none of the hoped-for traffic of skills. Ras Ali had been right.

Plowden performed his consular tasks as best he could. He wrote to London with reports on slavery, on the activities of the French, on missionaries. Every quarter he drew his salary: 'I have the honour to state that I have been at my post, and in the execution of my duties . . .'

But it wasn't much. 'I am consul in name only,' he wrote, 'having no consular powers, no foreign commerce, no mercantile interests, and no British subjects to protect.'

He hated Massawa. He hated its climate, its humidity and haze. He called it the 'slave depot of Turkey'. Successive Ottoman governors had tied him down with petty restrictions, hoping to drive him and other Europeans away. The last *pasha* was a particular menace to the consul, who complained frequently of his 'misgovernment, bribery and oppression'. When Plowden wanted to repair his well, the *pasha* told him not one stone could be moved without permission from Constantinople. Within days the leaves of his shrubs and vegetables crunched to dust between his fingers.

Whenever he was able during those years, Plowden travelled up into Ethiopia. There he breathed the mountain air, climbed beneath a puff-clouded sky to ridges where you could gaze for a hundred miles or more. He bathed in bracing streams, slept easily in the cool nights. He visited John Bell, hoping to hear that the rebels were on the run, that Ras Ali was victorious and that he might at last take up residence in the highlands.

In 1850, Ras Ali suddenly made headway. Two of his greatest enemies – Dejazmaches Kasa and Wube – fell into line behind him. When he called them to campaign on his behalf, they came running. They brought their thousands of followers. A strange peace began to settle over the country, and many believed that the years of the *Mesafint* might just be over.

But in January 1853 Plowden wrote to his masters in the Foreign Office: 'One of the great vassals of Ras Ali named Dejazmach Kasa . . . has rebelled.' He reassured them that 'at present the position and power of the Ras will be in no wise endangered'.

Four months later, he reported: 'This rebel chief has gained another decisive victory over the combined forces of Ras Ali and Dejazmach Wube.'

Two months later: 'Dejazmach Kasa is increasing in force.'

Three days later: 'Dejazmach Kasa has completely defeated Ras Ali.'

The tufty-cheeked mandarins of the Foreign Office were not impressed. All they'd ever heard from their consul to Ethiopia was bad news from the interior and endless squabbles with the Turkish *pasha*.

'Her Majesty's government,' wrote the permanent secretary, 'were led by the representations made by you to expect that advantage would result to British interests from the conclusion of a treaty with the Rulers of Abyssinia . . . It appears however with your reports now before me, that there is little reason to expect such will be the case.'

Plowden was forced to agree. On 10 July 1854, six years after his original appointment as consul, he asked for his first leave.

Yet even as he was waiting, a new possibility emerged. As more news came in about Kasa, Plowden began the same *volte-face* that others had already performed in the highlands. Dejazmach Kasa, the wrecker of peace, was becoming the bringer of peace. Plowden delayed his departure.

On 3 March 1855 he wrote to tell Lord Clarendon that Dejazmach Kasa had defeated his last enemy, Dejazmach Wube. 'There is at last some chance that Abyssinia may be united under one Sovereign, and such an one as shall merit the support and friendship of Her Majesty's Government.' The more Plowden heard of the new ruler, the more excited he became. Dejazmach Kasa had already abolished the slave trade, spoken out against battlefield mutilations. He had written to Plowden himself expressing his interest in 'a sincere friendship with Europeans, more especially the English government'. When news reached him that Kasa had been crowned, Plowden was elated. He cancelled his leave and prepared to travel inland. He had waited nearly a decade for an opportunity like this. The Ethiopians had waited rather longer, and the promise of liberal reforms and foreign relations meant less to them than Kasa's choice of name. He had been crowned Tewodros II.

5

How Kasa Haylu rose to become Tewodros II is a tale so often told in the villages and highlands of Ethiopia that the details have become stretched, added to and reshaped to make them fit a grander pattern. Even during his own lifetime they began to take on the form of more familiar tales, those of ancient folk heroes, of saints or the giants of the Old Testament. In particular his chronicles tell a story similar in many ways to the early life of the greatest of all kings, the father of Solomon – King David.

It was King David who had achieved what Ethiopian Christians longed for: he brought to an end the *Zemene Mesafint*. His story and the psalms attributed to him were a touchstone for educated Ethiopians who had all learnt by heart their *'Dawit'*, the psalms of David. As a boy Kasa completed his *Dawit* with great speed. In later years it was the story of David and the beauty of his psalms that he turned to in times of reflection and need. Those who met him said he carried a copy of the psalms wherever he went, and were struck by his command of them. Henry Dufton, who came to Ethiopia in the early 1860s, concluded that 'he took for a standard – a model to which he could conform himself – his illustrious progenitor, King David'.

The strange thing is that many of the confirmed facts of Kasa's early life really do fit with the young David, as did the physical prowess, the military skills and the intensely human virtues and flaws that shaped each of their reigns. Like David, Kasa emerged not from the royal court, but from provincial obscurity. He was born in about 1820. His father was Dejazmach Haylu Welde Giyorgis, who died when Kasa was young. The truth about his mother troubled him all his life. His enemies taunted him with accusations that she was a camp-follower, a woman who had simply slipped into Haylu's tent. They said she sold *koso*, a much-used purgative, on the street corners of Gondar. To others she was a noble-woman of astonishing beauty. Either way, it was she, Atitegeb, who ensured that he received many years of Church schooling. In biblical matters he could outquote many of the European missionaries who came to the country. He became proficient in Arabic.

He was still a boy, studying at the monastery of Mahbere Selassie when it was attacked by a warlord. The novices were slaughtered or castrated, but Kasa fled unharmed. He joined that nameless tribe of outlaws who haunted the remoter hills of the kingdom. He lived in caves, off the berries of the forest.

Then David departed and came into the forest of Hareth.

His strength with the spear, his skills as horseman, his courage and luck attracted others around him. He was little more than twelve years old. Sometimes he and his band would rob a caravan, or ambush the soldiers of the hated Oromo, and then he divided the spoils as David had divided the spoils of the Amalekites.

And when David came to Ziklag he sent of the spoil unto the elders of Judah, even to his friends, saying, Behold a present for you the spoil of the enemies of the Lord.

19

The years passed. Kasa fought in the lowlands to the west. The number of his victories grew so quickly and with such mysterious ease that Kasa began to see them as part of a plan devised by God. Then a great drought came and famine swept through the highlands, and Ras Ali and his mother Empress Menen could do nothing for the people. Out of the wilderness rode Kasa and his men with looted grain. Kasa gave the people money to buy tools, and he himself helped cut back the forest to plant grain. He showed them how to make the wild places green.

And every one that was in distress, and every one that was in debt, and every one that was discontented, gathered themselves unto him; and he became a captain over them.

In Gondar, Ras Ali's mother, Empress Menen, saw the rise of Kasa and despatched an army to defeat him. It was too late. When her men came upon him, such was his reputation that they fled with hardly a fight.

Then Menen and Ras Ali and the Oromo chiefs became angry. Kasa's support among the people was greater than theirs. They summoned him, that he might make an alliance with them.

And the princes of the Philistines were wroth with him; and the princes of the Philistines said unto him, make this fellow return, that he may go again to his place which thou hast appointed him, and let him not go down to battle, lest in the battle he be an adversary to us.

Menen and Ras Ali said to him: We will forgive all that you have done against us, if you will join us.

Kasa refused. So they offered him the hand of Tewabach, the daughter of Ras Ali.

*And Saul said to David, Behold my elder daughter Merab,
her will I give thee to wife; only be thou valiant for me.*

Kasa was astonished; the daughter of Ras Ali was celebrated
for her beauty. He accepted their offer.

*And David said, Who am I? and what is my life, or my
father's family in Israel, that I should be son-in-law to the
king?*

It was a marriage that should not have worked – a bride
from the dynasty Kasa was determined to destroy. But in the
years to come, though they were often apart, the two developed
an understanding that survived the desperate turbulence of
their times, the wilder fringes of his personality, even, when it
came, his decisive rebellion against her own father and grandmother, Ras Ali and Menen. She remained loyal to him, and
he to her. She was probably the only figure in his adult life he
ever learned to trust.

6

Nothing but the chronicles and legend survives of Kasa's early rise to power – except four brief letters. They were written during his years in the lowlands of the west. They are all in Arabic and all addressed to local rulers in the borderless land between Ethiopia and Sudan. A boisterous confidence gushes from them. They were clearly dictated from the centre of a camp that never knew defeat, in which a powerful aura had already gathered around its leader.

In the letters Kasa refers to himself as 'His Excellency, the honoured, the bravest of the brave and the greatest of horsemen, the mighty, the exalted, the praiseworthy, the owner of all the land, that is Shaykh Kasa . . .' Demanding tribute from the Muslim rulers, he threatened: 'Now, if you bring it, well and good. But if I come, then you'd better crawl back into whatever space is left in your mother's womb . . . I am Kasa. No man can face me.'

At about this time, towards the end of 1846, Kasa made his boldest move. When Empress Menen left the old capital of Gondar with her troops, he marched in and claimed the city for himself. Kasa was now in control not only of the imperial capital but also of all the land to Lake Tana and beyond. On 18 June 1847, Menen met Kasa in battle. Kasa was victorious.

He captured Empress Menen and her husband, the King of Kings, the Solomonic ruler, Yohannis the Fool.

In 1852, Ras Ali sent an army against Kasa. It was commanded by the great Ras Goshu, father of Biru Goshu. The two forces assembled on the plains of Gur Amba. Goshu's men were pleased to find the rebel Kasa in such open country, so outgunned and so outnumbered. Goshu's *azmari*, Tewfech, stood before the troops and sang a scurrilous song about Kasa to encourage them further:

Have you seen this scatterbrain
Coming down to Gur Amba, escorted by five hussies,
Fondling them
And followed by his usual band of loose women?

Kasa was again victorious. Goshu was killed, his men fled. Many were captured – including the *azmari* Tewfech.

'Please,' asked Kasa, 'recite for me this rhyme of yours.'

When the *azmari* had finished, Kasa had him flogged to death.

Ras Ali then summoned all the military force of his kingdom. From Wollo to Gojjam, Lasta to Begemder, the *negarits* sounded. He asked Wube too to send an army. He placed them all under the lucky command of Biru Aligaz. They marched against Kasa, and in April 1853 met at Takusa. In the ranks there was great confidence. 'This man of the lowlands,' scoffed Ras Ali's men, 'this grower of red pepper – at last he's come to fight us!'

'How does he dare? We are ten to his one!'

'Shush! How can you know what the Lord has decided?'

The Lord had decided on triumph for Kasa.

Kasa then began to move more quickly. He marched south. In May he burned Ras Ali's capital at Debre Tabor. On 29 June 1853, Kasa finally clashed with Ras Ali himself, his own father-in-law, on the flat land around Ayshal. The chronicle tells of terrible bloodshed. Ras Ali's troops fell like leaves from a wind-shaken tree. Those who were wounded and were unable to move perished from cold. Ras Ali fled the battlefield. He never recovered his power. The *Zemene Mesafint* was over.

Kasa still had some regional problems to sort out. A lightning march on Tigray wrong-footed its ruler and secured for Kasa the transfer to his camp of Abune Selama, the most senior cleric in the country. Kasa moved south, against Biru Goshu in Gojjam. For years Biru's men had resisted Ras Ali's vast army. But now the enemy was not led by the Oromo. Biru's men refused to fight the invincible Kasa, with the figure of the *abun* behind him. Biru was captured without a shot being fired. He was dragged in before Kasa, a penitential stone pressing down on his shoulders.

'If it had been me before you,' asked Kasa, 'what would you have done?'

'Executed you,' he murmured.

Kasa's men wanted his blood, but he spared Biru. The rebel chief remained in chains for the next fourteen years. In the meantime Dejazmach Wube, said to be the wiliest man in the whole of Ethiopia, still ruled in the north. His regime had begun even before that of Ras Ali. Kasa sent a messenger to Wube, demanding tribute. 'Who are you,' responded Wube, 'that I should pay you tribute?'

'You shall see, great Goliath.'

In January 1855, Kasa marched north. He moved rapidly into the Simien mountains. Day after day, without rest, he drove his troops until they reached the great basin at Deresgie. High brown peaks ringed the skyline. A city of white tents was massed below them. Kasa turned to Yohannis, his *liqemekwas*, his chamberlain, and asked him to look at the tents through his glass.

Yohannis was the Englishman John Bell. With the defeat of Ras Ali, Bell had neatly swapped his allegiance and joined Kasa. Bell pressed the telescope to his eye and told Kasa – Yes, those are the tents of Wube.

Kasa's men were exhausted. They were daunted by the prospect of battle against the great Wube. When Kasa ordered the advance they did not move. He rode out in front of them. 'After all our victories, does this old man frighten you?'

The men did not budge.

'Do his guns, charged with rags, chill your souls?'

Nothing.

Kasa made one final plea to them. 'I will give you my name!'

Now one or two cheers rose from the ranks. Soon they spread and became a chorus, a battle cry. No highlander was immune to word-play, and Kasa had given them a pun. 'My name' in Amharic is *'simien'* – the name also of the native province of Wube.

The battle was not easy. It continued all day. Only when a group of Kasa's men stumbled on a resting Wube and captured him was it decided. Kasa now controlled all of Tigray too – and from Wube's treasury, safe on a high *amba*, he collected a great hoard of gold and silver. He handed out the money to his nobles, officers and soldiers according to rank. Such was the quantity that he continued to do so for months afterwards. The rifles he found were so numerous they were hard for his men to carry. There were also two cannon.

Two days later, in the presence of both Abune Selama and the *ichege*, the country's chief monk, Kasa was crowned.

Dejazmach Kasa did not take at this stage the title King of Kings, or claim to be the heir of Solomon. He did better than that.

'I will give you *simien*,' he had promised his troops days earlier. 'I will give you my name.' He promised an end to generations of oppression, to centuries of waiting – Kasa became Tewodros.

'At my birth,' he wrote, with echoes of King David, 'God picked me up from the dust, gave me strength, raised me up and by Divine power, I chased away the Galla.'

Tewodros's success lay not just in an astonishing series of

military victories. He had something of that curious mystique that gathers round certain men, the impression that just a little of God's energy flows directly through them. Although it failed to convince many of the old nobility, Tewodros's charisma was more effective than any number of big guns, and remained with him throughout all the heady years of his reign, surviving his caprices, his violence, his self-destructive manias, the eventual depletion of his forces, and even his death.

II

Jidda gorge

7

Down in the heat of the Jidda gorge, Walter Plowden waded across the thigh-deep river and began to climb. High above him, some 4,000 feet, were the cliffs of the Delanta plateau. Up there was Tewodros's camp, with his 50,000 soldiers and 100,000 followers. As the slope steepened, so the paths filled. The British consul passed scouts and sutlers, fell into step with water-carriers, wood-carriers, mules laden with grain, shepherds and stockmen driving their beasts to feed the emperor's troops. Once he reached the plateau a group of mounted generals came out to escort him in to camp. Flautists played beside them. Drummers beat their goatskin tympana. As the party approached the open ground at the heart of the camp, with its reception tent, a volley of muskets was fired.

Inside, the consul blinked in the sudden darkness. As his eyes adjusted, he saw the emperor for the first time.

Tewodros was sitting on a divan, dressed in gold-threaded robes. The imperial crown lay on a cushion beside him, hung with pendants of silver filigree. The sword of state was held above him. Abune Selama and the *ichege* sat on high chairs on either side. Standing in attendance were dozens of officers. Plowden lowered himself to the carpet.

The earlier portraits he gives of other nobles – Wube and

Biru and Merso, even Ras Ali – make them all larger than life. But none was painted with the same fascination as that of Tewodros. Plowden was at once struck by his physique – his fitness, his poise and his youth. His face was powerful and handsome, with thin lips and hair running back down to his shoulders.

Plowden stayed two weeks in the Delanta camp, and afterwards wrote an extensive report for his impatient masters at the Foreign Office. It remains one of the most detailed portraits of Tewodros at any stage, but certainly in this moment, in the first months after his coronation, flushed with his own success.

Tewodros, wrote Plowden, 'is young in years, vigorous in all manly exercises, of a striking countenance peculiarly polite and engaging when pleased, and mostly displaying great tact and delicacy'. Like most observers, Plowden noted his energy. 'Indefatigable in business, he takes little repose night or day; his ideas are clear and precise; hesitation is not known to him.'

Plowden's reception showed the value Tewodros placed on ceremony and form. Yet his personal instincts were towards simplicity and equality. 'He salutes his meanest subjects with courtesy,' the consul wrote, 'he is generous to excess and free from all cupidity.'

Tewodros's plans were common currency in the camp, and Plowden stressed to London how important he could become in the politics of the Red Sea. 'Next year he will devote to the settlement of Tigray, including the tribes along the coast, and meditates upon the occupation of Massawa.' He would reclaim Ethiopia's northern and western borders, the territory annexed by Egypt. 'Nor does his military ardour hesitate to dream of the conquest of Egypt, and a triumphant march to the Holy Sepulchre.' In this, as in all his actions, the emperor believed he was merely fulfilling the course of divine will: 'His faith is signal.'

Plowden's assessment of Tewodros was not blind to his faults. 'The worst points in his character are, his violent anger at times, his unyielding pride as regards his kingly and divine right, and his fanatical religious zeal.' It was, wrote Plowden, 'impossible for him yet to believe that so great a monarch as himself exists in the world'.

Plowden proposed again the establishment of official relations between the two countries. He offered Tewodros the chance to send an embassy to London, in return for recognition of himself as consul. The treaty signed by Ras Ali contained in it clauses for his successor. So now Tewodros too could claim its benefits: *There shall be a firm, mutually cordial and lasting friendship between the king of Abyssinia and his successors and Victoria, the queen of England and her successors . . .*

When Plowden began to talk of this treaty, Tewodros said he knew nothing of it. 'I am young and inexperienced in public affairs,' he explained coyly.

So Plowden sketched out the mechanics of a consulship, the rights it gave Tewodros to send his own representation to Queen Victoria, to the court of St James's, and the principle of mutual exemption from local laws. He spoke of the benefits of such an arrangement, the military aid that would accrue, assistance, trade. Plowden recognised in Tewodros an openness, a yearning for new ideas and contacts. But the emperor's generals were impatient to return to battle. Every minute Tewodros wasted with this foreigner gave the enemy an advantage.

It was John Bell who relayed the emperor's reply: I cannot consent to a consul, said Tewodros. I cannot allow anyone in my territory, consul or not, to be free from my jurisdiction. Plowden was devastated – even Ras Ali had agreed to that.

'For anything else you wish for,' Tewodros assured him, 'now and hereafter, for yourself or other English, I shall be happy to perform your pleasure.'

Plowden felt sure that Tewodros would relent in time. He was used to waiting – he would wait a little longer. He travelled to Gondar to sit out the rains.

Tewodros moved his army south, towards the Christian kingdom of Shoa. The king of Shoa died the night before he was due to fight. The arrival of Tewodros with Abune Selama combined with the sudden death of their king to persuade the Christians of Shoa that a new age lay before them, and that Tewodros was its fiery exponent. Shoa was added to Gojjam and Wollo, Begemder and Gondar, Simien and Tigray. The territory of Ethiopia was now larger than it had been for over a thousand years.

8

Tewodros signalled the start of his reign with a series of stirring proclamations.

'Go now,' he told his followers, 'lay down your arms, return to the country of your fathers. Take up the tools of your former trade.' The merchant will abide in his store, the farmer in his field. He himself – Tewodros, Elect of God – will keep an army and they will be trained matchlockmen, and he will drill them and train them in the use of their arms. Soldiers will be paid and they will buy food from the peasants and no longer plunder farm stores. All guns not in their hands will be smelted into plough-shares and sickle-blades, and in the markets across the land the price of the plough-ox will exceed that of the war horse. Seek out the habits of peace, said the new emperor, live with your family, continue your old peacetime occupation unless it was as a *shifta* in which case, like Adonibezek who was pursued from the city of Bezek, you will have your hands and feet chopped off.

There shall be no more slavery. Existing slaves must be sold, the money given to charity, and the slaves baptised. Tewodros himself showed the way by buying slaves from the Muslim traders and sending them to priests for baptism. He encouraged others to follow him in formalising their marriage before the priests and to remain faithful to their chosen partners. Women of the camps and of the towns and of *tella bets* must no longer sell themselves to men. Murderers will not be handed over to the bereaved families for retribution, but dealt with by his own executioners. Tewodros revived the right of all citizens to approach him as the point of final appeal. Long before dawn, the cries of the persecuted surrounded his tent: *'Jan Hoi! Jan Hoi!* Your Majesty! Give me justice!'

He wanted roads. He planned a transport system with Debre Tabor as its hub and spokes pushing out to Gondar, to Meqdela, south to Gojjam. 'Hitherto,' wrote one observer, 'not a single road had ever been constructed.' The first stages, of route-planning and blasting, were carried out by German missionaries.

Nor did he remain silent on matters of dress. Under the old regime, clothes for the upper body – for man or woman – were a privilege. 'Childish customs,' scoffed the emperor, and introduced the wearing of a loose cotton shirt for all. If it reached below the knee, or was of silk, or was brightly coloured and had slashed sleeves, it meant that the wearer had earned the garment in service to the state.

Tewodros's vision for his country was undeniably a righteous one. Even a man like the Catholic missionary Mgr Justin de Jacobis, driven out of Gondar by Tewodros, recognised, as he fled, the heroic scope of his persecutor's ambition. Tewodros is 'extraordinary', he admitted, the bringer of 'laws and admirable ordinances of public prosperity and morality'.

Tewodros wanted national unity, and tackled the problem of regional power. During the *Mesafint*, the provincial rulers had become too powerful, corrupted both by the habit of rebellion and by their alliance with the Oromo rulers. Tewodros (who himself was innocent of neither) ousted these hereditary rulers, and many now shuffled harmlessly around the flat-topped mountains, their hands and legs in chains. Tewodros appointed his own governors.

He was one of the first Ethiopian rulers to take any notice

at all of the world outside. He had felt the full force of Egyptian expansion in 1848 at Debarki when a few men had devastated his forces with their guns; Ottoman power in the Red Sea, far to the south of the Bosphorus, was on the wane, and the British and French made no secret of their desire to fill the gap. European politics intrigued him, and he developed a fascination for the war that broke out as he rose to power, that concerned the shrinking of the other end of the Ottoman Empire – the war on the Crimea peninsula. Every visitor was asked for news, for stories of Balaclava and Sevastopol. But Tewodros was baffled by the allegiances. Why in God's name had France and Britain, who spent their time squabbling around him, been allies in the Crimea, helping the Muslim Turks against Christian Russia?

The future for Ethiopians would no longer be decided only within their own borders. They must learn not only to spare the lives of visiting foreigners, but to see that these strangers might actually bring benefits. He himself was frequently in debate with the two Englishmen, Plowden and Bell.

Plowden left a great deal of written material, but little is known about Bell. Yet it was he who was closest to Tewodros. He had been appointed his *liqemekwas*, involving among other things dressing as the emperor did in battle, to act as decoy. Bell was given his own detachment of cavalry and married a cousin of Tewodros, Wurqnesh Asfa Yilma. On campaign he often shared a tent with Tewodros and was known to read to him from a copy of Shakespeare with such devotion that the emperor referred to it as 'Bell's Bible'.

Tewodros wanted a modern state, a Christian state, without slavery, without feudal fiefdoms, defended by a standing army equipped with up-to-date weapons. More than anything he wanted a Church that did not hold the people in thrall, nor dictate to the crown, nor hoard the tithes from the third of the land it controlled, nor peddle its mysteries in a long-dead language. Plowden in his writings frequently mentions parallels between Ethiopia and medieval Europe. In his quest for unity and centralised rule, Tewodros was attempting 'a task achieved in Europe only during the reigns of consecutive Kings'; in his taming of the Church his own Reformation. His ideals of worldly power were forged in the heat of the Books of Samuel and Kings yet tempered, with assistance from Bell's 'Bible', by a little European humanism.

But God grants no easy victories. Tewodros's people had lived for too long in darkness to appreciate at once the light he brought. In Tigray, Niguse and Tesemma, of the family of Wube, rose up against the new regime. In Gojjam, Tedla Gwalu rebelled. Kinfu's son rebelled. Nor could the Oromo of Wollo yet understand that their years of rule were finished. Across the country, priests too had reservations, strangely slow to see that in Tewodros's victories was the manifest will of the Almighty.

9

Standing barefoot on the stony earth, with his plain *shamma* around his shoulder, Tewodros would say: 'Without Christ, I am nothing.' He understood his worldly role in terms of biblical precedent. He understood his particular duty as saving Ethiopia's Christians from extinction by Muslims. He would first convert the Oromo to Christianity, then put the choice to all remaining Muslims in his realm: follow Christ or leave the country. He was not above superstition, seeing portents when they were obviously put in his way. But his zealotry was Christian. He was a crusader, the heir of David, the Elect of God, the dutiful Slave of Christ.

Yet Tewodros didn't much care for priests. During the *Zemene Mesafint* many of Ethiopia's clergy had, according to the chronicles, become 'polygamists, sorcerers and drunkards'; by day they performed the rites, by night they visited women without husbands. Even worse, they had confused and divided the people with their arguments, squandering the comforts of orthodoxy for baffling schisms. As in the *Mesafint* of old, when the children of Israel forgot Jahweh and went a-whoring after Baal and all the false gods, so the priesthood had forgotten the one truth.

Foreigners were to blame, at least in part. The Portuguese

in the sixteenth century had brought their own interpretation of Christ's nature and convinced many Ethiopians to adopt it. These ones became known first as *Kidat* – 'Unctionists' – then as *Yesaga Lij* – 'Son by Grace' – and finally as *Sost Lidet* or 'Three Births', because they said that Christ was anointed in a 'third birth'. To their detractors the Three-Birthers had therefore to admit the inadmissible: that there was a time when Christ was not fully divine. For traditionalists of the Alexandrian, non-Chalcedonian persuasion, that was a heretical slur on the pure divinity of Christ. These ones referred to the Three-Birthers as *Karra Haymanot* – Faith-in-the-Knife – because they had sliced the third birth from their teaching.

Tewodros was not interested. He wanted conformity. If the Church was to help in re-unifying the country, it must be unified itself. In 1854, in his first act of statesmanship, he called a council of clergy in Gondar. He was not yet emperor, but having defeated Dejazmach Wube, he now stood with an important ally at his side – Abune Selama.

The *abun* was the head of the Ethiopian Church, the only bishop in the entire country. The post was never held by an Ethiopian, but always an Egyptian, a Copt appointed by the Patriarchate in Alexandria. Often the incumbent was elderly, unable to speak Amharic, and ignored. In the 1820s, writing about Selama's predecessor, Dejazmach Sebadagis complained to the Alexandrian patriarch: 'Was it because you hate Ethiopia that you sent him?' And as Egypt expanded south under Muhammad Ali, and spread the terror of invasion in Ethiopia, so suspicions of the Coptic *abun* grew.

Arriving in Ethiopia in 1841, the new Abune Selama was young and ambitious. He was appalled at the spread of Catholic missionaries in northern Ethiopia, and was keen to protect the traditional conformity with Alexandria. In the rise of Tewodros he found someone of like mind, and as vigorous and as determined as himself. At the meeting of clergy in 1854, he and Tewodros outlawed the Three-Birthers, demanding a choice between confession of the Alexandrian creed, or death. They also ordered the expulsion of Catholic missionaries. Shortly afterwards Abune Selama crowned Tewodros and sanctified in church his marriage to Tewabach. Their alliance found its most powerful expression in the invasion of Shoa some months later, when they arrived together at the head of an army.

The fertile alliance between the two men did not last. Abune Selama was too ambitious, too strong-willed, too much like Tewodros himself, for it to be an easy relationship. Antagonisms between them began to multiply. The clergy too began to grumble about the speed of Tewodros's reforms. After the rains of 1856 he called another gathering of clergy in Gondar, to persuade them of the need to tax some of their vast wealth.

'Our enemies are many,' Tewodros told them. 'It is only fair that some of this should go to feed those who protect us all.'

The clergy also needed to eat, he was told. And anyway, there were more of them than of his soldiers. 'What you should do,' said one priest, 'is take your army from one province to the next, allowing each one to recover its reserves of grain.'

'That's how it's always been, Your Majesty,' explained another. 'It's the custom.'

Neither side conceded anything. In the end the priests fetched the *Fetha Negest*, the 'Book of the Law of Kings', and read: 'That which is taken to the Holy of Holies should not be taken out.' From which was understood, it was not in anyone's power to relinquish Church land.

'This book,' fumed the emperor, 'has been translated a thousand times and interpreted in a thousand ways! If you want to put another on the throne, do so. And like the Oromo rulers I will continue to plunder the beasts and the fields of the people!'

He turned and left, and the priests watched his guards close around his back.

As quick as Tewodros's anger was his remorse. Later he called Abune Selama to him, and the two men agreed a compromise. The priesthood would accept Tewodros's right to tax them, and Tewodros would agree not to exercise the right.

And the next day the priests led a joyful procession through the streets of Gondar. The city was filled with the sound of the *kebbero* and the *debteras'* sistra and the songs of Moses. Tewodros had failed. The expansion of his rule had, for now, reached its limit at the gates of the church. He returned to campaigning.

10

Several months later, on 27 December 1856, the Coptic Patriarch Cyril IV – spiritual father of the Ethiopian Church – rode into Gondar. He had travelled for months from Alexandria. His men ran ahead of him, through the stony streets of the old capital, in and out of the juniper shadows, shooing all women from the slightest possibility of meeting his gaze.

The patriarch's journey to Ethiopia was one of the most significant moments of Tewodros's early reign. Cyril turned out to be the highest-ranking foreigner ever to reach the emperor, and his visit forced the imperial hand in his initial choice of overseas allies. It also revealed in public for the first time the extremes of Tewodros's personality.

It began well enough. Tewodros received His Holiness in Debre Tabor with great ceremony and genuine deference. But as the days passed the emperor began to spot blemishes in the heavenly mantle of the primate. He heard Cyril's muttering about his daughter Church, the inappropriate worship of the cross and of the saints, about how full the Ethiopian calendar was of fast days and holy days. For a man whose thoughts seldom strayed from matters of the spirit, the patriarch also appeared very keen to inspect the imperial forces. At the same time Tewodros received reports that Egyptian war-camels were gathering on his western border, and that Said Pasha himself, viceroy of Egypt, was in the Sudan. Suddenly all became clear to Tewodros – the patriarch's visit was a ploy by the *pasha* to check Ethiopia's weakness before invading. What should he do?

Tewodros imprisoned the patriarch. He locked him up in a house with his bishop Abune Selama and placed a hedge of thorns around it. During the days that followed, loyalties polarised sharply. Many Ethiopians were horrified at Tewodros's sacrilege, and were quick to blame the other foreigners, the European Protestants. In turn, Tewodros turned to his 'children', Plowden and Bell, for support, and they saw a chance to press for a direct approach to Queen Victoria and Britain.

But the suggestion angered Tewodros. 'Do you suppose me capable of fear, that I would use such a moment?'

'I don't believe the *pasha* would ever become the aggressor in the face of our protests,' stressed Plowden.

Tewodros clung to his belief in the Protestants. With the Copts still imprisoned, he stood in court one day trying to explain his stance. Pointing to a pair of Protestant missionaries, he addressed the sceptics: 'They seek our welfare, and have brought us Bibles and Testaments in our own language. But the holy father has come as a merchant and ambassador, asking us for wax and ivory and mules and *zebal*, and for friendship with the Mohammedans.'

He reminded them of the urgency and integrity of his own mission. 'I am Christ's servant. He gave me victory over all my enemies. I am labouring for His honour, to protect our Church against Muslims.'

They should trust him as their leader. 'As long as I have life, I will keep down the patriarch, the *abun* and Said Pasha – even the Queen of England, should she help him.'

Yet between Tewodros's suspicions and the detained churchmen, his people had made their choice. Both Tewodros and his Protestant friends found themselves marginalised.

Some days later, the emperor called a much larger assembly – courtiers, ministers, missionaries, foreigners. A thousand priests and *debteras* joined them, thousands more of his own troops. This time he stood before them not in defiance, but to confess: it was the devil who had made him abuse the churchmen in this way. He sent a message to the thorn-rounded house, pleading for reconciliation. When it was granted, he went to kneel before the patriarch and the *abun* and begged their forgiveness.

Before returning to Egypt, Cyril IV left a tiny seed to take root in Tewodros's mind. Europeans, he said, were not to be trusted, their motives were selfish. Earlier he had urged Tewodros to expel the Protestants. Now he told the emperor quite plainly that the English merely wanted his friendship in order to 'undermine his power and conquer his country'.

At the time Tewodros refused to believe it. But in years to come, as he tried to understand the ambiguous signals of British diplomacy, he often found cause to recall that patriarchal warning.

11

When Cyril left for the lowlands, Tewodros sent him off with personal gifts of ivory and, for Said Pasha, 'three excellent and four average horses', as well as some spears and a dagger. He also enclosed two letters in his saddlebags – one to the *pasha*, the other to Queen Victoria. It was his first foray into foreign relations.

Within eleven days the letter to Said Pasha passed from Amharic to Arabic. Its date changed from the Ethiopian 5 Hidar 1850 (13 November 1857 in the Gregorian calendar) to the Hejira 25 Rabi' al-Awwal. The address was buffed up from the plain Amharic of Tewodros – 'my friend Sa'id Pasha, the ruler of Egypt' – to the Arabic: 'to His Highness, the most noble, the magnificent pleasure, and the true lover of God, Muhammad Sa'id Pasha, Protector of the Land of Egypt. May he continue to be preserved through the care of the Lord of Creation.'

The text itself reflected the turnaround in Tewodros's attitude to Egypt. Glossing over his own furious imprisonment of Cyril, he wrote: 'When I was told by my father the patriarch that you love me and want my friendship, I was very happy . . . May God increase our friendship.'

The letter to Queen Victoria was unembellished, and more

neutral. He probably wouldn't have sent it at all had Plowden not encouraged it. The consul was keen to preserve his own ambitions in the light of Tewodros's new friendship with Cyril and Egypt:

May this letter sent by the King of Kings Tewodros of Ethiopia reach the queen of England, Biktorya. How are you? Are you well? I am well, thank God ... I have received your envoy Buladin [Plowden] with love and friendship. It is because I have not found rest and [matters] have not settled down for me that I have not written until now. Now, you are the child of Christ and I am the child of Christ. For the love of Christ, I want friendship ...

It was Plowden who was now isolated. He accompanied Tewodros's letter to the queen with an explanatory one of his own. He stressed how finely balanced not only Tewodros's interest in the British was, but also his entire rule. It was imperative to offer material support to Tewodros. Plowden was aware that only a year earlier the Egyptians had granted a licence to the French to build a canal at Suez. Now the French were trying to wrest Ethiopia from Tewodros: 'The French and the Roman Catholic mission have already spent large sums to enable, if possible, his adversary Dejazmach Niguse to rival him and three cannon are now at Massawa for that purpose.'

To help save the Red Sea from French control, Plowden suggested to the Foreign Office that they send Tewodros a few hundred muskets and percussion caps – also a 'handsome piece' for the emperor's own use.

In London Plowden's long letter received a scribbled, single-word minute from Lord Clarendon: *Approve. C.*

The first reply to the two letters came from Egypt. An ambassador from Said Pasha arrived in Ethiopia with a long train of mules behind him, heavy with gifts for Tewodros – one hundred double-barrelled guns, numerous tents and silks and bolts of cloth – and four large cannon.

Meanwhile, from Lord Clarendon's desk, Plowden's plea for arms snailed its way to the War Office. A year passed. The War Office amended Plowden's order, and a docket was filled out by a Mr Moore at the Tower:

Rifle with rammer and implements 1
Cone and screw-driver for Deane's revolver 1
Case 1

That was all. The War Office considered it 'inappropriate' to send arms to Tewodros at that moment. On 5 October 1859 – two years after the letters had left Ethiopia – Plowden at last received news of the request from his agent on the coast: 'The rifle has been received, but no ammunition.'

Plowden's position had become precarious. Four and a half years previously he had come up to the highlands on a brief visit to the new ruler. As British consul he was not only friendless now but surrounded by murmurs of hostility. The Ethiopians had reverted to their old suspicion of European Christians, and his way out of the country was blocked by the rebel Niguse. Walter Plowden was trapped.

12

After His Holiness Cyril IV left Gondar in 1857, Tewodros marched to Delanta. He defeated a rebel governor there, then crossed the Abbai into Gojjam, where a force had risen against him. He captured the wife of one of their leaders and stripped her naked before having her shot. The rebels themselves he released; some were later captured again, and this time had to be executed. In Gojjam he found a slave market and ordered all the slaves to be freed, and many of them married each other. Then he moved north and did battle with the Agew and captured their leaders. The governor of Wegera rebelled and Tewodros moved his forces west to fight him, but the governor escaped. Tewodros had his prisoners' hands and feet cut off, and hanged them from an acacia in Gorgora. He then marched to Zur Amba, and to Gondar, then back to Wegera and down to Zur Amba again.

That year, the year of St Mark, turned out like the others. Tewodros drove his men back and forth through the high plains, putting down rebellions. 'He is coming – he is coming!' hissed all before him, but the rebellions flared up again as soon as he had left. In three years of rule, nothing he had done had yet become solid: not the defeat of the Oromo, nor the appointments he made from among his own people, nor the alliances with Abune Selama, the Egyptians, or the scheming Europeans. His kingdom was little more than the province where his army was camped, his palace his campaigning tent, his power the last battle he had won. Only his strange record of success bound his territory together, and hope – less the hope in his new reforms than in old notions of peace through power, unity of Church and crown and common cause beneath the tattered Solomonic banner.

Between Wollo and Begemder there stood a mountain. Its dark cliffs were like the sides of a great ship, its flat summits decks on which cattle grazed and crops grew. No man could approach that mountain without being seen; it could be defended with the tiniest force. It was called Meqdela. In time Tewodros saw it as the still point of his turbulent world: 'Meqdela shall be the storehouse of my treasures; those who love me will come and settle there.'

Only Tewodros would have favoured such a location, surrounded by his enemies. 'Believing I had power,' he wrote years later, 'I brought all the Christians to the land of the heathen.'

Meqdela became garrison, treasury, prison, stronghold and home. Over the years, everything that was most valuable to him ended up on Meqdela – his captured cannon, his precious stones, his looted manuscripts, his most important and belligerent prisoners. Biru Goshu was chained there, also the 'rightful' Solomonic ruler Yohannis the Fool, who was always treated with deference by Tewodros. HH Cyril IV and Abune Selama had attended the dedication of the mountain as a place for Tewodros's treasures, at which there was 'extraordinary rejoicing'. He erected a church dedicated to his favourite sacred figure – Medhane Alem, 'saviour of the world'.

Up there too he had sent Tewabach, his beloved wife. He visited Meqdela when he could, and those around him noticed the calm that settled upon him when he was with her. She was one of his 'guardian angels', it was said (the other one being

John Bell). She prepared his food, read the Bible with him, and though no heir had yet been given them, God would choose the moment in His own time.

That year, 1858, in the early days of *keremt*, the season of big rains, Tewodros rode up the mountain and was with Tewabach. She washed the dust of battle from his feet. He was still for a moment and went nowhere and sat reading the Psalms – *Lord, how are they increased that trouble me! Many are they that have risen against me . . .* Each day the clouds gathered over the peaks, and after the storm, the sun shone on the plains far below and its web of silvery streams.

While he was on Meqdela, Tewabach fell ill. With each day, the emperor's anxiety grew. He ate only *shurro*, fasting food. He spent the nights in Medhane Alem church praying for her. He begged the small group of Protestant missionaries to apply their medicine to her. His army, so used to movement, began to plunder the villages around Meqdela, and Tewodros was forced to drag himself from his wife's bedside and lead his troops southwards where they were able to attack the Oromo. There they could plunder all they liked.

On the evening of 13 Nehase, the day of *Rob*, in the year 7350 since the creation of the world, Itege Tewabach died. Tewodros was still with his forces. He returned at once and had her body put in a coffin, and the coffin put on a stretcher. From his fortress at Meqdela, Tewodros took her embalmed body from camp to camp. She lay in her own tent and Tewodros spent hours sitting alone with her. She was taken to another mountain, Amba Gishen, whose flat-topped summit faced the heavens in the shape of a cross. While her funeral was being arranged, Tewodros composed a lament:

I pray, ask her before she goes
If Itege Tewabach was wife and servant
She of such wisdom, such industry, died yesterday
She served me and treated me by ploughing the earth.

Many miles away, deep in Oromo country, was another mourner. Banished to his native province of Yejju, Ras Ali wrote a bitter verse for the double loss of his daughter. He had not seen her since Tewodros had robbed him of his power and driven him into exile:

When I said to her 'I love mead!' she brought me
    honey.
When I said to her 'I am hungry!' she brought me my
    chosen fruits.
When I said to her 'I am cold!' she sent me *shammas*.
Taken by my thief, she is now carried on a coffin;
I grieve not, as long ago she disowned me.

Some weeks before her burial a comet appeared in the heavens. Each night Tewodros went out and sat in the stillness of the mountain to watch the arc streak across the sky. On the fortieth night it was gone. He marched his forces to the Oromo region of Wollo and massacred many people. He captured thousands of animals, and meat became cheaper than cabbage. He appointed a new governor, a loyal man, and went south and killed all those Oromo he could find between Gimbia and Geneta. The children he distributed among his nobles.

In Shoa, someone whispered of the governor's secret dealings with a rebel. Tewodros had the governor chained and another appointed. That one revealed his treachery before Tewodros left Shoa. He had him chained too. Then he heard that the new governor of Wollo had rebelled. He rode north again, tens of thousands behind him. He rode in silence.

13

Walter Plowden now cut a sorry figure. He had few supporters left in the highlands. He had nothing to offer Tewodros. London had lost interest in his mission. He was desperate to reach the coast, to return to Britain, but the road was still blocked by Niguse. Plowden never doubted that Tewodros would move against Niguse, take Massawa from the Turks and gain access to the sea. But in four years he had been oddly slow to do so.

He was with the emperor on another campaign in Oromo country. 'Leave the Oromo,' he urged. 'Move on Niguse in the north.'

Tewodros resented the interference, but reassured the consul: 'Nothing but my death shall prevent me from placing you at Massawa.'

It was the last time the two men ever saw each other. They had met in 1855 in a flurry of mutual hope – the newly-crowned Tewodros with his attendant military angel; Plowden and his epistolary link to the powerhouse of the British Foreign Office. Tewodros's reforms had been stalled by his hydra-headed enemies. Plowden's paper link had proved just that. In recent years they had grown apart.

In the 1840s, when Plowden had first stumbled into the

Ethiopian highlands, the world was a bigger place. British interests were less compromised. Palmerston in 1847 had been able to share Plowden's enthusiasm for an entire new territory, an ancient half-forgotten kingdom. Trade and thwarting the French added a little pragmatic purpose to Plowden's carefree project.

By the time of Tewodros's coronation in 1855, the Foreign Secretary Lord Clarendon remained thrilled by Plowden's assessment of the emergence of Tewodros and the prospect of opening up relations: 'Have read his very able report with great interest, and entirely approve his language and proceedings.'

But in the following years it had been impossible for Plowden even to leave the country. In the meantime the convergence of interests in the Red Sea – French, British, Egyptian and Ottoman – had made foreign policy a much more delicate exercise. Involvement in overseas territories was also seen as having a much greater price: the Indian Mutiny had revealed the strange truth that native peoples did not always appreciate the presence of the British. Ethiopia and Tewodros were an equation that didn't work out; they were risk without profit.

To the Foreign Office, Consul Plowden slipped from view. There was no more talk of receiving an ambassador. By 1860 Lord Russell, Clarendon's successor as Foreign Secretary, was fed up with this emperor and his endless struggles; all that mattered was the coast. Plowden was wasting his time in the highlands: 'You will therefore return to Massawa, which is your proper residence, and you will not leave it, unless under very exceptional circumstances.'

But he could not even reach Massawa.

The only duty the Foreign Office now asked of Plowden was to tell Tewodros to stop his persecution of a group of Ethiopian Catholics. Very reluctantly, Plowden sent their letter on to Tewodros: 'We would advise you earnestly to be like ourselves, that all people shall have religious liberty in your country.'

Not for the first time, Tewodros was baffled by the Europeans. What was his old friend Plowden doing, speaking up for his enemies? The French were supporting Niguse in the north, and Niguse had promised to convert to Rome when he had defeated Tewodros. Yet through Plowden, Tewodros was being asked to accept the Catholics. Was Plowden in league with the French?

Tewodros read the letter on campaign. He handed it to an aide. Six hours later he gave the order to break camp. He never replied.

Seventeen years had passed since Plowden first arrived in the country. 'The love of change and of the wildest freedom first led me to Abyssinia and made me feel as imprisonment the least restraint.' Now in Gondar, in and out of fever, lying on another *alga* in another season of highland rains, he recalled those early days – the excitement of Biru's camp with just a thaler to his name, the week of 'song and merrymaking' after killing an elephant, then rushing to war; hunting hippo on the shores of Lake Tana, or the sunset scene, 'so strange and novel', of watching thousands of Oromo swimming the Blue Nile in its mile-deep gorge.

There was the time spent in a mini-fortress with the eighteen-stone Oromo chief Ahmed Huru – 'the rain prevented us from going out, so we drank *tej* without ceasing', and without eating, for six days, while Ahmed 'eyed me askance in a most ludicrous way'. (He also made an offer to Plowden of his daughter 'to be my lawful wife, and of a fat portion of his dominions'.)

Plowden had always had luck – leaving his residence in Monculu just hours before the arrival of an army that burned the village to the ground. He had won over the right people – Biru and Wube and Abune Selama and the dangerous Haile the Devil – 'with my usual good fortune in Abyssinia, I made him my friend'. His friendship with Tewodros was, in its best moments, of great significance to them both. Once on parting for the battlefield the emperor had taken Plowden by the hand and said: 'All men are mortal; if anything happens to me, befriend my son. Write to your country; say you had a friend who loved you all, and who intended to send an embassy to you for your friendship, and beg them to support my son.' When Plowden agreed, Tewodros told him: 'I love and trust you – goodbye!'

Plowden heard the echoes of English history in the country's arcane customs and codes and its battle lore. He saw Ethiopia on the road of progress, behind Europe, but on the same road, in its own Middle Ages. He admired too the defiant strangeness, the beauty of the landscape, the sights that the people in it would suddenly produce, like *gugs* – 'a fine animated game' of feigned battle: 'with their scarlet saddle-cloths and glittering *benaicka* flashing in the sun, and long sheepskins on their shoulders, the hair streaming as they gallop, they present a picturesque and wild appearance'.

From the time that he became consul and signed the treaty, something of Plowden's initial joy was lost. Even the excitement of Tewodros's early reign soured. Five years he had been stuck in the highlands. Now his luck seeped from him. In November 1859, playing a game of *gugs* himself, his horse rolled and he broke his leg. For two months he was 'entirely incapacitated'. When he wrote again to Lord Russell, and apologised, it was to tell him that he had heard that the French had sent an embassy to Massawa – further backing for Niguse. For some time the rivalry between Niguse and Tewodros had reflected the growing rivalry for the Red Sea between Britain and France. Niguse had the advantage, having blocked Tewodros from the coast. Tewodros now appeared the loser.

In fact, he had already made his move. The very next day, Plowden received the news he had waited years for: from Shoa, Tewodros had suddenly marched his forces to Tigray. It was an astonishing feat. Only Tewodros could have achieved it. Six hundred miles through mountainous terrain in forty-odd days. With 60,000 men he had confronted Niguse. Niguse fled to the west. After five years, Tewodros had at last added Tigray to his realm. His territory now stretched from the Awash river in the south to the mountains above the Red Sea coast. It included Aksum, seat of the first Ethiopian empire. It revived for many the stalled hopes of Tewodros's early years. Plowden was among them.

In Gondar, he hopped to his feet. He packed his belongings and prepared for the journey. He would see Tewodros in Tigray, then continue on to the coast. In Britain he could have his leg set properly and, with Tewodros's new strategic advantage, present his case for the first time in person to the Foreign Office. Raised up onto a mule, he was escorted out of Gondar.

His small party was crossing the River Keha when a group of four hundred men attacked them. They were led by Gared, a nephew of Tewodros but a follower of Niguse. Plowden's side was pierced by a spear. He died nine days later.

Later that year, Tewodros avenged the death of his old friend. He drew Gared into battle at Debarek. It was Yohannis, John Bell – in the uniform of the *liqemekwas* – who spotted Gared and shot him dead. But as he fired his pistol, Gared's brother killed Bell, and was himself killed by Tewodros.

Tewodros knelt beside the body of John Bell. First Tewabach, then Plowden, and now Bell.

'Yohannis! Poor Yohannis,' he wept. 'You saved my life, but at the expense of your own.'

Witnesses saw him sit there for some moments, overcome by grief. Suddenly he rose. He leapt onto the fallen figure of Bell's killer, thrusting his spear again and again into the corpse's head. 'You wretch, you have taken from me my best friend, my only friend!'

Some months later, a visiting missionary showed the emperor a 'stereoscopic image'. It showed a soldier weeping at the grave of friends fallen in recent fighting at Melegnano. When Tewodros saw the picture, he gazed at it a long time.

'Let me also weep,' he told the missionary, 'for I have lost my best friends.'

Tewodros at the Gefat foundry, from a mural in the bar of the Hotel Tewodros, Debre Tabor

14

One of the first letters Tewodros sent after his coronation in 1855 was to Samuel Gobat, Anglican bishop of Jerusalem. Gobat had been a missionary in Ethiopia some twenty years earlier, but had been forced out by the country's paralysing instability. Like others, he had watched the emergence of Tewodros and felt the chance had come again – not for him, but for a new generation of evangelical workers.

Tewodros, however, was asking him for artisans and craftsmen. He certainly did not want priests. 'You know the situation of our country. It is where you lived. It has been divided, one against another, even into three. Now, by the power of God, I have unified it, so now let not priests who disrupt the faith come to me . . . of workers, let one who ploughs with a fire-wheel come, bringing the engine with him to me. I have heard people say that it exists.'

Eight months later, Samuel Gobat stood before the Anglican congregation on Mount Zion in Jerusalem. Seven fresh-faced, Swiss-trained missionaries gazed up at him.

'Beloved brethren,' he began, 'the hour has come for which you have for some years been preparing yourselves, the hour for parting with the Christians in whose circle your spiritual life has been developed.'

The bishop was a solid and portly man. A great bib of a white beard hung down his chest. In his address, he drew on his own experience in the field years earlier.

'Now, you will have to lean on the Lord in your weakness, in a land that is covered with darkness, and among a people who are still in the shadow of death. If you have ever felt and understood your infinite weakness and helplessness, as every one must into whose soul a ray from the Sun of Righteousness has penetrated, you must increasingly feel it in this solemn hour, as you see before you the difficulties of the journey and the deep degradation of the people to whom you are going . . .'

But with their own deviant version of Christianity, the Ethiopians were a people not entirely without redemption.

'According to the ideas of the present king, who himself reads the Bible in his own language, and according to the practice of the Abune Selama, I do not think you will have any obstacle in spreading the Word of God. Judging by my own experience, I believe that many an Abyssinian will receive the Bible with thankfulness.'

He did warn them of the ambiguity that lay behind their mission.

'Do not put to the king direct questions, so as to get decisive answers, as to whether you may settle in his country as messengers of salvation. The better plan will be not to bring the matter forward, nor seem anxious about it, but try first to persuade and convince the king through your behaviour, that you are true Christians who are led by the Spirit and the Word of God.'

Gobat believed that in Africa a great new world of evangelism was opening up. He and his committee planned an 'Apostelstrasse', a series of twelve stations between Egypt and Ethiopia which would help supply the Ethiopian mission, as well as radiating the Word of God from each station.

'The field that lies desert before you, and must be worked and turned into a garden of God, is a wide, almost immeasurable field. It not only includes all Abyssinia, but the neighbouring heathenish Galla tribes, and the whole centre of Africa, of which Abyssinia is only the entrance. There the devil has his kingdom, and for thousands of years it has been allowed to go on quietly and undisturbed beneath his government.'

He concluded by reminding them that they were invited as artisans, and that their missionary activity should be covert.

'You may feel it strange and disagreeable to hear that instead of preaching and baptising you are asked to work with your hands, and partly to earn your own living. The devil will whisper to you, and your own hearts will answer him loudly enough: "Work and earn our bread, live and die, we could have done in Germany, without the long preparation, and without going to wild Abyssinia."'

Three of the men were so alarmed by Gobat's portrait of wild Abyssinia that they pulled out. Among the others there were reservations. Only two out of the seven – Mayer and Kienzlen – set off for Ethiopia with anything approaching enthusiasm.

15

For a few years the mission ran smoothly. Tewodros was too busy campaigning to pay the missionaries much attention. But in 1858 he asked them to treat the dying Tewabach, and though they could do nothing, it marked the beginning of a closer relationship. As his own clergy revealed themselves to him as hidebound fools, so Tewodros took to spending time with the south German Pietists, and developed a respect for their brand of unadorned faith. They in turn overlooked his brutal sorties against the Oromo, and came to admire him.

'He is,' wrote Kienzlen, 'the only man in Abyssinia who possesses the fear of God.'

In 1859, a new missionary arrived – Theophilus Waldmeier, a young Swiss of deep humility and an almost saintly gentleness. Tewodros always had favourites among the foreigners, and as the years passed Waldmeier came to fill the gap left by John Bell.

Theophilus Waldmeier had had a strict Catholic upbringing. As a boy he soon realised that 'the priest is a bigger sinner than other people'. His grandmother beat him with a stick for saying so and he ran away from home. He rejected Catholicism and ended up at missionary school, at the famous St Chrischona

College. There Samuel Gobat came and selected him for service in Ethiopia.

He travelled to Ethiopia with another recruit, Saalmuller. With them too was the German missionary Martin Flad and his new wife, Sister Paulina. As a concession to Tewodros's secular ambitions, they were also accompanied by a man named Schroth and his son. They were gunsmiths. In the last days of 1858 the party set out across the Egyptian desert. A long line of camels stretched behind them – thirty-two, loaded 'mostly with Amharic Bibles and Testaments'.

The journey itself was a great excitement for young Waldmeier. He was interested in seeing Egypt because it was the land of the pharaohs and the children of Israel had lived there in exile. The desert looked like 'a past world burned by the wrath of God', and desert travelling was hard, he warned in his own innocent way, because 'water is scarce'.

It became harder, and hotter. The sperm-candles in their baggage oozed through the crates and onto the flanks of the camels. Everyone but Mrs Flad fell ill, and they camped for days slumped in the heat, in the shadow of mounds of Bibles. When Schroth and his son died, the others could barely drag themselves out to scrape at the sand to bury them. They all believed that they would soon go the same way. But the Lord spared them, and soon they found themselves climbing into the highlands, surrounded by wild roses and fresh water.

At that time, in 1859, John Bell was *liqemekwas,* and greeted them in the royal camp. He in turn presented them to Tewodros. Waldmeier thought the emperor very civil. With great charm he asked about their journey, and expressed regret that Schroth and his son had died on the road.

'It is on account of my sins,' Tewodros told the missionaries, 'that God took these two men away from me.'

Tewodros sent them to Meqdela. It was for their own safety. Theophilus Waldmeier settled easily into his new mountaintop home. He shared a hut with five of the other missionaries, studied Amharic and taught some basic mechanical skills. There were long debates about the Bible with the royal scribe Debtera Zeneb, who in time came to see the true light of the Gospel.

Waldmeier was delighted by the country of his calling. After the rains, he wrote, the entire land turned into 'a beautiful flower garden'. The people were 'nice-looking' and 'clever in everything when taught'. Like Plowden before him, he dreamed of Ethiopia's development, of its prospects if it could 'only have good government, and its own old sea-port of Massowah'. He believed too in Tewodros's good intentions. 'Where is another king to be found, who in spite of his power and greatness in self-denial disdains all comforts, luxury and good living – he lives very poorly, while he rewards and gives royally – who in living trust in God's help lays before his feet heathen and wild nations?'

In turn, Waldmeier came to the attention of Tewodros early on by repairing some of his great store of broken muskets.

By December, Waldmeier had even married into his family. Among the community on top of Meqdela was Tewodros's cousin Wurqnesh, the wife of John Bell. Waldmeier married their eldest daughter, Sarah (Saalmuller later married her sister). For the wedding Tewodros sent Waldmeier an ornamental saddle embroidered with gold thread, a silk shirt of rank, eighty oxen and five hundred sheep. The feast continued for a whole week.

But Waldmeier felt Meqdela was too isolated for their evangelical work. He told his father-in-law, John Bell, that they needed to establish a mission. Tewodros gave them Gefat, a small hill a little to the north of his capital at Debre Tabor. Plowden had lived here for a while. It was a beautiful place. Accounts of the early days at Gefat, with the young families clearing brush to build lodgings and huts, opening a school for children of the poor, shine with a pioneer zeal.

In time Gefat became a great centre of technical skills. The missionaries built a water wheel. Tewodros sent hundreds of people there for instruction – 'all the clever men of Abyssinia were brought thither by order of the king'. Tewodros himself paid visits more and more frequently. 'I often sat for hours with the king,' wrote Waldmeier, 'engaged in religious conversation and speaking about the welfare of his country and its people.'

Then John Bell was killed and Tewodros's world grew darker. The high-minded conversations became less frequent and the emperor made it clear what he wanted from the missionaries at Gefat. He wanted them to build guns, bigger and bigger guns.

16

Tewodros first tried to build artillery before he became emperor, during a campaign against Ras Ali. He hollowed out a log, coiled wire around the outside and filled it with stone shot. It wasn't a great success. His victories enabled him to capture a few cannon. He received four more from Said Pasha, but other gifts of guns tended to be seized by the Turkish governor at Massawa. Lacking a coastline, Tewodros realised that if he was to have proper artillery, he would have to make it.

In 1861 a man named Monsieur Jaquin arrived in Ethiopia, and word spread that this Frenchman was something of an expert in metal casting. Tewodros sent him an order: Go to the community of Gefat, where Theophilus Waldmeier and the Protestant missionaries will assist you in casting a cannon. In turn he told the missionaries that they must provide Jaquin with all the materials he required. They must organise labour for him and support him in every way in the construction of 'deadly weapons'.

'We could make no objection to this,' wrote the ever-forgiving Waldmeier.

Jaquin arrived and the missionaries recruited hundreds of workers. Some were despatched with mules to the iron mines. Others collected boulders of tufa to be broken and graded.

Within days the walls of a blast furnace began to rise on the small knoll of Gefat. Ox-hides were sewn together to make bellows. Charcoal was burnt, and Jaquin inspected the work with some anxiety. The day came when he decided that it was complete, and a great crowd gathered to watch.

The furnace was lit. The bellows pumped. Blasts of air shot through the clay tuyère. The fire inside flickered, then whooshed into life. Nervously Jaquin stood watching. The fat leather lungs swelled . . . emptied . . . swelled . . . emptied . . . The temperature climbed higher. The ore inside took on a yellowish glow. Still the bellows worked. The heat rose still further, the ore glowed brighter – and then, very slowly, the outer walls of the furnace began to crumble.

'The Frenchman,' observed Waldmeier, 'began to lament and weep; he went half-mad, cried wildly and finally asked the king's permission to leave. After obtaining it he left the land.'

Some time later, Tewodros himself came to Gefat. He summoned the missionaries. He told them they must carry on with the work of Jaquin, and endeavour to forge a large gun.

'Your Majesty,' they said with all due tact, 'we have neither knowledge nor experience in this matter, and are quite ignorant of it, and we are afraid to try what is above our strength.'

'That does not matter,' replied Tewodros. 'If you are my friends, then try. If God allows it to succeed, it will be well; if not, it also will be well.'

They found that no argument could be made against that statement. Before leaving, Tewodros encouraged them by ordering their servants to be imprisoned. Waldmeier and the others came together to discuss the matter. Building guns to terrorise the people was not what Gobat had in mind when he sent them out. But they agreed that the work of the Gefat mission – the school, the informal teaching they dispensed to the hundreds of workers – was of great value. They must obey Tewodros. But how? They prayed for guidance. They debated.

They prayed again. They tried to remember all that Jaquin had talked about. They made several attempts at rebuilding the blast furnace with stronger walls. All failed. They did not know what to do – and also all their servants were locked up. The missionaries agreed that they should go to the emperor and explain to him that they were willing to undertake any work for him, anything – building of roads and bridges, teaching – but not casting metal. It was too difficult.

Tewodros told them to make him a cart.

Mayer set to work. He produced a vehicle hauled by four mules, but the wheels were useless without roads. The farmers found it a great joke, because it had to be taken to pieces to go any distance. Waldmeier spent days fashioning a gunstock for Tewodros, and when he saw its beauty the emperor ordered the release of the missionaries' servants.

But he was no closer to building cannon.

For some years there had been in Ethiopia a Pole named Moritz Hall, a deserter who had fled the tsarist strictures of the army of Nicholas I for the boundless south. By trade he was a caster of bells, and as the Protestants at Gefat struggled even to build the means for casting, Hall performed a small miracle in another part of Tewodros's kingdom. He made a gun. It was strangely bell-shaped, but propped on its side it appeared heavy and robust and warlike.

'When the king saw it,' said Waldmeier, 'he jumped with happiness and thanked God.'

For some time Tewodros felt the same joy every time he looked at the gun, but then, gradually, he became less satisfied. He sent for Hall and told him this one was too small. He wanted a larger one.

'I alone am unable to undertake such a work,' replied Hall, 'but if the Europeans at Gefat help me I hope to be able to oblige Your Majesty.'

'Waldmeier and all the Europeans shall be put at your disposal; consult together and work together in mutual love.'

With the emperor's blessing Hall went to Gefat. When he told the Europeans what they must do, they all became nervous. Many times Tewodros's messenger came to Gefat, and every time they had to tell him there was no progress. Never mind, the emperor told them. Begin again at the beginning, and do each thing with care.

Then another European, an Austrian named Baptist, arrived at the court of Tewodros. He had heard of the emperor's longing for munitions, and said he had managed to make high-quality gunpowder from local components. He produced a small pouch of it and, time and again, when he ignited it the powder exploded in a most beautiful manner.

Tewodros was delighted. He gave the man honey and sheep, and butter and cash, and asked him to prepare a larger batch. But it soon became clear that Baptist was not what he appeared. The powder he had been demonstrating was English powder. He had brought it in from abroad, and now it was finished. When Tewodros again asked him to demonstrate, Baptist really did use local components, and it failed. Even when it was thrown in the fire, nothing happened. Baptist fled. Some time later, the missionaries heard that he'd been accused of murder in Mecca, and executed.

At Gefat, success was no closer for Hall and the missionaries. Whispers reached the ears of Tewodros: these Europeans are liars, they're just deceivers like Baptist. The emperor was shamed in the eyes of his people, and in his shame the missionaries realised their own danger. They gathered together and prayed. One last time, they collected ore and prepared the furnace.

'We made a final despairing attempt,' wrote Waldmeier. 'And behold, for the first time, we were successful.'

At once everything changed. The local people stopped laughing at them. They marvelled at the gun and congratulated them. 'The king,' wrote Waldmeier, 'was pleased beyond all measure with our little piece of metal, kissed it and cried,

"Now I am convinced that it is possible to make everything in Habesh. Now the art has been discovered. God has at last revealed Himself!"'

He arranged a great feast for the missionaries and asked, 'What, save my crown and my kingdom, can I give you?'

'Your Majesty,' replied the missionaries piously, 'we wish for nothing but to remain in constant possession of your love and friendship.'

Tewodros gave them a thousand thalers each, and for a while all sides were happy.

Then the emperor asked for a larger mortar.

Once again the missionaries were afraid. They retired to Gefat and prayed and prayed, and were successful. In response, Tewodros wrote one of the longest and most effusive of all his surviving letters:

> My friends and my children! God, who can do everything, and does it, has not allowed us to be shamed in our work. Many people who hate us in this country as well as abroad, have derided and mocked us, but now they have been disgraced, since God is moved in all things by the prayers of those who believe in Him and he helps them in time of need.
>
> You have opened the eyes of us Abyssinians, whom others have abused as blind donkeys.

(Tewodros himself, for one – 'My country is like a paradise,' he once told Waldmeier, 'only I am sorry to say it is inhabited by donkeys.')

Hard work and perseverance had rewarded the Protestant missionaries:

> Since God said to Adam, 'In the sweat of thy face shalt thou eat bread,' it would be a sin to lie down like a

sluggard and not care about a country like this, which still lies in such disarray.

The letter was clearly written in one of the emperor's more excitable moods – when his imagination raced across the centuries:

Napoleon Bonaparte, the emperor of the French, who defeated other kings with many guns and mortars, at last fell from his high position and died. Although he was a strong ruler, Nikolai, the emperor of the Russians, was defeated by the English, the French and the Turks, and died soon after, without being able to carry out the plans of his heart. Sennacherib of Assyria was proud of his power and relied on himself. In the pride of his heart he abandoned the Lord and died. The pharaoh of Egypt was proud of his power, hardened his heart against God, and perished in the Red Sea. But what more shall I say to thee? You yourselves are learned and well versed in the Bible. 'Do not cut meat for a lion and do not teach a learned man.'

At the same time, Tewodros displayed a touchiness about his own parentage and ancestry – a theme which preyed on him more and more:

Finally, I have to note that people have slandered me, saying that I am not the rightful heir to the throne, but only the son of poor parents. It is possible to prove my ancestry and my right to the throne from Abraham to David and Solomon, from there to Fasil and Fasil to myself.

One day a few months later, the emperor came to Gefat and asked for a demonstration of the guns. The party assembled in front of Saalmuller's house. A carpet was spread out for Tewodros and he tucked his legs under him and took his place. The others gathered to one side and behind him. The most recently-cast mortar was brought out. It was the largest the missionaries had built so far. It was charged and primed. Brother Bender, House Father of the mission, leaned down to fire it. For a moment there was silence. Then the mortar lurched back out of its carriage, and Bender had to leap aside to avoid it. Distant slopes repeated the shot in ever-decreasing reports. Tewodros was silent.

Several more shots were fired. All the while, Tewodros said nothing. The missionaries were apprehensive. His lips were pressed tight together, his brow pressed down over his eyes. He appeared to be in some sort of trance.

But as soon as the last shot had been fired, he put an arm around the shoulder of one of the missionaries' children and began a lively conversation about military strategy, asking about the powers of Europe and their use of cannon. Once again he admired the new gun, telling them all what a fine job they had done and what a beautiful gun it was. But it was too small. Now, according to the will of God, they must build him a bigger one.

IV

Ethiopian shield, silver on buffalo skin, nineteenth century. (Reproduced courtesy of Gail Warden)

17

On 7 October 1862, two and a half years after Plowden's death, Tewodros ordered his ministers to put on their silken *lemds*, their lion's-mane cloaks, their finest *shammas*, and to gather in his salon tent. He himself settled on a silk-covered divan. He placed a double-barrelled gun beside him, and two loaded pistols. The boom of twelve cannon bounced back and forth from the surrounding slopes.

The tent flaps lifted, and the new British consul ducked through them. He was unwell. He asked to sit down. Tewodros sensed at once that here was a different sort of man to Bell and Plowden. Charles Duncan Cameron was a little older than them. For many years he had obeyed his orders as a soldier, then served as consul in the Black Sea port of Poti. For eighteen months, he had delayed his departure from London. Tewodros's late British friends had loved Ethiopia and none other. For Cameron it was another posting, and an uncomfortable one at that.

Tewodros began by explaining exactly what had happened to his predecessors. He listed the details of Plowden's luckless death, and how it had been avenged. He explained that after Bell was killed he had taken five hundred prisoners and had them decapitated in Debarek market. The heads made such a large pile, the chronicler said, that they could only be counted in rows. 'This was done,' explained Tewodros modestly, 'in order to win the friendship of Her Majesty.'

A couple of days later Cameron had another interview. Tewodros's principal concern was 'the Turks' (meaning both Ottomans and Egyptians). In recent years, his good relations with the Egyptians had broken down. Annexing Tigray had also brought him up against the Ottomans of the Red Sea coast. He wanted to attack, to push the Egyptians back from the lowlands of the west, to march on Massawa. Before doing so, he was keen to have the support of the Christian powers of Europe.

Ethiopia, stressed Tewodros, was being encroached upon on all sides by Muslims, and he would do all he could to see off their incursions. 'If not,' he said, 'I will die preventing it!'

All this talk of war and defiance worried poor Cameron: it was 'not the sort of temper I was sent to encourage'. He made the position clear to Tewodros: if you maintain peace, we can invite your envoys to London and ensure their safe passage. But if you fight, it will be impossible.

'Skirmishes?'

'No.'

Cameron returned to his tent. He had done his duty. Diplomacy must follow its proper course.

Over the coming days, he noticed that the food delivered to his tent became worse, and less frequent. When he tried to see Tewodros, it was not convenient. Those charged with looking after him became curt and careless. They began to ask how long he'd be staying. When the requests were made 'hourly', the consul grew impatient: 'I will stay six months if that's what it takes to finish the work I was sent by my government to do.'

Tewodros was furious. 'Leave for the sea at once!' he ordered the consul.

But Cameron knew that Her Majesty's diplomats were not

dismissed like that. He stayed, and his patience was rewarded. When he did leave camp, a month or so later, he carried a letter of friendship to Queen Victoria.

Tewodros did not only write to Great Britain. He told Cameron he wanted to inform 'all Christendom' before making any move against the Egyptians and Turks. He wrote to France, and also possibly to Holland, Germany, Austria and Russia. Only two of these letters survive – though the common ground between these two suggests that they would all have said broadly the same thing. To Queen Victoria: 'The Turks [Egyptians] refused to leave my father's land when I told them to. Therefore, by the power of God, I shall fight [them] now.'

To Napoleon III: 'The Turks [Egyptians], however, resist the will of God, and since they refuse to surrender the land of my fathers, I am going out to fight with them.'

The basis of his appeal for friendship varied a little more. To Napoleon III, he wrote: 'The splendour of your reputation as the emperor of the French and the prince of the Christians has reached us. I rejoiced and desired that, by the Grace of God, bonds of friendship would unite us, that you would look upon me as one of your relatives, and that you would love me.'

To Queen Victoria, he recalled that 'Mr Plowden and Liqemekwas John used to tell me that there is a Christian king, a great man, who loves Christians, with whom they would acquaint me.' (The confusion of Victoria's gender lay more with the scribe than with Tewodros.) He also asked to send embassies. Plowden had always made it clear that, when peace permitted, the two countries could exchange envoys. Peace was still pending. 'Since the Turks deny me passage by sea,' he told Queen Victoria, 'I have been unable to send my envoy with Consul Cameron.'

To Napoleon, he said: 'I wish to send you ambassadors. Please, Your Majesty, let me know if you will indeed receive them.'

Tewodros had made his appeal. He now settled back to wait. The threats from the Egyptians increased, but, placing all his hopes in European support, he kept his forces in camp.

18

Ten months later, Tewodros was sitting in a small recess in one of Gondar's ancient palaces. Around him was the scatter of vellum and parchment, the nap of leather-bound books. Behind him rose a tall, glassless window. Below was the palace compound and the walls, and beyond that the town and the tents of his army and in the distance, streaked by early sun, stretched the plains, green and fertile after the rainy season. It was early on the morning of 28 September 1863, and the wild celebrations of Mesqel, the Feast of the Finding of the True Cross, were over. The great pyres had all burnt down. The city dozed.

Tewodros did not doze. He had summoned the Europeans to a meeting. Out of the half-darkness of the palace interior came Consul Cameron in his blue diplomatic uniform. He had returned, as had Monsieur Bardel, the French envoy. A number of the missionaries were with them – Theophilus Waldmeier and Reverend Henry Stern, who had been trying to convert the Falashas, the Ethiopian Jews. They all arranged themselves at the emperor's feet, on a semi-circle of rugs.

While waiting for a reply to his letters to European capitals, Tewodros had been attacked by the Egyptians. Musa Pasha had looted Metemma, burned Dunkur, marched on Wehni.

Tewodros's hold on the lowlands was destroyed, his native Qwara overrun. He had done nothing. During his visit, Cameron had convinced the emperor that European support was too great a prize to risk with an impulsive attack. Tewodros waited for a reply to the letters.

Yet by June not one response had come back. When Cameron returned to Ethiopia just before the rains, he was empty-handed.

'Your Majesty,' he promised, 'I will give my head if after two months the answer to your letter is not here.'

Tewodros was already angry with Cameron. He had not taken Tewodros's letter himself, but sent it to London by a messenger. He then went off to travel through the eastern Sudan, the very lands that the Egyptians had overrun.

A couple of months later, Tewodros received better news. A response had arrived from the French, and he had now called the Europeans to hear it read out. He turned to M. Bardel and asked him about his mission – Bardel, who at least had had the courtesy to go to Paris.

'Your Majesty, I met with a most uncourteous reception at the court of France.'

'Did they provide you with a house, food and all you required?'

'No, *Jan Hoi*. I got neither a house to dwell in, nor food, nor money to supply my daily wants.'

'What did the emperor tell you when you presented my letter?'

'He dismissed me with the sarcastic sentence, "I will have no direct intercourse with a sovereign who cuts off the hands and feet of his subjects."'

Several things were at once clear to the others listening. Bardel and Tewodros had rehearsed this exchange, Bardel was making it up – he had never had an audience with Napoleon III – and Tewodros was struggling to control an unholy rage.

He told Consul Cameron to read out the letter from the

French. It was not even from Napoleon, but from the Minister of Foreign Affairs, M. Drouyn de Lhuys, dated 23 March 1863. Just as the British government had through Plowden, the French urged Tewodros's protection of Catholic missionaries: 'all those governments worthy of calling themselves civilised have adopted the principle of freedom of belief'.

Like the British too, the French found it necessary to lecture Tewodros on his war plans. 'Before going to war against powerful neighbours, it is as well to take note of their forces, and to guard against losing any advantage already acquired in rushing into such a hazardous undertaking.'

Tewodros had placed great faith in the Christian powers of Europe. This is what came back. The more he saw of Europeans, the more disappointed he was. In their world there seemed no clarity of alliance – Christian and Muslim fought on the same side. Privately the French envoy said one thing to him, the British another; when he asked for their support in defending himself, they said the same thing: don't. He had taken a personal dislike to the two envoys, Bardel and Cameron. 'The Frenchman is a madman, the Englishman an ass,' he was reported as saying. The individuals now sitting at his feet were not, in his eyes, of the calibre of loyal John Bell or Walter Plowden.

He snatched the paper from Cameron's hand. 'Is this an answer to my letter? Napoleon may think himself great, but I am greater still. His genealogy is only of yesterday, mine I trace back to David and Solomon!'

Each of those sitting before the emperor, watching his anger, realised that something had changed. They had come to Ethiopia for their own reasons – duty, vocation, adventure. Many now decided that the time had come to leave. Those who did not looked back to that morning in the old palace at Gondar and remembered the sight of the raging Tewodros, and realised it had been their last chance.

19

Just over ten years had passed since Tewodros rebelled against Ras Ali and began his dazzling march to the throne. He had defeated Ras Ali and his mother Menen and Wube and Goshu and Biru, all the giants of old. The Yejju dynasty was no more, the kingdoms of Wag and Lasta were under his rule, Shoa and Tigray too. With the support of Abune Selama he had rid the Church of hundreds of years of division. He had purged and conquered, and put in place reforms to elevate the ancient kingdom back to its rightful place in God's order.

In 1859, Tewodros had admitted to Plowden that it was all taking a little longer than he'd hoped. 'Providence,' he explained, 'wills that some delay should interpose between my coronation and my perfect success.'

Four years later, he saw things more darkly. 'It is evident I have deceived myself. This is a stiff-necked people, and it is necessary to chastise them before they enjoy the blessings which Providence has intended for them.'

The missionary Henry Stern saw the change in Tewodros as sudden: 'he boldly burst the barriers which had hitherto restrained his impetuous temper, and threw aside the garb of sanctity which had disguised his true character'. Likewise in 1863, the acting French vice-consul Guillaume Lejean watched him rid himself of 'the last scruple which had restrained him on the edge of a terrible brink'.

In truth, the emperor's behaviour had been pretty extreme for several years. With Tewodros, there were always spells of good humour, acts of forgiveness, moments of generosity, gestures that surprised everyone around him with their humility and grace. Yet they were more infrequent, and interspersed with such savage rage that few trusted him any more.

Many put it down to grief. The moderating counsel of Bell and Plowden had gone, though most pointed to his losing the intimacy of Tewabach, his 'good genius'.

In 1860, Tewodros had married again. Tirunesh Wube was the daughter of his former rival Dejazmach Wube – meaning that the daughter of each of his great enemies had become his wife. When Tirunesh produced an heir, Alemayehu, five hundred prisoners were freed in celebration. But the marriage was not a happy one. Tirunesh resented her husband, the upstart conqueror of her father's kingdom. Little is known of their time together, in part because there was not much of it. But a story tells of him walking into her tent, and her failing to rise. 'I am conversing with a greater king than you,' she muttered, continuing to read from the Psalms. Tirunesh – and Abune Selama – were now the only two who dared stand up to Tewodros.

He sent Tirunesh and their son Alemayehu to Meqdela, and took his pick from the women of the camp. 'Since the death of my good queen,' he said, 'I have been leading an unChristian and disreputable life.'

If there was, as Stern and Lejean suggest, a moment that marked Tewodros's decline, it was the first few months of 1863. On 10 February, the emperor rode out of Debre Tabor. He was heading for Gojjam, where Tedla Gwalu, scion of the old ruling family, had recently built up a formidable band of rebels. Tewodros riding at the head of his vast army was still an impressive sight. A traveller's description of him at this time gives a sense of his striking presence:

'The forehead is high, and tends to be prominent. His eye is black, full of fire, quick and piercing. His mouth is perfect, and the smile, which during the conversation continually played upon it, was exceedingly agreeable, I may say fascinating ... His manner was peculiarly pleasant, and even polite, and his general expression, even when his features were at rest, was one of intelligence and benevolence.'

For several days, the army marched south. When they approached the Blue Nile, Tewodros stood in the fort by the old Portuguese bridge and watched his forces pass. Hour after hour they flowed down the rocky slope. With Tewodros was Lejean, who recorded the sight: 'Cavalry, infantry, baggage and followers all descend, or rather roll, like a thick cloud of dust, amidst the glittering of thousands of lances.' Lejean estimated that 40,000 crossed the small bridge. Tewodros, 'that indefatigable marcher', then bounded up the slope. Lejean struggled behind him.

Tewodros's forces met those of Tedla Gwalu in the Injabarra valley. Although the imperial army was triumphant and managed to capture 7,000 of his men, Tedla himself escaped. Tewodros was furious. More bad news reached him – Musa Pasha and an Egyptian army had swept into the lowlands. At the same time he heard that his appointed governor in Shoa had declared the province independent and himself its king. At the height of his power, Tewodros looked around and saw in every direction a precipitous drop. After all his years of struggle, the territory around him was no less full of his enemies, while beyond the boundless highlands, the Europeans in whom he had placed his hopes appeared less keen to support him, a Christian, than the Muslim Egyptians and Turks.

He issued an order – kill every one, kill all 7,000 prisoners.

From then on, dissent mounted in his own ranks. In February he discovered a plot against his life among a number of high-ranking officers. One morning he had them dragged before him, and a hand and a foot were cut from each one: 'all of them died, after suffering agonies more or less prolonged, some few of them being devoured by hyenas'.

A few months later, with his men hungry and mutinous, Tewodros allowed them to plunder, and solved two problems in one. Eat all, he told his forces in the lands of the rebels, eat all! Fourteen provinces were stripped bare.

He never doubted his calling, but he realised now that he had misunderstood what it said. The years of tireless criss-crossing of the country were not intended to stamp out rebellions and establish a beneficent peace. God meant him to punish his people: *'The righteous shall rejoice when he seeth the vengeance; he shall wash his feet in the blood of the wicked. So that a man shall say, Verily* there *is a God that judgeth in the earth.'*

According to Lejean, Tewodros now declared himself 'the Judgement of the Habesh'. As the Gefat mortars rolled towards Gojjam during the *belg* rains of 1863, a motto could be read carved into the sides of the squeaky-wheeled carriages: *The Flail of the Wicked – Tewodros!*

Until now, Tewodros had confined his retribution to his own people. But one day, on campaign against Tedla Gwalu, he lost his temper with Lejean and put him in chains for twenty-four hours. The emperor's suspicion of Lejean was deep-seated – his collusion with the Egyptians, his squabbling with Bardel – but what triggered the outburst was something more basic. Lejean had asked to leave.

20

13 October 1863 was the feast day of Kiddus Giyorgis. Two weeks had passed since Tewodros stood in the half-darkness of the Gondar palace, yelling at the foreigners. The missionary Henry Aaron Stern was one of those who had then decided to quit the country.

He rose early. He said goodbye for the last time to his friend Abune Selama. He felt satisfied that the missions he had established 'would prove centres of light and truth to irradiate far and wide the thick darkness of Abyssinia's superstitious gloom'. Consul Cameron rode with him out of Gondar. At the banks of the River Keha, where Walter Plowden had been fatally wounded as he'd tried to leave, M. Bardel joined them. The three men rode on happily together, 'beguiled by pleasant converse about the future destiny of the country, of whose beauties and capabilities we could judge by the surrounding scenery'.

Stern said farewell to Cameron and Bardel, and hurried on with a couple of retainers. His baggage had gone ahead. The road was filled with Tewodros's xenophobic troops. Stern had to steer his mule through them, and they leered at the missionary as he passed, throwing out 'coarse jests and gibes'. As the road steepened and his progress slowed, so the crowd increased.

Stern felt the press of their number, their hostility. At about noon he reached the wide plain of Wegera. The road stretched far into the distance, northwards towards Tigray and the coast.

On one side of the plain was a collection of tents. Stern was suddenly alarmed. In the middle of them stood the bright white pavilion of Tewodros. He knew that he was obliged to stop.

The emperor and his chiefs were celebrating the feast day of Giyorgis. Stern reached the tents with his companions, and as they watched, a number of men lurched out. They had been drinking. They stood for a moment focusing on Stern. Their abuse was directed at all the Europeans.

'Why do you fight with cannon and musket?' they mocked. 'What is wrong with sword and lance?'

Then the flaps of the pavilion were peeled back and a group of officers ducked out into the light. With them was Tewodros himself. Stern's servants threw themselves to the ground. Stern bowed low.

Tewodros gazed at him without expression. 'What do you want?'

'I saw Your Majesty's tent,' he said, according to his own account, 'and came to offer my humble salutations and respects to Your Majesty.'

'Where are you going?'

'I am, with Your Majesty's sanction, about to proceed to Massawa.'

Tewodros's gaze drilled through him. 'Can you make cannon?'

'No.'

'You lie.'

The emperor turned to the first of those with Stern. 'Are you the servant of this white man?'

'No, Your Majesty, I am in the employ of Consul Cameron, and only accompany him down to Adwa, where I will see my family.'

Something snapped in Tewodros. The calm that he had shown vanished. 'Vile carcass!' he roared. 'How dare you bandy words with your king? Down with the man and *bemote*, beat him till there is not a breath in his worthless body.'

Several men seized him and threw him to the ground. With sticks they mashed his body to a pulp.

'There's another.' Tewodros pointed to another of Stern's men. 'Kill him too.'

He was dragged beside the other's corpse – and without a murmur, he too was beaten to death.

Stern looked on in horror. He turned away, pressing a finger between his teeth, unaware that this was a gesture of revenge in Ethiopia. At once Tewodros rushed at him. He thrust his pistol in the missionary's face. Stern expected to be shot – but the emperor cased the gun. 'Knock him down!' he ordered.

Stern was thrown to the ground and beaten. He lost consciousness. Writing later, he was not shy in pointing to this moment as the real turning point in Tewodros's reign: 'His power began to wane from the very hour that a scarred, lacerated, and bleeding missionary lay insensible at his feet.'

Stern narrowly survived his beating. He was taken back to Gondar. Manacles were hammered into place around his legs and hands. He was close to death, and in the coming days, suffering greatly, found reassurance in the suffering of another: 'At such a period – I say it solemnly – the punctured head, the riven side, the pierced feet, and the heavy cross of Redeeming Love, is a sight that calms the nerves and supports the dropping and despondent spirit.'

21

Stern's capture looked impulsive. Had he not stumbled on Tewodros's camp that morning, had his passing not coincided with the Giyorgis-day *tej*-bout, or had he chosen a slightly different route, he would have escaped Tewodros, ridden out beneath the wide skies of Tigray and reached home.

But in the days to follow, Stern learned the truth. He was due to have been caught and arrested anyway.

Henry Aaron Stern's particular zeal for rescuing lost souls stemmed in part from his having been rescued himself. He had been born to a Jewish family in Hamburg. At nineteen he found a job in London, but the company collapsed and he was left destitute. For months he wandered the streets, hungry and alone. One evening, at the Palestine Place Chapel, his life changed. He was told that the second coming of the Messiah would only come about when the Jews had all accepted the first. He became a Christian. He studied for ordination, and began mission work for the 'London Society of Promoting Christianity among the Jews'. He also took up British citizenship.

In Jerusalem he was intrigued to hear about the 'lost tribe' of Jews in Ethiopia, and early in 1860 headed south along the Nile. The great extent of error in Africa was at once apparent.

In desert towns he saw mixed 'the repulsive vices of Moham-medanism with all the revolting pollutions of Paganism'. The Ethiopians were no better. 'I had from the first day noticed that they were a false, treacherous and insolent race – absurdly superstitious in their religious belief, and revoltingly obscene in their domestic relations.'

He set up a mission not far from Gondar, then returned to Britain to raise funds. There he wrote a book entitled *Wanderings among the Falashas* before coming back in 1862 and resuming his work. Having seen the new severity of Tewodros's anger, he decided that 'the object of my mission was by this time completely attained' – and hot-footed it towards the coast.

Tewodros's resentments were spreading. Everyone was under suspicion. Abune Selama, once an ally in his great project, was now an enemy. Europeans had failed in all they'd promised. They were scheming and duplicitous. Stern had become suspiciously friendly with Abune Selama. His book was found among his papers, and in it Stern had written that Tewodros was the 'son of a *koso*-seller'. Now, the emperor was told by his courtiers, the lie was published in England for all to see.

But the rawest wound had nothing directly to do with Stern. He was British, and Queen Victoria had still failed to answer the emperor's letter. Harder to bear than the scoffings at his origins was the official indifference. In the silence Tewodros imagined the whispering plots of his enemies, the Egyptians and the Turks. Why was it that British subjects moved so easily in and out of their territory?

So Stern lay manacled in a tent. Over the coming weeks he knew only the pale light of his goatskin prison, and his guards – the vengeful ones who hammered his chains so he couldn't stand up or lie straight, and told him he would soon be executed, and the others who treated his wounds and loosened his chains. But in time things began to improve. His wounds healed; it was clear that he would not lose his arm or his hand.

A message even reached him from Tewodros, asking after his health. Good news too came via Consul Cameron: a steamer had docked at Massawa, and on it was what Tewodros wanted – two letters from the British government.

On the morning of 20 November, after more than five weeks in chains, Stern heard the gathering of a distant crowd. At noon, guards stepped into the tent and ordered him up. He stumbled out into the light, blinking. A vast assembly lay before him. Was this the reception of the queen's letter? Was there to be a public reading, as with the French response?

He shuffled along between two rows of people. They watched his progress in silence. The white of their *shammas* dazzled him. Many of them he knew. Not one showed a trace of recognition. In front of him, at the far end, was another line of *timtim*-wrapped priests. In the middle, in the shadow of two vast silk umbrellas, sat Tewodros.

To one side of him, the Europeans were sitting on carpets – Consul Cameron, the Gefat workers and the missionaries. The sun pulsed down on Stern's bare head. He stumbled on across the dirt.

As he came to a halt before the throne he was shocked to see beside him another of the missionaries – Rosenthal – also in chains.

The letters had not arrived. The meeting, the great assembly of the top hierarchy of Tewodros's state, was their own trial.

'You Europeans came into this country,' announced Tewodros, 'and I loved, honoured and respected you, because I thought all Europeans were like my beloved John Bell who always spoke the truth; but you are liars.'

In the piercing midday light, a scribe stepped forward and addressed the crowd. From the pages of the *Fetha Negest*, he read out ten violations of the sacred law. The specific charges laid before Stern were slanders – that he had said that none of Tewodros's counsellors was worthy of the title, that Ethiopian marriage was invisible in the sight of the Lord, that the emperor had plundered several areas, had slaughtered between seven and eight hundred defenceless citizens, that he was in league with the Metropolitan and that, in his book, *Wanderings among the Falashas,* he had ridiculed Tewodros's genealogy. Rosenthal was accused of similar irreverence, suggesting in an intercepted letter that the country would be better off under Egyptian rule.

From the ranks of white-robed clergy, a monologue began. It was a recitation of Tewodros's true bloodline – from David and Solomon, through Menelik and the great Aksumite kings to Zara Yaqob and Lebne Dengel and Susenyos. But when it came to the seventeenth century and Fasilades, the voices lost their unison, and a murmuring dispute began.

Tewodros shouted at them. 'I shall teach you to remember who I am!'

The priests fell silent.

Stern could now make out Tewodros's face in the shadows. With horror he watched its 'tiger gaze' turn on him for the first time.

'If you are not a woman,' the emperor said, 'will you take the choice of weapon – sword, spear, pistol, or even cannon, and fight me?'

'I am a priest,' Stern said, 'and do not fight.'

Stern began his defence. The supposed defamation was merely the malicious distortion of his translators. Likewise, the passage from his book was taken out of context, and if read as a whole, would reveal the high regard in which he held His Majesty.

It fell to Consul Cameron to perform the head juror's task. He was obliged to pronounce the accused guilty. Stern and Rosenthal were sentenced to death. They were led away, back to the tent. For the next few hours they waited for the sentence to be carried out – but no summons came.

22

Two days later, the letters from the British government finally arrived from the coast, and were delivered to Cameron:

> I have received your despatches from no 18 to no 24 of last year and from no 1 to 7 of the present year, and with reference to your no 18 of 31 October last [the one enclosing Tewodros's letter] I have to state that it is not desirable for Her Majesty's Agents to meddle in the affairs of Abyssinia.

That was all. The letter from Tewodros asking for support, asking to send the embassy he had always been promised by Plowden, was not even mentioned directly. Lord Russell also ordered Cameron back to the coast. But Tewodros refused him leave to go: he still had not received a reply from Queen Victoria, and Cameron would stay until he had.

On 4 December 1863 Tewodros ordered the condemned Stern and Rosenthal to attend another trial, this time not their own but that of a group of peasants. They were tried and sentenced, and the punishment was carried out at once. As they were whipped to death with a *giraf*, and their blood splashed on the skin and rags of the missionaries, Tewodros turned to them and snarled: 'Are you afraid now?'

The prisoners' conditions improved a little. Their fetters were removed and they were allowed Bibles. Their guards told them that Tewodros had planned to kill them with the peasants, but had relented. Now he might even release them.

On 3 January 1864 Stern and Rosenthal were again summoned before the emperor. This time it was a Sunday, and the missionaries knew that the *giraf* at least was not swung on the Sabbath. Their guards too were encouraging, hinting that they would soon be freed. They stepped into the tent. The emperor was on his throne with the customary carpets scattered beneath his feet. Cameron and four or five of the other Europeans were sitting to one side. Their expressions were stony.

Stern and Rosenthal took up position beyond them. As they passed the group, a message was hissed to them. It was not what they'd expected: 'We are all prisoners now!'

At that moment they all heard the heavy chink of chains, and the guards began to hammer them onto their legs.

Two things had tipped Tewodros against the Europeans. A priest reached him from Jerusalem with the news that the Copts had driven the Ethiopians from their rightful corner in the Holy Places. The British consul in Jerusalem – long the protector of the Ethiopians – had this time done nothing. Cameron had also again received orders from London to leave Ethiopia. 'On my asking the necessary permission,' wrote Cameron, 'the storm burst on us all.'

Tewodros concluded that the British government cared more for Turkish power than for Ethiopia, and did not even intend to reply to his letter. In both these assumptions, he was right.

Five months later, a pencil-written note reached London. It had been smuggled down to the coast and bore the initials of Consul Cameron. It was headed *Gondar, 14 February 1863* (haste had made him put the wrong year):

Myself, Stern, Rosenthal, Cairnes, Bardel, McKravie, and McKilvie are all chained here. Flad, Staiger, Brandeis, and Cornelius sent to Duffat [Gefat], to work for the King. No release until civil answer to King's letter arrives . . .

V

Tewodros's seal: 'King of Kings Tewodros of Ethiopia. He who is Victorious, Tewodros, king of Abyssinia'. From his letter to Queen Victoria, 29 October 1862, document FO 95/721 no. 126

23

What had become of Tewodros's letter?

It left the emperor's camp in the hands of Consul Cameron. In Adwa it passed from him to a messenger with a note for the British Resident at Aden – 'I can hardly estimate the importance of the Despatches herewith enclosed, or that of the appeal to Great Britain among other countries which accompanies them.' It was taken down to Massawa, and from there sailed by dhow across the Red Sea. In Aden it entered for the first time the labyrinthine world of British imperial administration, following its own narrowing course through a series of sealed leather pouches and sleepy offices, passing before the eyes of dazed and responsible clerks, its passage logged in dozens of marbled registers. From Aden it steamed to Bombay and from Bombay back across the Indian Ocean, up the Red Sea – past Massawa – to Suez and across the desert to Alexandria, by ship to Marseilles and by boat-train up to the Channel coast and England. From the terminus of Victoria it was taken to Whitehall and the Foreign Office itself, a block of four or so townhouses knocked together to form a muddle of sunless corridors, spiral staircases and cramped rooms which served as the administrative hub of a fair slice of the world's territory.

It was closed. One of the residential clerks signed for the letters and sent them up to the Consular Division.

Over the months, Tewodros's original letter had snowballed through the system, picking up as it went a number of Cameron's other recent reports and expense claims. By the time it reached London the whole package amounted to more than a hundred pages of foolscap.

The Permanent Under-Secretary Edmond Hammond, Assistant Under-Secretary James Murray, the Parliamentary Under-Secretary Austen Henry Layard and the Foreign Secretary Lord Russell all considered the despatches from Ethiopia. Their conclusion was the same. The minutes and notes they wrote all suggested that Consul Cameron and his mission were doing no good:

'He seems to me to be far too busy and meddling . . . Our consul seems disposed to meddle a great deal too much . . . we can expect no advantage from meddling with the politics of Abyssinia.' There was only one useful bit of meddling that could be performed by Cameron regarding Ethiopia, and that was to inform them of any risk 'to British interests from French meddling'. And that was the sort of meddling that could be done perfectly well from Massawa. They ordered him back to the coast.

Lord Russell wrote simply 'India Office' on the package, and there it went, on 5 May 1863. Lacking any further instruction, it sat there unread and ignored for a year.

In May 1864, Cameron's desperate pencil-note reached London: *No release until civil answer to King's letter arrives . . .* and Lord Russell asked innocently: 'Are there any letters from the King of Abyssinia unanswered?' He had forgotten.

The letter was at once recovered from the India Office. Now there was a diplomatic crisis. The irritable Murray took the matter in hand. He drafted a reply from the queen to Tewodros, one which he hoped might 'tempt the savage to let our people go':

We do not require from your Majesty the further evidence of your regard for ourselves which you propose to afford by sending a special Embassy to our Court. The distance which separates Abyssinia is great, and the difficulties and delays which would attend the journey of your Ambassadors might be hard to overcome, and much unavailing disappointment and regret might result from any accident which might befall your Ambassadors.

Accounts have, indeed, reached us of late that your Majesty had withdrawn your favour from our servant, and had subjected him and many others in whom we feel an interest to treatment which is inconsistent with your professions . . .

Your Majesty can give no better proof of the sincerity of the sentiments which you profess towards us, nor insure more effectually a continuance of Our friendship and good-will than by dismissing Our servant and any other Europeans who may desire it from your Court . . .

The letter was signed at Balmoral on 24 May 1864 by 'your good friend Victoria R', countersigned by Russell using the Large Signet, and on 16 June despatched with all haste to Egypt. The translation was overseen by another British consul, Frederick Ayrton, and as he looked more closely at the wording, he saw it for what it was – contemptuous, bullying and counterproductive. It made demands which could not be backed up with force (no gunboats could be deployed in the distant highlands); it offered 'friendship' but denied Tewodros an embassy, making it clear that the British wanted nothing to do with them.

Ayrton wrote to Lord Russell, spelling out the risks – over thirteen pages – of sending such a letter: the evaporation of the emperor's last drops of goodwill towards England, the likelihood of his turning to France, the opening up of trade and growth of a French Red Sea steam company with the subsequent loss of access to India. Russell agreed to give whoever delivered the letter to Tewodros full permission to offer him an embassy verbally. This added yet more weight to the task of going up to Tewodros, a task which fell to a young and resourceful Iraqi Christian named Hormuzd Rassam.

If no gunboat could reach Tewodros's territory, at least it could reach Massawa. From there the emperor's spies would relay to him a sense of the military might that lay behind British diplomacy. Unfortunately there were no gunboats available: the Indian Navy had been abolished. A large transport steamer named the *Dalhousie* was found, and five guns swiftly bolted to her decks.

A year and a half had passed since Tewodros's letter passed quietly through Massawa on its way to Aden. Now in late July 1864 came the reply. With its single-envelope cargo, the *Dalhousie* slid into the waters off Massawa, and fired its five-gun salute.

24

After their arrest in January 1864, Cameron and the half-dozen other European prisoners spent several months in the royal camp. They rose at dawn, drank coffee, gathered for Matins and read the Psalms. At midday, they crouched around a basket of *injera* and *wat* served by a woman who had once worked for Plowden. Every movement they made was laboured, accompanied by the slow clank of their chains. Cameron in particular was badly affected, and kept himself apart from the others. Stern conveyed their mood in his own melodramatic way: 'Hope, that greatest blessing of man, almost ceased to irradiate the gloom of our captivity, and, in a state of apathy bordering on reckless indifference, the sun rose and set upon the isolated captives in wild Africa.'

Although their tent was just 'a stone's throw' from the royal suite, they had little direct contact with Tewodros, and were glad of it. But on 12 May 1864, they overheard an argument – a 'Billingsgate scene', according to Cameron – between the emperor and Abune Selama. Tewodros accused the *abun* of telling Stern that his mother was a *koso*-seller, which Stern had then published as fact in his book.

Abune Selama had long ceased to be on good terms with Tewodros. Ten years ago they had established an alliance that each believed would fulfil his own hopes for Ethiopia's Christians. Even by the time of Tewodros's arrest of the *abun* and the patriarch in 1856, their relations had soured. As the emperor's circle of trust narrowed, Selama found himself further outside it. He was a Copt, and it was the Copts who had just driven the Ethiopian monks from the Holy Sepulchre. Selama had also appeared very quick to defend the hated foreign prisoners, and had been very friendly too with Stern.

After the argument Tewodros leapt on his horse and Cameron 'saw him galloping like a madman over the plain'.

That evening the prisoners heard a sudden rattle of spears, and Tewodros and his guard appeared outside their tents. The emperor himself grabbed Stern and yelled, 'Give me the name of the man who reviled my ancestors or I'll rip it from your heart!'

Stern, Rosenthal and Cameron were shoved to the ground. Rosenthal's wife was with them, but not in chains. Shielding their young son Henry, she also fell before managing to slip away. The men were bound with sisal cords around their upper arms, wrists and chests. The cords were tightened until they felt the blood swelling in their fingers.

'Stern!' groaned Cameron, 'we shall soon be in heaven.'

The guards threw cold water at the prisoners. The fibres of the rope contracted, squeezing tighter.

'Stern! Stern! Say what you know!' begged Cameron.

Stern prayed.

Then, just as suddenly, the ropes were removed, and the guards were tending their wounds.

The next evening the same thing happened. This time, by his own account, dizziness overwhelmed Stern, his sight darkened, his mind became 'confused, bewildered, and mad' – and he confessed.

'Yes!' he cried. 'The *abun* often told me that the king was more dreaded, and possessed more power than any of the former sovereigns of Ethiopia, but that his ambition and cruelty had depopulated the country.'

Tewodros himself then left, and they heard nothing more. But for Abune Selama it confirmed his disgrace. He was never actually imprisoned or chained – Tewodros's faith held him back – but nor was he ever again really free.

The Europeans had their hand-chains removed and replaced with manacles. Cameron's were so tight that his legs swelled. After complaining and begging he had the manacles filed off – which took a day of 'the most horrible suffering'.

The rains were approaching. Tewodros moved his camp nearer to Gondar, and there the Europeans spent the next few months. Their shirts had been reduced to rags during May's night of torture, and their tent was ripped; their daily food was a handful of dried peas.

'Naked and starved,' wrote Cameron, 'and almost out of our senses with pain and suffering, we passed a tropical rainy season.'

25

On the evening of 22 July 1864, Hormuzd Rassam rowed ashore from the SS *Dalhousie* and landed at Massawa. The town had first been seized by the Ottomans three hundred years earlier. It slipped out of their control in the eighteenth century, into Egyptian hands, and then back to the Turks in 1850, when Plowden was based there. None of these changes was momentous. Massawa was a slow and torpid place, supported by the trickle of trade from the Ethiopian interior and characterised by one thing above all – its heat.

'Even Aden seemed a paradise compared with Massawa,' grumbled Rassam.

With him as he stepped ashore that evening were the ship's captain, Lieutenant Morland and Dr Henry Blanc. The Turkish *kayim-makam*, Massawa's lieutenant-governor, received them in bed. His gut had been destroyed by years in this Ottoman backwater, but his spirits lifted a little on seeing that there was a doctor with these visitors. Rassam told him they had come to deliver a letter from Queen Victoria to Tewodros.

'I am a friend of the English,' the *kayim-makam* explained gravely, 'and an admirer of the British government, so it is my duty to do everything in my power to prevent you going up into Ethiopia. The king is mad.'

'I am merely fulfilling my orders,' explained Rassam with confidence. 'In any case, Dr Blanc and I hold no particular anxiety for our mission.'

The sickly governor had made his point. He now bowed as best he could. 'As an official of the Sublime Porte, the ally of the British government, I shall be most happy to render you every assistance in my power.'

Hormuzd Rassam understood such Ottoman ambiguities; he too had been born in the sultan's empire. Now in his mid-thirties, he was a Chaldean Christian from the town of Mosul. As a young man he had assisted Austen Henry Layard during the excavation of Nineveh, and proved a brilliant pupil. In 1852, working alone for the British Museum, it was Rassam who discovered the palace and great library of Assurbanipal and the famous lion-hunt bas-reliefs, among the most remarkable finds of the Ancient World. Layard sent Rassam to England for formal education, and he soon became both a Protestant and an anglophile. He made many friends. 'England,' he wrote, 'became a home to me.' His languages earned him the appointment of first assistant secretary to the British Resident at Aden, and it was there that he received the summons to deliver the letter from Queen Victoria to Tewodros. Layard – now Parliamentary Under-Secretary to the Foreign Office – confirmed that Rassam was a 'very faithful intelligent man, thoroughly well acquainted with the Arabs'.

Others opposed his appointment. They worried that he 'lacked pluck', and that a strapping British officer would be much better for the job than an 'Oriental'. Some in the Foreign Office thought Rassam's origins an advantage; if anything should happen to him, his foreign-sounding name might not stir up the same public outcry as that of a native Briton (the others in the three-man team – Dr Blanc and Lieutenant Prideaux – likewise had foreign-sounding names, though they were British citizens). Rassam proved excellent in every way –

patient, resourceful, brave and pragmatic. As the drama unfolded, it was clear how much worse things could have become if another man had been in charge.

After all the delays, Rassam knew it was important to act swiftly. He would write himself to Tewodros, announce his precious cargo, and seek permission to deliver it himself. What he needed was a messenger. The efforts of the ailing Ottoman governor yielded nothing. Making the journey up to Tewodros was not something anyone was keen to do, however much was offered as payment. In the end, Rassam did manage to persuade two Muslim Ethiopians to take his introductory letter to Tewodros, on the condition that there was nothing in it of any offence.

He settled down to wait. Massawa's climate was like a sickness. Dr Blanc kept a constant record of conditions. At night the temperature rarely dipped below 95 degrees Fahrenheit. When Rassam and Blanc developed a heat rash they jumped in the sea to escape. But the sea too was 95 degrees, and it made the rash worse.

The town was haunted by the spirit of former British envoys. The widow of William Coffin arrived to speak to Rassam; since his death some years earlier, she had been left destitute. Then the consulate's landlord demanded his rent arrears, and one day Rassam rode out to Monculu to find Plowden's old home. He had been told it was 'a fine building' where the consul had planted fruit trees and vegetables, and that the water at Monculu was the best for miles around. What Rassam found was a shack. The well was brackish. Thorns tugged at his hair as he pushed through the wilted shrubs. He gazed at the rat-chewed walls of the residence, the beetle-weakened timbers. None of the British representatives to Ethiopia who had been based at Massawa had returned home. William Coffin had died at Massawa of a broken heart, it was said (his son had been tortured to death by Wube). Plowden had been killed at Gondar, and now Cameron was in chains. What were Rassam's own chances?

The three men camped in Plowden's garden. It was cooler than on board the ship. They dug the old well down to bedrock and drew clear water. But the daytime was unbearable. Even in the porch of the residence, with the ground watered, the temperature bottomed out at 103.

Two months passed. No reply to Rassam's letter came from Tewodros. Many in Massawa had lived under the shadow of his rule and believed that even here, in Turkish territory, far from the turbulence of the highlands, every word spoken would find its way back to him. Others were less shy. Markos the Armenian (who had briefly been locked up by Tewodros) scoffed at the mention of his name. 'The fellow who calls himself a king would not fetch a farthing if put up for sale in the Constantinople slave market.'

The French vice-consul told Rassam that Tewodros was not the monster many suggested – the Europeans had simply not shown him due respect. He felt sure that Tewodros would release the prisoners once he saw the letter from Queen Victoria. The powerful local ruler Naib Mohammad Abd al-Rahim was another admirer. Tewodros, he said, was naturally kind, but his better instincts were swamped by the blood-lust of his people.

'Of course,' smiled the Naib, who had himself spent forty-one days as Tewodros's prisoner the previous year, 'he is also insane.'

Some told Rassam that Tewodros was losing power to the rebels. Others believed he was invincible.

'Master,' stressed Rassam's fourteen-year-old Tigrayan cook, 'rest assured that he only has to move against them and they will be scattered to the winds.' (This boy, Desta Giyorgis, was a brilliant linguist, and Rassam kept him for some years as an interpreter.)

Monsignor Bianchari, self-appointed Bishop of Eastern Abyssinia, had been forced to give up his inland residence and its 'delightful climate' when he heard Tewodros was about to seize him. Rassam found him in a most agitated state. When speaking of the emperor he sat pummelling his fists together: 'If I had the power I would pound the despot to atoms.' The prelate died a few weeks later from heart disease.

A large group of Banian merchants made a special visit to Rassam to assure him that Tewodros was a vicious man. Khoja Bedros, a long-term resident of Massawa, came and said the Banian merchants could not be trusted. 'Do not believe what you are told in Massawa,' he warned Rassam.

Another hissed the name of the emperor. 'Let me tell you about Tewodros,' said Hajji Adam Korman, once Ethiopia's leading trader. 'Let me tell you. I was married to one of the country's most beautiful women, now I'm an exile. The *negus* took my money. He took my wife. He converted her to Christianity and elevated her to the first among his hundred concubines.

'Tewodros,' he warned the British envoy, 'is the scourge of humanity ... the arch-enemy of humankind.' (In fact, Hajji Adam had been smuggling arms to the rebels; Tewodros confiscated all his goods, and put his wife to work in his kitchens.)

In October, the temperature in Massawa eased a little ('Oct 16 *sunrise – 83; 9am – 91; 2pm – 98*'). Rassam, Blanc and Prideaux had been there nearly three months, and still had had no word from Tewodros. Rassam wrote a second letter, reminding Tewodros that his longed-for reply from Queen Victoria was waiting for him in Massawa.

'I beg you to honour me with an answer soon ...'

26

When Stern and Rosenthal were sentenced to death, Tewodros had received a petitioner. Theophilus Waldmeier knelt before him. In tears he begged for leniency towards his two fellow missionaries. Tewodros 'looked fixedly' at Waldmeier, took his hand and said: 'Do not be afraid, my friend, my child. For your sake, and Mr Bell's, I will not kill them.'

The friendship that had grown up between Tewodros and Waldmeier was both touching and improbable. Somewhere in the clouds of Tewodros's anger remained an idealism, a simple faith that the Swiss missionary, almost alone now, was able to glimpse. The emperor, meanwhile, surrounded by sycophants and two-faced foreigners, responded to Waldmeier's open-hearted honesty.

'You are true,' Tewodros told him, 'and I love you.'

Some years earlier, Tewodros had sent Waldmeier a present. It was forbidden for anyone but the emperor to own a lion, so Waldmeier was doubly surprised when a soldier arrived at Gefat with a small lion cub cradled in his arms. Waldmeier fed him milk. In time he grew bigger, and as he grew, so did his appetite. He wanted flesh. Soon a whole sheep was required each day, provided by Tewodros himself. Waldmeier and his wife Sarah named the lion 'Hagos', meaning 'happiness' in

Tigrigna. On the small hill of Gefat they kept him on a chain but often 'gave him liberty to run about'. Their daughter Rosa loved to ride on his back.

'But I was obliged,' wrote her father, 'to be at her side to hold her with my right hand, while I led him with the left.'

Waldmeier wrote that Hagos was 'a beautiful, fine animal'. With an unconscious glance to Tewodros, he added that he was 'really a kingly lion' with a roar 'so powerful he made the air tremble'. Only one thing made Hagos angry: he hated being watched while he ate.

After the rains of 1864, the European prisoners were brought to Debre Tabor, within an hour's walk of Gefat. They hoped for support from Waldmeier and the community.

Little came. The prisoners smelt of death and the contempt of Tewodros. Waldmeier and the others did what they could: they sent potatoes and bread and milk, and a short note which confirmed the prisoners' fears. When Tewodros visited them at Gefat, they reported, he would not even suffer a mention of them.

The prisoners remained in their tents, chained and fearful. Their fate depended on events far beyond their control – a chance remark, a drinking session in Tewodros's tent, or the letter now waiting in Massawa. On 5 November, they heard that Tewodros was sending Kentiba Haylu, former governor of Gondar and one of the emperor's most loyal ministers, to escort them to Gefat. There they would be granted their freedom. Their chains were removed and they waited for the *kentiba*'s arrival.

But the next visitor to their tent told them Tewodros had changed his mind. He had heard rumours: a British general and his troops had landed at Massawa; another European force was reported at Sennar. Then they heard the name Meqdela.

'My whole frame,' wrote Stern, 'shuddered at the idea of a deportation in chains to that very rock.'

Just before they left, Theophilus Waldmeier rode over to

see them. He was forbidden to enter the compound. They were not able to speak. Stern watched him beyond the brush fence gripping his horse's reins. The animal was skittish beneath him, stepping back and forth and conjuring up for Stern 'visions of freedom and liberty, that made the irons burn like fire around the wrists'.

The European prisoners now numbered more than a dozen, plus two of their wives and four children. They all joined a convoy of other prisoners on the road to Meqdela – rebel chiefs, disgraced officials, murderers and thieves. Tewodros and his people came with them. For seven days they tramped east across the plains, dropped through tumbling gorges, climbed up from the rubble-bed of Wurq-Waha to the slopes of the mountain itself. On the first night there, the Europeans slept out, while the two hundred other prisoners were pushed into a hut. It took three days for the resident blacksmiths to hammer chains onto the new batch of prisoners.

Cameron, Stern and Rosenthal were considered among the most dangerous of all the prisoners, but were spared the cramped prison and given huts close to the royal compound. The flat of the *amba* stretched to cliffs a few hundred yards to the south. Just twenty yards behind the foreigners' huts were more cliffs, dropping sheer to the distant plain. The entrance to the *amba*, a series of rock-cut steps leading down to the main gatehouse, lay some fifty yards to the west. Their guards warned:

'The *negus* charges us to guard your persons, and not to watch over your health and comfort. If you die we shall not be blamed, but if you escape, we lose our heads.'

Could they not see, puffed the indignant Stern, that their prisoners had no wings to fly out of the *amba*, nor claws to climb over perpendicular precipices?

27

For the remainder of 1864, and into 1865, Rassam, Blanc and Prideaux sat waiting on the coast. The heat became 'so intense at times that we could hardly breathe'. Now there was famine too: drought and locusts had kept the highland traders away, and the market stalls were empty. People stripped the meat from cattle and camels as they fell, then boiled the hide and bones. On the shoreline, crowds scavenged in the shallows for shellfish. Many died from eating them. A number of those who left for the *haj* did not return; cholera was reported in Mecca.

Massawa, moaned its ailing Turkish governor, was a place fit only for monkeys and hyenas, and 'would eventually serve as an appropriate suburb of Gehenna'.

Rassam had had no reply to his first letter to Tewodros in July 1864, and no reply to his second in October. He had written a third time in March 1865, expressing 'great anxiety' that there had been no response. Might His Majesty not have received the first two letters? (Rassam had confirmation that he had received at least one of them.) Might he be suspicious of the real motives of his mission? 'I can confidently assure you that the British Government takes a sincere interest in the welfare of your empire.' Rassam made it clear that his time was not unlimited. 'If your Majesty will not honour me with an answer soon, I shall be obliged to return to my duties at Aden.'

Dr Blanc left such dealings to Rassam. He and Lieutenant Prideaux were there because a doctor, a soldier and a diplomat were considered the bare minimum for such a mission. Blanc filled his days with science. He took regular meteorological measurements and in Massawa's markets and back alleys uncovered an exotic sub-culture of growths, ailments and infections. Scurvy was less common than he'd expected, fevers only a problem after the very rare rains. Venereal disease was rife in the garrison. Smallpox broke out brutally and suddenly and, obtaining vaccine lymph, Blanc managed to inoculate against it, but it didn't take 'owing, I suppose, to the extreme heat'. Childbirth was the biggest killer.

In the meantime, Rassam heard direct from the hostages. They had managed to smuggle letters out of Meqdela. Cameron said he had consulted with the other prisoners, particularly the Flads and the Rosenthals, 'who have not only their own lives, but those of their children at stake' – and they were unanimous. Only military action, they thought, would make Tewodros act. 'For God's sake,' Cameron concluded, 'do not come up here, he will cage you sure as a gun.'

For Rassam, doubts were now added to the anxiety of endless waiting. He was not short of advice. Hajji Adam told him: 'You should have listened to me. You have made the mistake of treating Tewodros as a human being. If you handle him like the donkey he is – with a stick – he will act.'

The Naib told him that he had once sent two very important letters up to Tewodros, and received no reply; only when he sent a third, on some trivial matter, did an answer come. He is fickle, said the Naib, like a spoilt child.

The whole mission was in limbo. The weeks passed. It was now the hottest time of the year again. Another batch of letters arrived from the captives, 'very desponding in tone'. The three men went on an excursion inland from Massawa to escape the heat, but found it even hotter. They pushed on further, crossing salt plains to the hills, where they found some relief. On 8 August, returning to the coast, they were sitting in their tent with heads wrapped in wet towels (Dr Blanc had explained the danger of their brains overheating). Suddenly they heard a voice outside crying, '*El-Basharah! El-Basharah!* Good news!' Pulling up the flaps, they saw one of the nephews of the Naib climbing down from his camel. 'Good news!'

Emperor Tewodros had written.

28

For some years now, Tewodros had been losing what he had once gained with such ease: regions, generals, soldiers, allies and support. Now he lost a campaign. Shortly before the rains of 1865 he returned from the south, back from dealing with the rebellion of Bezzabih, his own appointed governor in Shoa. He had been beaten. His soldiers hung their heads in defeat, beset by hunger and exhaustion. They could not return to Gondar, as it had fallen to the rebel Tiso Gobeze. They could not face entering Debre Tabor.

Tewodros led them to Meqdela. The mountain was his chosen asylum, his treasury and his dungeon. 'Half the aristocracy of Abyssinia is here,' wrote Cameron. A year earlier Tewodros had emptied Zur Amba of its political prisoners, and brought them to the mountaintop with the Europeans. They joined looted treasures from a hundred churches, synaxaria, hagiographies, patristic tomes, copies of the *Kebre Negest*. The emperor's wife Tirunesh was here, and Alemayehu, their infant son. In semi-captivity on Meqdela were the wives of prisoners, also the *abun* and the last Solomonic ruler, Emperor Yohannis III, Yohannis the Fool. Tewodros had also collected several heirs to regional kingdoms, including the Oromo prince Ahmed. He was currently negotiating with Ahmed's mother, the local Oromo queen Wurqit, whose men had, according to Cameron, 'been cutting off the arms of the King's soldiers and hanging them about their necks'.

Also on Meqdela was the Shoan heir, Menelik. When he first captured the kingdom of Shoa ten years earlier, Tewodros had brought back the eleven-year-old Menelik and raised him with Meshesha, his own son by an earlier marriage. He'd shown them both the same affection. Menelik himself said that Tewodros was like a second father to him, and on Meqdela he had married Tewodros's own daughter, Altash. But with Bezzabih's victory over Tewodros, Menelik grew restless. When he heard that Bezzabih had declared himself king of Shoa, he felt forced to act. On the night of 30 June 1865 he gathered his mother and other Shoans – but not Altash – and slipped away from the mountain.

In the morning Tewodros stood on the edge of the cliff and watched the progress of Menelik's party through a telescope. He saw them arrive in the camp of Queen Wurqit. He pressed the telescope shut, locking each section into the next with a metallic click. 'Wurqit has found a son who is free,' he said. 'She can dispense with the one who is chained.'

Mounting his horse Koutama, he rode across the flat summit to the prison.

He called for the son of the Oromo queen: 'Where is Ahmed?'

'Here, Your Majesty,' called the boy warmly.

Neither affection nor pity was in the soul of Tewodros that morning. He sent Ahmed and a couple of dozen Oromo chiefs to the edge of the Meqdela cliffs. There they were slashed with swords, their feet cut off to save the chains. The men were then tossed over the cliff, and rocks hurled down on their broken bodies.

Later, when Tewodros saw the *abun* sitting outside his hut, he cried out, 'Why did you not come and absolve me?'

'I saw your face stained with blood.'

In fury, Tewodros rode up and thrust his spear at the prelate.

The *abun* yanked his headdress from where it covered his neck. 'Kill me, then!'

Tewodros let his spear drop. As he rode away, he told those with him, 'If he wants to die, let him live!'

At about this time, with Meqdela's community reeling from the horror of the massacre, two merchants arrived from the coast. One was Welde Selassie Gobeze. Tewodros had asked him to go and meet the English envoy, Hormuzd Rassam, and take the measure of him.

'He is a good man,' Gobeze now told the emperor, and went on to give such a glowing report that his companion scoffed: '*Wai, wai*, Welde Selassie, you have been bribed by the *farenjis*!'

Welde Selassie turned and struck his companion – and Tewodros laughed.

Until then, he had 'not the slightest intention' of allowing Rassam up to Meqdela. But the favourable account of the envoy, shock at the loss of Shoa, and the wrench of Menelik's desertion all helped persuade him to move the hostage question forward. Tewodros summoned his two scribes.

29

Rassam read the Arabic version of Tewodros's letter a month later. It was the first glimpse of the man who, even at such a distance, was beginning to control his life. The letter came unsigned, and without the royal seal:

> Why I do not write my name to you is that Abune Selama, the Falasha called Kokeb [in Amharic *kokeb* is, as *Stern* is in German, the word for 'star'] and Cameron whom you appointed and sent as consul, insulted me when by the power of God I had settled them in a friendly way in my own city, because I wanted the friendship of the queen of England. When the Englishman called Plowden and John [Bell] were attacked in my country and when I avenged their blood, by the power of God, they insulted me for this, calling me a murderer.

The letter continued with Tewodros's grievances against Cameron, how when he had been sent off 'to make me the friend of the queen, he came back after staying some time with the Turks', then came again without a reply. Tewodros had not at the time reacted to the hurt he felt. 'Wondering what I had done that they should dislike me, by the power of my Lord, I kept quiet.'

He ended the letter not so much with an invitation as advice on how to reach him:

> Since rebels have risen in Tigray, by the power of God, make a detour and come round by Metemma. When you reach Metemma, inform me and by the power of God, I shall send people to receive you.

Rassam was confused. Should he go up? Cameron had advised him strongly not to – and he felt 'intense chagrin' at the absence of a seal and signature. Tewodros's attitude also appeared 'neither courteous nor becoming'. But the messengers told him that Cameron was free (which was not in fact true). Having waited for a year to try to resolve the crisis, Rassam wanted to see it through. Seeking guidance from London, he settled back to wait.

One evening he was out rowing in the *Dalhousie*'s gig. He watched the sun darken over the town of Massawa, and disappear behind a great curtain of dust. He hurried to the nearest shore and took shelter beneath the boat. The sand scoured the gunwales as it dashed before the wind, out of the desert and over the bay. Only after dark was he able to come out. Then he saw lightning 'so constant and vivid that night seemed turned into day'. In over a year, wrote Rassam, 'it was the first strong wind we had experienced from that quarter' – the direction of the Ethiopian highlands. When he returned to the island, the gig's bottom-boards were covered in fish.

A few days later he received bad news. The British government, giving in to the murmuring doubts about himself, had appointed another man to go and visit Tewodros – an Englishman, William Palgrave. Rassam went to Egypt. From Suez he took the train to Alexandria, stayed in the comfort of the Hôtel d'Europe and, by means of the new submarine telegraph, communicated daily with the Foreign Office. Telegraph messages bounced back and forth between Alexandria and London, with such speed that all doubts and misunderstandings evaporated. Palgrave was recalled, and Rassam went shopping in the *suq*. He bought presents for Tewodros.

Within a couple of weeks, at twilight on the evening of 19 September, Rassam was leaning on the rail of the SS *Victoria*, heading south for Massawa again. He had clear instructions from London. He had the right permissions from Cairo, and boxes of gifts. Below him, the steel bows of the ship split the waters of the Red Sea with imperial confidence. Rassam was in buoyant mood. The weather was good, and the wind was behind him. It was 'a happy omen, as I then hoped, that the tide of Abyssinian affairs had turned in our favour, and that henceforward it would all be plain sailing'.

VI

Hormuzd Rassam (City & County of Swansea: Swansea Museum Collection)

30

On the afternoon of 15 October 1865, as cholera picked off its victims with ever greater speed, the British mission left Massawa for the court of Tewodros. To avoid the rebel-held regions of Tigray, they headed north-west, towards the Sudan, following a great arc through the lowlands. With Rassam, Dr Blanc and Lieutenant Prideaux was a guard of Turkish irregulars, a clutch of Portuguese and Indian servants, a nephew of the Naib, and sixty camels laden with stores and gifts.

Having exhausted his analysis in Massawa, Dr Blanc now found the temperature varying again, and new climates meant new patterns of disease. Prideaux, the mission's military man, was content to be on the march at last.

They passed through a region desiccated by years of drought. Locusts had stripped the surviving scrub of any greenness. The camels started to stumble and wheeze; the weakest were unloaded and left for the hyenas. Kasala was practically deserted. Local troops had recently risen against their officers, 2,000 had been killed in retribution and the remainder lay dying from disease in the town's jails. The town, wrote an animated Dr Blanc, was 'haunted by its few remaining ghost-like and plague-stricken citizens'.

For a month they trudged on through the sand. They saw hardly a soul – neither ill nor healthy.

'Extremely dreary and fatiguing,' recalled Dr Blanc.

'Too few features of general interest to be dwelt on,' wrote Prideaux.

Towards the end of November they reached Metemma. Tewodros was now just a few days' march away and, as instructed, Rassam at once sent him a letter.

A week passed.

A German in the town, who had just been with Tewodros, encouraged them: he thought that delivery of Queen Victoria's letter would see the release of the prisoners. They continued to wait. Dr Blanc found plenty to do: chronic diarrhoea (castor oil, followed by opium and tannic acid); dysentery (ipecac-uanha, followed by astringents); 'large-cake-like spleens' (locally applied tincture of iodine). He was curious too about the prevalence of ophthalmic complaints, skin diseases and glandular swellings.

Lieutenant Prideaux looked at the physique of the men and found them 'fine, powerful fellows with well-knit limbs and excellent horsemen'.

Rassam, though, thought them a 'lazy, indolent race', as they refused to take messages back to Massawa for him.

The local sheikh returned from visiting Tewodros and sent the town into a wild frenzy. He embraced Rassam 'almost too affectionately' and cried, 'Tewodros is a great man, yes, a great man,' and 'good-hearted'. Then he went off to get drunk.

A letter was discreetly pressed into Rassam's hand. It had been smuggled from Meqdela, and was from Consul Cameron, who presented a more measured picture. A new urgency had gripped the prisoners. The European community at Gefat thought that if Rassam did not come at once, it would mean the end for the foreigners on Meqdela, then the end for the foreigners at Gefat. The Meqdela prisoners were still bound hand and foot, movement was crippling, though Tewodros had sent them each a cow, which was a good sign.

Another three weeks passed.

'I now began to fear,' said Rassam, 'that Theodore intended to keep me waiting at Metamma as he had done at Massowah.' Christmas was terrible in such an 'outlandish and pestilential place'. Missing his adopted England, Rassam lamented that 'the necessary ingredients for a plum pudding were not procurable'. His Indian servants did though manage to make some mince-pies.

On Boxing Day, a letter came from Tewodros, in Arabic:

To the beloved and noble Huruz Risam. After greeting you and inquiring after the soundness of your health – we are, a thousand times praise be to God, well to the extent of the summit of health and well-being – what we inform Your Excellency is that your letter, dated 22 November, has reached us; we understand it word by word and we thanked the Creator for your friendship.

Despite its effusive greetings, this letter proved to be another vent for Tewodros's bitterness. As he held it and reread it, Rassam grew nervous. Once again, at its foot, was no signature and no seal:

And now, O beloved, as we have explained to you this letter is without our name as it has been withdrawn from such people as those whom I used to love, and who were permitted to sit on my divan every day, but who reviled me.

The day after writing this letter, Tewodros had had a change of heart.

'How can I continue to treat Rassam so badly,' the emperor had addressed his court, 'after his anxious efforts to cultivate my friendship? Call the scribe . . .' He had then dictated a second letter:

While those wicked people have reviled me, what evil have you, O beloved, done to us?

The two letters arrived together, and Rassam saw that on this one, looking out at him from beneath his cross-topped crown, was the stamped emblem of Tewodros's rule, a paw-raised, high-tailed, rather chubby-looking lion.

For the first time, Rassam had felt the bump and rise of Tewodros's seesaw diplomacy.

A couple of weeks later, the mission stood before a vast and shadowy cliff. They had reached the edge of the Ethiopian plateau. They began to climb. Frequently they were forced off their mules to scramble up the cliff. At the summit, they paused for breath.

'We congratulated ourselves,' wrote Blanc, 'as much upon having at last reached the land of promise as for not tumbling into the fearful chasm below.'

The weight of his task was briefly lifted from Rassam's shoulders. He looked around him in wonder. 'Such an extraordinary prospect ... I had never witnessed. Before me, extending nearly a hundred miles towards the north and west, were ridges of lofty mountains, with deep ravines of varying slopes and hues, here seeming to run parallel with each other; there to cross each other's lines.'

Lieutenant Prideaux made no mention either of the climb or of reaching the top.

The three men carried on towards the shores of Lake Tana and the royal camp. In each district they were joined by more and more baggage-carriers. Soon, as well as their own escort of some two hundred, another twelve hundred followed them. 'It was quite ludicrous,' wrote Rassam, 'to see a couple of powerful men supporting a small chair between them; others again made a load of a stick, two or three tent pegs, or a mallet.' News of the convoy spread far before it, driven above all by one thing: among the *farenjis* was a doctor.

31

On Meqdela, the days crept past the prisoners. The rains of 1865 were late; even in the middle weeks of July little had fallen. But by September dozens of tiny flowers speckled Meqdela's flat and rocky summit, while far below, crossed by shining strands of water, barley plots and fields of *teff* wheat glowed emerald green in the morning sun. The cliffs which fell away on all sides of the plateau remained as black as ever.

After Menelik's escape in July 1865, Tewodros had given new orders for the European prisoners: a clasp must be added to their right wrists, with an eight-inch chain linking it to the ankle fetters. The ensemble weighed twenty pounds. Walking was only possible as a crouching shuffle. Unable to straighten up, Stern and Cameron developed severe spinal pains. Their lives, wrote Stern, 'became more burdensome and afflictive'.

But they were at least allowed their own huts, and one or two servants. For the Ethiopian prisoners, crammed together in a number of buildings on the eastern side of the *amba*, conditions were terrible. From time to time, at Tewodros's whim, one or two would be pulled out and executed. Disease accounted for many more.

After the rains, Tewodros took his forces away to deal with the little rebellions that sprouted up like the season's flowers.

With him went a good deal of the fear that had hovered over the *amba* since his massacre of the Oromo prisoners.

By this time the Europeans knew that Tewodros had invited Rassam up to deliver the queen's letter. Their feelings were mixed; in part they clutched at the slim hope that this news gave them, but they were also uneasy about more foreigners arriving to lay themselves open to the emperor's anger. They spent their days stumbling around the compound of their huts, glimpsing the distant ridges and the sky beyond. Among them only Mrs Rosenthal in her long grey skirts, and her three-year-old son Henry, moved freely. They had followed the others through all the stages of their twenty-month detention – the arrest, the torture, the trial, the journeys with the shifting city of the royal camp, and now their imprisonment on the high, cramped summit of Meqdela. The Rosenthals had arrived in Ethiopia as missionaries in 1862. For much of the journey from England Mrs Rosenthal had been pregnant, and Henry was born shortly before his father was arrested. With his own wife and children back in London, Stern turned the full sentimental force of his pen on the child: 'The tender creature just began to be conscious of a mother's loving smile, when, driven from house and home, he had to feed on tears, and to repose on a bosom often, very often, throbbing with the anguish of a breaking heart.'

According to his father, Henry Rosenthal's brief, troubled life had left its mark on his development. Compared to others his age he was 'not so forward in body, nor speaking'. Two months earlier he had become dangerously ill. In his chains, Rosenthal sat up every night with his wife and son 'in constant apprehension lest our little darling should not see another daylight'. When the boy recovered, Stern knew who was responsible: 'the great physician has cured him without scientific men'. He watched Henry regain his strength: 'Like a bird released from a cruel cage, he was always in motion, running, unhindered by guards.' The younger Ethiopian prisoners played with him, teaching him to plait grass or to knot rags into a ball to chase across the open ground. Other members of Meqdela's strange shipwrecked community, those neither free nor strictly prisoners, encouraged him to come to their quarters. Ras Ali's mother, Empress Menen – once Tewodros's greatest adversary – received the boy. Abune Selama let him examine his glittering crosses and colourful vestments, of which he had a great many.

By day, most of the hundreds of prisoners were allowed to hobble around the mountaintop. But at night they were counted back into huts in which there was scarcely room to lie down. Sooty webs hung from the thatch; spiders dropped from them. Rats converged on the huts to scavenge among the closely-packed bodies. Every week or so there was a brief burial.

The European prisoners earned a good deal of favour and privilege by treating the mountain's sick. Between them there was not a hint of qualification, but they did have a good supply of pharmaceuticals, and a medical book. According to Stern they cured some three hundred cases of eye disease. Stern himself developed his own brand of tablet blending colocynth and tartar emetic, and made even more appealing by the addition of opium. His partner was a young Irishman named Laurence Kerans who had, Stern claimed in his defence, 'imbibed a profound knowledge of the pill-manipulating process beneath the parental roof'. Kerans's father was a famous surgeon from Co Galway who some years earlier had allowed young Laurence a spell of character-building travel. He had arrived in Ethiopia as a messenger, delivering from Massawa the unfortunate letter from Lord Russell to Cameron in November 1863. Kerans also brought Tewodros a carpet. The gift had been selected to appeal to the emperor, showing a picture of the celebrated French hunter Jules Gerard about to kill a lion. Tewodros understood it rather differently. What the foreigner meant, he realised, was that he was the victim, the lion, about to be conquered by the Egyptians. As a result of this insult, Kerans was chained with the others. In July 1865, from Meqdela, he had written a wonderful piece of filial correspondence:

> Now dear father and mother, you must be very anxious to know how I'm getting on. To begin with I am now a year and six months in prison, in chains of about 20lbs weight on the legs and now the right hand is attached to the feet. You cannot imagine what fearful sufferings I have to go through every day; it has been much worse before than it is now, but still it is torment . . . I was glad to hear that Tom has got his lieutenancy.

Cameron now watched Kerans at work on his Meqdela patients, amazed by the zeal with which he took to surgery: 'Arrah! By St Patrick, but he shows the family talent still in drawing teeth and cutting up tumours like oranges.'

But none of the Europeans or their pills could do anything about the smallpox that reached the mountain that autumn. In the prison it proved impossible to contain, and the cries of the dying filled the night. In time the epidemic passed and the weeks continued in their spirit-numbing way. Stern hobbled around outside his hut, dispensing drugs, while Kerans, with his chains ringing as he worked, tugged and cut at his patients. Young Henry Rosenthal was their envoy to the partially free world beyond the compound, ranging further, skipping and ball-chasing across the summit, welcomed in every hut. One day Abune Selama was watching him play in the dust, and said: 'This child bears the impress of heaven, and will not continue long upon this earth.'

Not long after, with his father and the others finishing their prayers, Henry suddenly stood still, struggling for breath. He cried out. Just a few days later, with their free left hands, the missionaries scooped out a yard of soil and buried him.

It was at about that time that a single word began to be

uttered among the warders and visitors. Driven by the ceaseless anxieties for their health, it spread through the mountain's entire bunched-up community. '*Hakim! Hakim!*'

Far to the west, from the direction of Sudan, a doctor had arrived in Ethiopia, and news of his cures had spread from village to village, from valley to valley, even to the slopes of Meqdela.

32

What started as a trickle became a stream. 'I had no more privacy,' wrote Dr Blanc. 'I had no rest.'

As the three envoys hurried through the highlands towards their appointment with Tewodros, Dr Blanc found himself in demand. He had begun by seeking out cases – now they sought him. Many were treatable swiftly – the skin complaints, the eye infections. There were other patients, though, whom he could not cure, and they stayed, hopeful that the English doctor would eventually work his magic. *'Abet, abet! Hakim!'* they called, hobbling after the mission as it pressed first eastwards, then south down the western shores of Lake Tana. Each day more joined them, the abandoned, the crippled and the tumoured, the cases of advanced syphilis and epilepsy, wretches with ankles swollen by elephantiasis, fingers eaten by leprosy, necks weeping with scrofulous sores or limbs truncated either with the random slashes of battle or the more deliberate mutilations that followed.

Soon Dr Blanc was unable to leave his tent. When he did, the uncured swarmed around him. The Ethiopians in the end placed guards to drive them all away. But soon the guards started sending their own family and friends to see him, and the numbers grew until Blanc's tent was surrounded again.

Then, slowly, the crowds began to subside. With each day's march, Blanc noticed that even the most persistent were falling away. Soon the party found itself on its own. A strange silence settled over the land. The crops grew thinner and the herds scarcer. Moving down the edge of Lake Tana, in the province of Damot, they found everything destroyed, huts abandoned, storehouses emptied and earth blackened by burning.

'Here and there,' recorded Blanc, 'amongst the ruins of former prosperous villages, some half-starved, almost naked peasants were seen erecting small sheds on the ashes of their ancestral huts.'

They were drawing close to Tewodros's camp.

In the last week of January 1866, the British mission and their fourteen hundred porters reached a place where they saw neither beast nor man, where the ash still blew fresh over the torched stumps of dwellings. One afternoon, during the calm after making camp, they made out a faint sound, a 'distant hum', said Blanc, 'such as one hears approaching a large city'. Rassam went on ahead. As he came out on top of a low ridge he saw beyond thousands and thousands of tents. In the middle, a white dot in a sea of black, his guide pointed to the pavilion of Tewodros himself.

33

Eighteen months had now passed since Rassam left his sleepy office in Aden. He was exhausted. He had been worn down by the waiting, by a year of 'vain efforts to reach the most impracticable man that ever swayed a sceptre'. But he knew that the most delicate part of his mission still lay before him. On every detail of his conduct, the slightest misjudged comment, rested not only the success of the mission, but the life of each of the few dozen Europeans in the country.

Plowden had had flautists and generals, Cameron twelve cannon. Tewodros's reception of his third British envoy was even more elaborate. On the morning of 28 January 1866, as he approached the emperor's camp, Rassam felt events taking on a strange pattern, directed by a remote and unseen hand.

First, a messenger arrives early at the British camp, relaying Tewodros's greetings. *How is your health? How is the health of your companions?* Within a couple of hours, two more come, asking the same thing. Officials arrive to escort them to the camp. The road fills with chiefs of staff and officers, each dressed in the silk shirt of rank; each comes up saying, *How is your health? How is the health of your companions?*

Two miles short of the royal camp itself, the foreigners are shown into a tent where they change their clothes. Rassam puts on a blue diplomatic uniform with ceremonial sword; Dr Blanc, as a medical officer of the Indian Service Medical Corps, and Lieutenant Prideaux of the Bombay Staff Corps, each button up their scarlet coats.

As they leave the tent in the midday heat, they see two hills ahead. On one are massed musketmen and spearmen. All are dressed in brightly-fringed *shammas*, their weapons are flashing in the sun. On the other hill is the group of black tents and the white tent of the emperor. Between the hills are two rows of cavalry, several men deep. The horses' heads shine in their silver-plated bridles, their riders carry panelled shields and wear the *bitawa*, the armlet of valour. Rassam and Blanc each estimate the size of the cavalry as 10,000.

Far ahead, between the lines, a group of Ethiopian officers is coming towards them, headed by the prime minister, Ras Ingida and Ato Samuel, the legation's *balderada*, their assigned escort. The two parties approach each other on foot. When they are within speaking distance, they all stop.

Ras Ingida: *His Majesty asks, how is your health? How is the health of your companions, how is it, really?*

Ras Ingida presents Rassam with a mule. It is equipped with a royal saddle and an embroidered cloth. He apologises on behalf of His Majesty that he has not more to offer. Such are the strictures of campaigning.

They reach the hill below the royal tents. Ras Ingida says, 'Please dismount.' He escorts them to a red flannel tent. Inside he shows them to a seat.

Rassam: *We cannot possibly sit while a Minister of State remains standing.*

Ras Ingida (calmly): *By the death of the* negus, *sit down. You are tired and are guests.*

Rassam (sitting): *It is not fatigue that makes us submit, but the honoured* ras's *order.*

Ras Ingida leaves.

Ten cows are brought, ten sheep, food and some jars of very strong mead. The smell alone of the *tej* is drowsy-making. They sip at it. An hour passes, two hours. In the mid-afternoon a letter is delivered, written in both Arabic and Amharic and sealed with the royal seal:

In the name of the Father and of the Son and of the Holy Ghost, one God. Praise be to him forever. Amen.

From the Negashite king of kings, Sultan Tewodros. May this, by the power of God, reach our beloved Hormuzd Rassam today, since you have forwarded a request to us in the interest of friendship.

Shelter and rest should have been imperative, and the talk the next morning. But we have been quartered on the land and it has been eaten bare, waiting for your arrival. The troops are starving; they have become unruly. So the meeting has been ordered for today – and in the morning the journey. And now come to me.

They leave the tent.

Ato Samuel: *Stop!* (points at Rassam's ceremonial sword) *The* negus *receives no foreigner with a weapon.*

Rassam: *My uniform is not complete without it.*

At the top of the hill is a double line of musketeers, and at the far end the entrance to a *durbar* tent.

An officer approaches Rassam: *His majesty asks: How is your health, really?*

The gunners raise their muskets and fire a volley, then another, and another. The three foreigners follow Ato Samuel between the men. As they step into the tent, the shots cease.

It is warm. The light is falling through a canopy of striped silk. It gives a muted sense of shade and dark. Tewodros is sitting on a divan. On each side, standing, are his ministers. A guard stands with them, with a twin-barrelled pistol in each hand. The King of Kings himself is dressed in an ordinary *shamma*, but it is wrapped around his head. Only his eyes, partly shaded, are visible.

Rassam: *I have the honour to present to Your Majesty this letter from my sovereign, her Most Gracious Majesty the Queen of England, wherein you will find expressions of friendly feeling and goodwill towards you.*

I receive it with pleasure – the *shamma* drops away from the emperor's mouth as he speaks – *and I am glad to see you.*

Tewodros places the letter beside him, unopened. He invites the envoys to sit, on the other side of the letter. Rassam introduces Blanc and Prideaux.

Tewodros then begins a speech. He explains the grievances he holds towards Cameron and Stern, how he had treated them with courtesy but had then been betrayed. He berates his own people: he had tried to give them peace, tried to pull them towards the ways of the civilised peoples, to give order to their lives, hope for their children. But they are a 'wicked people'.

Rassam makes few comments. He listens. He does not correct Tewodros on various points of detail during his complaints about Abune Selama, Cameron or Stern. But he realises too that silence is both suspicious and a sign of weakness. What can he say? He cannot confirm the guilt of the hostages, and risk their continued detention; nor can he deny their guilt and accuse Tewodros of injudicious cruelty. He chooses to confront Tewodros's worries directly – the personal nature of the offences, and the problems of his reign.

'In your Majesty's position as a King,' he reports himself saying, 'you ought not to be oversensitive, but should bear and forbear. A private person has only to look after his own affairs; but monarchs have to attend to the affairs of millions, and in thousands of cases they have to forgive even those who have committed heinous crimes. Is not your Majesty, as a sovereign, a father? And ought not a good father to be patient with his children, and teach them to do what is right, instead of continually employing the rod? I trust that after your Majesty reads the letter of our Queen, and takes into consideration the friendly mission on which I have been sent, you will forget the past, and try to establish amicable relations with England, which I, as a humble servant of her Majesty, will use my best endeavours to forward.'

Tewodros smiles, but returns to the slights.

Before the initial interview comes to an end, Rassam asks a favour.

'Please remember that my companions and I are strangers. We do not know either the customs of the country nor the etiquette of the Court. I trust therefore that your Majesty will overlook any mistake we may commit through ignorance during our sojourn in your dominions.'

'*Isshi, isshi*. Of course.' Tewodros laughs, and into that charming laugh is released much of the tension between the two men.

34

That night, Tewodros was in such a state of excitement that he was unable to sleep. At dawn he called his scribe, Aleqa Ingida.

Posturing, boasting or self-justifying, Tewodros's letters rarely fail to disguise the frailer emotional states behind them. What he dictated that morning was driven by a raw humility so extreme it might have been false. But it appears genuine, a paean to a distant and revered monarch.

May this letter from God's creature and slave, the son of David, of Solomon, King of Kings, reach Victoria, queen of England, whom God has chosen from among all men and exalted and made to reign, who loves friendship and religion and defends the oppressed and poor.

As for what you tell me, that you have sent Hormuzd Rassam, concerning the matter of Cameron, would I say no even if the slave of your slave, let alone you yourself, wrote to me?

. . . I am not worthy of corresponding with you who are great. However, a great person and the ocean are the same, they can bear anything.

Bear with me, the ignorant one of Ethiopia, for the

sake of God. It is myself whom the people I had imprisoned humiliated and reviled, I, the son of a daughter of Israel who became poor when, as a result of the rule of the Galla, the children of Israel had been brought to naught, and were itching and begging. But God has granted me power and restored my father's kingdom to me.

You must have heard of the ignorance and blindness of us, the Ethiopian people. If you find offensive what I was bold enough to write to you because it seemed appropriate to me, do not be angry with me, but advise me, for you the queen whom God has chosen, have had your eyes opened.

Written in the year 7358 after the creation of the world, on the twenty-second day of Tirr; in the year 1858 after the birth of our Lord.

A little later that morning, he sent for Rassam and the others. They found him standing outside his tent, waiting for them. He greeted them with warmth. Once inside, he dismissed his attendants and officials:

'For the sake of my friend, the queen, and in return for the trouble you have taken in the matter of Mr Cameron, I will pardon all the European captives.'

He had already ordered their immediate release. They would be brought from Meqdela, and handed over to Rassam for free passage out of the country.

Rassam's eighteen-month wait had yielded its result in less than twenty-four hours. There was no mention of conditions, nor of the embassy which had caused such agonised debate.

That same afternoon Rassam presented Tewodros with the presents. The envoys sat outside his tent while the emperor unwrapped the trinkets bought by Rassam in the *suqs* of Cairo. Rassam was not to know the contempt that Tewodros felt for gifts that were not weapons. Silks from Napoleon III he only half-opened before sending them to his women. A pretty box-organ brought by Cameron for him made him scoff: 'What's the use of Europeans sending me these nonsensical things?'

But Tewodros was now in a more appreciative mood. 'I am sorry for the trouble that bringing such heavy objects must have caused you.' He looked carefully at each gift before having it arranged with the others on the grass.

Rassam held out a vanity mirror. 'For your queen.'

Tewodros sighed. 'Since the death of my good queen, I have been leading an un-Christian and disreputable life.' He made no mention of Tirunesh, and told Rassam the gift would go to his favourite concubine, Yetemegnu.

35

Early the next morning, Tewodros's 45,000 fighting men took up their spears and muskets, swung themselves up into the saddle, or threw the corners of their *shammas* over one shoulder and set off for the north. Behind them, their temporary grass shelters crackled and burned. Tens of thousands more followed – baggage-carriers, muleteers, water-carriers, sutlers, cooks, concubines.

In Wollo and Shoa, Simien and Wegera, Tewodros had lost control. Tedla Gwalu had restored his rebel rule of Gojjam. Wagshum Gobeze was in Tigray. To the north of Gondar Tiso Gobeze had taken over. '*The king's only domain is Begemder,*' ran a contemporary report. '*All his soldiers have deserted. The king has grown weak.*' But here at the heart of his regime, he remained master.

'Everything,' wrote Rassam, 'was conducted with such perfect order that it was a pleasure to travel with the royal army.' In his account, he is quick to condemn Tewodros for his delusions, his poor administration and his brutality, but Rassam saw many things too that impressed him.

When the army reached a ravine, the order was broken. Everyone rushed to be the first across; the stream, dammed by half a million feet of man and beast, swelled into lakes above them. The *belg* rains had begun. Most settlements they passed were deserted. Villagers had long since fled the advance of the army. In long lines, foot-soldiers crouched in the fields slicing the stalks of abandoned crops with swords.

One morning, Tewodros called in person on the British mission. They were packing up for the day's march. *How did you pass the night? How is your health? How did your companions pass the night? Are they well? Are you well, really?* He then suggested that, for their comfort, the three travel with him.

Straight-backed on his groomed mount, Tewodros rode out in front. He was wearing a shirt given to him by Rassam. A pair of pages followed the emperor – one with his shield and the other with a gun and a telescope. Flanking them, and fanning back in two lines, were courtiers clutching Rassam's gifts. Two cases of curaçao had been divided up so that single bottles could be displayed. Behind Tewodros's pages came his prime minister Ras Ingida, then Rassam, Blanc and Prideaux. Other ministers followed, and then, stretching out behind them, its end far out of sight, and broken by islands of mounted warriors, was the sea of bobbing heads.

The royal party stopped in the hot mid-morning. They were on a wide plain. A messenger told Tewodros of a rebel force nearby, and he led the cavalry off against them. Soon the sky above the forest was filled with dark smoke. The crowds pressed on, bunching up and spreading out, an unstoppable tide flooding across the high plains.

They disturbed a number of grazing antelopes. The animals raised their heads, then leapt off into the forest. But there were more people there. They bounded on, between the trees. They could find no cover, no end to the line of men. They raced back and forth through the crowd, unable to break free. They panicked. In the end it was exhaustion that killed them. Their bodies were delivered to the feet of Tewodros, who sent the meat to Rassam.

The next day, only a short march from its source, they

reached the Abbai, the Blue Nile. Tewodros dismounted, crossed the river and sprang up the far bank. His toes pressed into the rain-softened soil. At the top he turned and shouted to Rassam. 'On the mule! Cross the water on the mule!'

Once across, Rassam too climbed the bank on foot. As he reached the top, his feet slipped and Tewodros grabbed him. Rassam felt the strong grip on his forearm, and the emperor's gaze inches from his face.

'Cheer up,' Tewodros whispered, in Arabic. 'Don't be afraid!'

On the far side, the banks were filling with men, and the front line was being pressed from the back. Tewodros saw that the bank on his side would collapse when they crossed. He grabbed his spear, plunged it into the soil and began to dig. The prime minister and others joined him. Rassam was 'astonished to witness his care'. Soon a solid way had been built. As the great crowd began to cross, Tewodros remained watching.

'Mind that poor child!' he called. 'No, no – carry him, help his poor mother.'

The journey continued. Sometimes they crossed the same river twice, or passed the dead ground of a previous day's camp. Everyone moved with practised purpose, but no one knew where they were going. Often they changed direction.

The king's only domain is Begemder. All his soldiers have deserted. The king has grown weak . . .'

36

One afternoon, Tewodros called for Rassam. They spoke, as Tewodros used to with Bell and Plowden, about world affairs. The emperor was curious in particular about different codes of war. They discussed the civil war in the United States, just ended, and the British action against the Ashanti, which was still going on. Then they turned to Tewodros's favourite war – the Crimean.

'Did the British execute Tsar Nicholas?'

'No,' replied Rassam. 'It is normal now for the defeated to ask for terms of peace.'

'Who pays for such wars?'

'It depends on the war. Normally each party bears the costs.'

Tewodros paused. 'Is there a country called Dahomey?'

Rassam said there was.

'I have heard that each year they sacrifice several hundred living humans in a religious ceremony. Why do the Christian powers not put an end to such barbarity?'

'In general,' explained Rassam, 'the civilised nations of Europe avoid direct interference in other states.' Rassam was pleased to be able to push home the point. 'They allow them to act as they please towards their own subjects.'

Tewodros nodded. 'Ever since the death of Plowden and

Yohannis [Bell], all the English and *farenjis* who have visited my country have proved lacking in sincerity, ill-mannered and ill-tempered.' But in Rassam, he said, he had found someone to trust. 'Your patience in waiting so long for an answer convinced me of your worth.' In his affection for Rassam was also an opportunity. 'I wish you to convey to your queen and to her Council my anxious desire to cultivate the friendship of the English.'

Rassam did not tell him that it was probably too late, that once the hostages were free, the British government was looking forward to having no more to do with him.

'It is an object,' concluded Tewodros, 'which I have been intent upon ever since I ascended the throne of Ethiopia.'

He renewed the conversation in the coming days. At one point he said he had ordered some 'curious articles to be sent to her Majesty, which, although worthless in England, would serve to show the skill and customs of his people'.

'But ah!' exclaimed Tewodros, 'Mr Cameron has spoiled the whole.'

He told Rassam and the others that they were to go to Qorata, a sacred town on the shores of Lake Tana. There they would wait for the freed captives to reach them before leaving the country. He himself would continue on his ceaseless quest to crush the rebels.

Before they parted, Tewodros summoned Rassam for a final audience. Rassam was beginning to enjoy these meetings; since his arrival at Tewodros's camp a week or so earlier, he had had nothing but good news and deference from Tewodros. Nothing had gone wrong. He watched Tewodros order two rugs to be spread, deep red islands on the yellowy grass, several yards apart. He sat on one, Rassam, Blanc and Prideaux on the other.

Tewodros stressed again his love for the English, his desire for their friendship. From his childhood on, he explained, he had been a successful commander. He liberated the land to the west taken by 'the Turks'. He pursued them into the Sudan and would have defeated them had they not hidden like cowards behind their cannon.

'You,' he said with sudden emotion, 'you are like brothers to me!'

Then, again, he returned to the insults of the missionaries. He spoke of a letter Rosenthal had written.

'In his letter, he called me "the King of the Wild Beasts". Do you know him?'

Rassam said he didn't.

Tewodros held his hand some four feet off the ground. 'The man who called me "King of the Wild Beasts" does not stand higher than this!'

Ato Samuel was translating. 'No, Your Majesty, you must raise your hand a little.'

He upped it six inches.

'A little higher, Your Majesty.'

Another six inches.

'A little taller.'

'No, Samuel. I cannot raise my hand any higher. I assure you, Mr Rassam, that he is not taller than *that*.'

His mood had suddenly darkened. 'I began to fear something disastrous was coming,' recalled Rassam. 'His face grew ashy pale and his hands shook.'

Rassam tried to reassure him. 'Why should His Majesty, who is a great sovereign, be vexed at what poor priests say?'

Tewodros smiled. 'I do not care about the past, but must only think of the friendship of you three.'

The sun was high. Tewodros had been 'so excited all the time' that he forgot to ask for umbrellas. Two hours they had been sitting in the rising heat.

Tewodros then recalled the treaty Plowden had presented to him on their first meeting in 1855. The treaty had been made with Ras Ali, and Plowden had asked Tewodros if he could raise a British flag at Gondar. 'What!' Tewodros had said at the time. 'Do you consider me like that menial servant, Ras Ali, that you can speak to me in this way? Can a renegade Galla slave enter into agreements with foreign nations?'

Now, Tewodros asked Rassam for a new treaty. Rassam explained that he did not have the authority. 'When I return to England, I will represent to her Majesty's Government how well-disposed your Majesty is towards it. Due consideration will be given to all your Majesty's propositions.'

As they parted, Tewodros said: 'I wish you to tell your queen that I consider her too great a personage for me to communicate with; but as I learn that she has a great number of governors in India, I hope she will appoint one of them to correspond with me.'

The British mission had achieved a great deal more, and more quickly, than they had ever hoped. Tewodros had received them with almost fawning honour and promised them all they wanted, the release of the hostages and their free passage from the country. Now they simply had to wait for the prisoners' arrival from Meqdela.

The next day Tewodros's mood was not good. He did not appear all morning, so the British mission slipped away for Lake Tana and the town of Qorata.

VII

Lake Tana

37

The mission spent a very pleasant two months at Qorata. They camped on the beach. The blue waters of Lake Tana stretched some forty miles to the north. The shoreline around their camp was rocky and wooded and full of birdsong. Lieutenant Prideaux propped his fowling-piece on a trunk and shot duck straight from his tent. A short stroll into the hinterland yielded whatever they chose from a menu of geese and guinea fowl, snipe and gazelle. Dr Blanc's patients were orderly, drifting in and out of the camp in twos and threes.

Ten miles across the water, to the west, was the forested rise of the Zeghie peninsula. There they could see the fires of Tewodros's semi-permanent camp. From time to time the *negarits* sounded and Tewodros led his forces off to do battle. But he never forgot the British at Qorata. He was infatuated with Rassam. The British envoy represented a world which was everything his own kingdom was not – stable, powerful, full of innovation and technology.

As the weeks passed a regular post of *tankwas* crossed the lake from the royal camp, pushing their soggy papyrus bows up onto the mission beach and delivering gifts: one single-barrelled musket, four double-barrelled muskets, five double-barrelled pistols, 5,000 thalers, two lion cubs, one antelope and a large number of letters.

The letters were deferential. Tewodros offered Rassam the honour of conferring the royal shirt on all of his Ethiopian servants. He wanted knowledge, 'so that my eyes may be enlightened, for I am blind'. He asked for Rassam's views on the relative buoyancy of fresh and salt water (he was trying to develop new boats for Lake Tana). He called Rassam variously 'my true friend . . . the great queen's great man . . . the servant of her whom God has exalted above all sovereigns, and glorified above all princes and peoples, and made Defender of the Christian faith, and the succour of the poor and oppressed, Hormuzd Rassam, who is, by the power of God, endowed with wisdom and a benevolent heart'.

Tewodros sent a message to Waldmeier and the others from Gefat: put aside your gun-making and go to Qorata, keep the honoured British guests company. Some days later, knowing 'how much Europeans appreciated the society of ladies', he told their wives to go too.

Dr Blanc, ever the rationalist, anticipated the arrival of these half-dozen Low Church missionaries without enthusiasm. But looking out across the plain one day, he was astonished by their approach. He had 'never been so taken aback as at the sight of these Europeans wearing the Abyssinian gala dress, silk shirts of gaudy colour, trousers of the same material'. The women likewise wore 'gorgeous attire', wrote Rassam.

With the Gefat community was a man called Wilhelm Schimper, a German botanist who had lived for years in Ethiopia. He knew how much in favour Rassam was with Tewodros. One day he took the envoy to one side to warn him. He showed him the palm of his hand.

'Abyssinia is like this.' He flipped his hand over, then looked around. 'But I must say no more, as the walls have ears.'

That same afternoon a *tankwa* arrived with three more gifts from Tewodros – squawking and scratching at the papyrus raft were two monkeys and a baboon.

38

On the afternoon of 24 February, Aggafari Golem – one eye lost to smallpox, famously bad-tempered – arrived on the mountain of Meqdela to announce the royal pardon. Cameron, Stern, Rosenthal and the others shuffled before him. Cameron was looking pale and ill.

'The *negus*, my master,' announced the *aggafari*, 'has charged me to inform you that he has received a letter from your queen, through her envoy, Mr Rassam, and that in conformity with the request embodied in it, he has been pleased to order your liberation.'

Captivity had instilled in the foreigners the etiquette of Tewodros's kingdom. Stern dropped to his knees and prostrated himself before the messenger; Cameron struggled to lower himself. Smiths at once set to work removing the shackles. They wrenched open the clasps, tearing the prisoners' flesh as they did so, driving wedges between iron and bone.

'Our gait on the removal of the manacles,' wrote Stern, 'resembled that of a thoroughly drunken man. We staggered, reeled, and sank down. All was swimming before the eyes or moving beneath the feet. To make a regular firm step was beyond the reach of possibility.'

Progress through the mountains towards Lake Tana was

slow. 'Our daily stages were long and fatiguing, but what did we care for exhausting marches when we knew that each step diminished the distance that lay between us and those dear faces, in whose smiles, chains and captivity, Theodore and Abyssinia, would be forgotten?'

On 12 March, at about two in the afternoon, the convoy of Meqdela hostages limped into the Qorata camp. Rassam, always correct, always alert and canny, had in the meantime noticed a slight cooling in Tewodros's attentions. According to Waldmeier, Rassam 'knew how to deal with the king better than any other foreigner'. Rassam understood that the arrival of the hated hostages in Qorata might in Tewodros's eyes colour the mission with their guilt. Tewodros would not tolerate seeing them leave if he thought they were forging an alliance.

So Rassam received the longed-for group with the detachment of a border official. He made a form of his own, filled out the twenty-three names (including three children), their occupation (HM Consul, servant, missionary, natural history collector . . .), the county and country of their birth and residency.

If the 'reception of the captives was cold and formal', he remarked, it was no reflection on the relief he felt on seeing them.

Two days later, an order was paddled across the lake from Zeghie. Rassam was to try the captives on Tewodros's behalf. Cameron – unable to stand up at the mock trial – was charged with dispensing with Tewodros's letter for Queen Victoria, then going to the emperor's enemies; the others faced a more general accusation of receiving Tewodros's friendship, and then abusing him. They were all duly found guilty, and Rassam wrote at once to Tewodros saying that they had confessed and begged 'the forgiveness due from one Christian to another'.

The mood again shifted in Rassam's favour. Tewodros granted his forgiveness, and thanked Rassam: 'I want to bow my head and kiss your hand and foot.' He sent Rassam fifty dairy cows. He granted him another 5,000 thalers. He wanted to give him a golden saddle, shields and medals. He proposed a new order of merit – the Cross and Solomon's Seal – to be minted and conferred on the three men of the British mission before they left for the coast. He sent four of his goldsmiths across the lake to consult Rassam on their design. The plan was to have a cross set inside the twin interlocking triangles of the Star of David. On the front would be inscribed: *The fear of the Lord is the beginning of wisdom*; on the reverse: *Tewodros, King of kings of Ethiopia*. Tewodros had thought it all through. The order would have three classes – of gold, gold and silver, and silver. Rassam, Ras Ingida and Tewodros's eldest son would receive the First Class. The Second would go to Blanc and Prideaux and Ras Tagga, commander-in-chief of all the musketeers, and the Third – well, candidates for the Third would be selected in due course.

Tewodros told Rassam to prepare to depart with all the Europeans. He would give his word and allow his honoured friend the servant of Queen Victoria to leave the country with all the captives – just as soon as the medals and the shields and the golden saddle were ready for him.

Rassam knew that every day risked bringing some message or rumour that might alter the emperor's mind. He maintained his cordial manner with Tewodros, but privately wished to consign 'all saddles and shields to the bottom of the sea'.

39

Easter was coming, and the great fast of *hudaddie* was drawing to a close. Tewodros sent for his women. Chief among them was Yetemegnu, whom he referred to as *'itege'*, 'empress', while his real *itege* and their son Alemayehu remained at Meqdela. Yetemegnu, famously large, stepped aboard the papyrus canoe. The emperor's other women settled in other canoes. The wives of the chiefs joined them and the flotilla, with its uxorial cargo wrapped in brilliant white *shammas*, headed out across the lake to the royal camp at Zeghie.

Tewodros had also asked for his horses. Unable to go by *tankwa*, they were led around the southern shore, where they ran the risk of falling into the hands of the rebels. So it was the horses and not the women whom Tewodros rode out to meet. Before leaving camp he wrote to Rassam on the thirteenth day of Meggabit, 21 March: 'I have been yearning to see you and meet with you. Now I have gone on business ... When I return, I shall inform you for, by the power of God, I miss your friendship.'

Clearly he did. While Rassam was at Qorata, Tewodros wrote him a total of twenty-three letters. As the day of the foreigners' departure approached, a certain tension settled over the Qorata camp. Rassam was aware that the affection he received from Tewodros could create its own problems. Tewodros himself was starting to feel uneasy about seeing the back of Rassam. He summoned Rassam to Zeghie, and also Blanc and Prideaux, Waldmeier and the Gefat artisans.

Tewodros greeted them above the beach. Seeing the official uniforms of the British mission, he smiled: 'I feel as happy as if I were visiting the queen.'

Crossing the compound towards the *adarash*, Tewodros held Rassam's hand. Inside they found an archipelago of carpets around the throne. Members of Tewodros's inner circle were there, with his own family. Taking his seat, the emperor called a young man.

'Meshesha,' he said, 'draw near.'

It was his eldest son, Ras Meshesha. He was dressed in a shirt made up from the bolt of Lyons silk given to Tewodros by Rassam.

'Shake hands with my English friends in the English fashion, as I want you to become one of them.'

Tewodros turned to Rassam: 'I wish this son of mine, and another at Meqdela [four-year-old Alemayehu], to be adopted children of the English. When you go back to your country, I want you to recommend them to your queen, so that when I die they may be looked after by the English, and not be allowed to govern badly.'

Tewodros then showed them some of his favourite guns – pistols, muskets, the pair given to him by Plowden and by Queen Victoria. He then reminded all present how deeply he had been let down by those who had been held captive.

The next morning there was a grand council. Eighty-five *shumoch* swept into the *adarash*, taking their place with the Europeans – Rassam and his mission, the Gefat group. Tewodros placed the letter from Queen Victoria in front of his throne and asked his close confidants, Ato Samuel and Welde Gabir, the question that lay behind the gathering. 'Should they be allowed to leave for the coast?'

'Your Majesty should send them to their country with joy,' they advised.

It was not the answer he wanted. 'Asses! Blockheads!'

Next he asked Waldmeier and the Europeans from Gefat the same question. To a man, they told him he should allow the Europeans to leave.

'But what surety do I have in my hand?'

The artisan Zander stepped forward and picked up the queen's letter. He pressed his palm against the wax seal and the two-year-old ink of the royal signature. 'Your Majesty, you should trust to these. They are a true sign of the word of the English queen – and she never breaks her word.'

Tewodros then dismissed all the Europeans. He turned to his chiefs. And all of them said: 'Let them go.'

'What does that leave me?'

Ras Tagga, commander of all the musketeers, made the plea on the others' behalf. 'We beg Your Majesty to let them depart in peace. If Mr Rassam is false to you after leaving, let God be the judge between you. Trust in God – He is enough for us.'

Another echoed the advice. 'If Your Majesty does not trust the English, make Rassam swear on the Bible. The English are very true to an oath made on the Bible.'

He dismissed them and recalled Rassam and the Gefat missionaries. It was clear as soon as they entered his tent that Tewodros was angry. He poured out a history of slights and slanders against him. The *abun* and his visits to the *itege* on Meqdela had made a cuckold of him. The Frenchman Lejean had insulted him in half a dozen ways. The Coptic patriarch had asked for his own crown. Basha Felika – an English adventurer called Captain Charles Speedy – had spoken of the Ethiopians as 'asses' after his visit.

'How can I know you will act differently?' Tewodros barked at Rassam.

Rassam struggled to reply. Tewodros himself filled the

silence, his voice suddenly quieter. 'You may not abuse me when you leave my country, but still you may forget me.'

Rassam said simply: 'I cannot praise myself by saying I shall behave better than others. But try me.'

Tewodros had exhausted his advisers. Everyone had said the same. There was a time when he would have made the decision without need of advice, by invoking the precedent of David to sanction his decisions. But those days were no more.

'*Isshi.*' His tone was measured. The anger had passed. 'Very well, I will try you. May you reach your country safely.'

40

On Friday, 13 April 1866, the camp at Qorata was packed away and the Meqdela captives began the journey to the coast. They pushed up the eastern shore of Lake Tana, crunching across the dust of dry-season riverbeds. Weeks of hard travel lay ahead, but that morning thoughts of liberation set their spirits soaring.

'Our excited imagination tinted every object with lovely colours,' wrote Stern, 'and we stumbled over holes and ditches, brushed along weeds and bushes, in the delirium of a most ecstatic dream.'

Meanwhile the three envoys crossed the lake to Zeghie for the last time. Rassam, Blanc and Prideaux were going to say goodbye to the emperor, then join the rest of the party on the northern shore of the lake for the journey home.

On landing at Zeghie the mission was greeted by the prime minister, Ras Ingida, and three caparisoned mules. Through flashing sunlight they rode up beneath the trees to Tewodros's compound. A midday silence hung heavy in the heat. No tents stood for their arrival. With a clatter of swords and buckles, they dismounted. Ras Ingida paused to bow before entering the *adarash*. Inside, they looked around the great hall and saw four hundred nobles – *rases*, *dejazmaches*, *grazmaches* and *kegnazmaches* – all dressed in their silk shirts. Between them, at the far end, was the throne. Rassam noticed it was empty. Something was not right.

At that moment, someone grabbed his arm. Then the other arm. A third officer took the tail of his coat. He looked around; Blanc was also seized. As Prideaux was taken, his military sash was wrenched from him with such force that his monocle shot out and landed several yards away. Blanc could not help grinning.

Ras Ingida turned to them. He looked surprised. 'Do not be afraid!'

At about the same time, some forty miles away across the lake, the escort of the liberated prisoners carried out their instructions. They turned on the foreigners and arrested them too. Then they began the two-day journey back round to Zeghie.

Tewodros had been thinking about Rassam's departure for months. Following the fifty-six-day Lenten fast of *hudaddie*, it was to be a grand farewell, the glorious resolution of an unfortunate incident, of mischief cooked up by scheming rascals. Then would begin a new era of Anglo–Ethiopian amity, a great Christian alliance to drive the Mussulmen back into the desert and away from the southern shores of the Red Sea.

Tewodros was going to present Rassam with the golden saddle. He would pin to his chest the new medal instigated for the occasion, the highest class of the Order of the Cross and Solomon's Seal. Tewodros had already selected from the royal stables some of the mules and horses to be given to Rassam. Detailed instructions had been issued for the escort to take the mission and the free captives away from Zeghie and out of his kingdom. Ras Ingida, the prime minister, would head the first stage. The emperor had summoned the chiefs and erected tents for the mission to use during the parting ceremony.

Even as the nobles began to enter the *adarash*, and while

Ras Ingida was waiting for Rassam and the others to change into their uniforms on the beach, they all thought they were to attend a farewell ceremony.

But in his own inner turmoil, Tewodros felt fury as well as doubt at the prospect of Rassam leaving. At that moment he was dictating a list of charges against him. Early that morning, before dawn, the emperor had instructed Bitwedded Tedla to cross the lake and re-arrest the Meqdela captives: 'We are angry with our friends and with the Europeans, who say, "We are going to our country," and we are not yet reconciled. Until we consult as to what we shall do, seize them.'

Tewodros had not slept that night. The day before, 12 April, he had been told that the re-gilded saddle would not be ready, nor the Order of the Cross and Solomon's Seal. It was also reported to him that Rassam had given the freed Meqdela captives guns.

In the crowded *adarash*, Rassam, Blanc and Prideaux, baffled and stumbling, their uniforms ripped, were now shoved before the empty throne. A scribe stood and recited Tewodros's ancestry, back to Solomon and Sheba, and King David. Rassam fielded a series of questions about why he had not brought the captives, why he had sent letters to the coast. The questions were 'vague and inconsequent', reported Prideaux; 'childish', said Blanc. Even the assembled officials dared to cry out in support of Rassam when he answered each charge with robust assurance.

All the while the throne stood vacant. Tewodros was sitting behind a door. It was said that he had been drinking for three days. To try to explain his reckless assault on Rassam, his prevaricating, is to enter a labyrinth of contradictory messages made more confusing by the emperor's growing paranoia. He had begun by asking Rassam to open relations with Britain; now he realised it was too late. All that was relevant was that he was unable to bear seeing the Europeans withdraw from his shrunken kingdom, knowing that they would take away forever the hopes he had once had of allying himself with the world beyond. To Tewodros, embittered and disillusioned, weakened by desertions, every departure was now an act of betrayal.

41

Three days later, Tewodros again summoned his court. This time he held it outside, on a piece of open ground in the hedged royal enclosure at Zeghie. He himself sat on a divan, while the throne stood empty beside him. In the early-morning sun, a great semi-circle of his establishment fanned out around him, a thousand men or more, some half-hidden beneath umbrellas, some sitting on carpets, some standing – priests and *debteras* with their faces shaded by ivory *timtims*, placid monks in yellow robes, seasoned ministers, chosen courtiers all arranged according to rank. In the warrior splendour of their coloured shirts, the silver-encrusted velvet capes, the tufting of lions' manes from their headdresses, the inscrutable faces, stood the generals, nobles and regional chiefs.

The court was an assize for the European captives. After the chaos of recent weeks, no one had any idea whether Tewodros now wanted to liberate or detain them. The Europeans arrived in the enclosure in order of current popularity. First came Waldmeier and the Gefat artisans, then, in uniform, Rassam, Blanc and Prideaux. Finally, an hour later, with the attendant *clank-clank* of fetters, the still-detested Cameron, Stern and Rosenthal and the other prisoners.

Cameron was too ill to walk, so Tewodros sent him a mule.

At about 9 a.m. he and the others shuffled through the gap in the hedge and approached the assembly. It was the first time Tewodros had seen the offenders for nearly a year. In the previous month, since they had reached Lake Tana, Rassam had done everything he could to keep them apart, to prevent risking Tewodros's anger by letting him see them. Now he could do nothing.

With hobbled steps, the chained prisoners approached the emperor. 'How are you?' he asked. 'How is your health?'

'We are well.' They dropped to their knees. 'We are well, thanks to God.' They touched the dust with their foreheads.

Tewodros asked Cameron to step forward. Watched by the crowd, the consul stumbled towards him. Sweat stuck curls of grey hair to his forehead and temples. Tewodros looked at him for a moment, a slight smile on his thin lips, then ordered his soldiers to hammer off the consul's chains.

'Take care not to touch him!' he warned. 'He has the syphilis.'

Cameron was told to sit with Rassam. Stiff and slow, he passed alone in front of the crowd, and lowered himself onto the carpet beside the envoy.

In his account of this court hearing, Henry Stern compares it with his own trial two and a half years earlier. Then, 'in the full flush of glory the infatuated man really began to believe he was the Tewodros of prophecy'. The contrast now was 'dire and rueful ... his extensive realm had shrivelled into a few provinces' and his 'army of 150,000 warriors dwindled to 50,000 ruffians'.

Stern overstates the case. Here at Zeghie, Tewodros's officers remained firm in their faith in him. Yet the shadows were gathering, and a hint of desperation surrounded the emperor. The witnesses called to declare his lineage were more numerous than previously, the repetition of the crimes of the Europeans more shrill. 'Never before,' wrote Rassam, 'had Theodore manifested such bitter animosity against the prisoners.'

That morning Rassam found himself accused directly for the first time. Tewodros called for him. Flanked by Blanc and Prideaux, he stepped up and stood before the emperor. The mid-morning heat was intensifying, and the principal question of the court was now addressed: why had the prisoners left without being brought to Tewodros?

For this, he blamed Rassam. 'You made the mistake, Mr Rassam. I told you to reconcile me with them. Why have you omitted to do so?'

Rassam explained that he understood such a reconciliation had been performed in March, after the trial he had been instructed to perform.

'But on the day when I sent to you that you might get ready for the road, did I not tell you that if you came you should bring the released prisoners with you, because I wished to give to those who had no mule, a mule; and to those who have no money, some money for the road: according to which you gave the answer that you have brought the mules for them, and that you have money enough for them to take to their country?'

'Yes,' said Rassam. 'But I did this only to spare Your Majesty to be troubled with them.' Rassam suddenly felt the chilling intimation of what was to come – not just Tewodros's enmity, but blame for the entire re-detention.

Tewodros gestured to those still manacled. 'Now you see for your sake they are again in chains. From the day you said you wished to send them by another road, I got suspicious. I thought that you wished to do so in order that you may say in your country you have released them by your prudence or by your power. Who are you? Are you a king?'

'No, Your Majesty. I am your friend.'

Tewodros assured Rassam, again, that had he brought the prisoners to him, he would have given them transport and sent them all on their way.

The emperor's anger was flaring. Everyone knew the signs. Whether it was the sight of Rassam himself standing before him that helped control it, or something else in the swirl of Tewodros's thinking, is impossible to say. But for now it died down. He gestured to Rassam to sit in the honoured place before the throne, and began a verbal assault on the rebels and the Turks.

'Ah!' he cried. 'If the English would only assist me, we could build a fence around Senaar!'

The session ended without judgement, but the embers of Tewodros's rage still glowed. Before rising, he said to Rassam, 'Is this your friendship, Mr Rassam, that you wish to leave me and take away those who have abused me?'

Rassam knew now that none of the foreigners was safe.

The next day the emperor called them to a private meeting in the audience hall. The Europeans were nervous. As they entered, each instinctively checked Tewodros's movements and expressions for signs of his mood. He appeared calm that afternoon, almost withdrawn. Almost at once he lowered his head before them. 'For the sake of Christ, forgive me.'

Nothing surprised them any more. They too bowed their heads and, in their relief, offered a congregational murmur of forgiveness. They too begged absolution, and Tewodros granted it.

Silence.

They all stood there, looking at the ground. Tewodros kept his head lowered.

It was one of the Gefat missionaries who hissed to Rassam the protocol of court forgiveness: 'You must tell His Majesty to sit up!'

42

The pattern of Tewodros's temper had shown itself again, as it had in 1856, when he imprisoned the Coptic patriarch. First were the suspicions, the offence taken and the reckless detention. Then, at the moment of greatest defiance, he would drop his chin and beg forgiveness. Rassam now 'hoped that after this formal reconciliation there would be no further hindrance to our departure'.

Later that afternoon, Tewodros sent away the Meqdela captives and kept Rassam with him. He called Aleqa Ingida to dictate a letter for Rassam to take to Queen Victoria. As the scribe scratched at the paper with his reed pen, Ato Samuel translated Tewodros's words into Arabic for Rassam.

The emperor began with his customary invocation of the Trinity, then the deferential address:

God's creature and slave, the son of David and of Solomon, the King of Kings Tewodros. May [this letter] reach the queen of England, Victoria, who God has elected and exalted above all men and enthroned; who loves religion and friendship; who protects the oppressed [and] poor.

Tewodros explained – repeatedly – how he had freed the prisoners:

Very well, look, I have, by the power of God, released Mr Cameron and handed him over to Mr Rassam. By the power of God, I have released all the imprisoned Europeans whom you asked me to release for you, and handed them over with all the Europeans who wanted to return to their country. Very well, by the power of God, I have handed [them] over.

Then Rassam heard his own name again in the Amharic. Aleqa Ingida took down the emperor's words, and Ato Samuel translated:

The reason I have kept your servant Mr Hormuzd Rassam is in order to correspond with you, having consulted with him in accordance with what you said, 'For all the things you want from us, consult with him.' Since we, the people of Ethiopia, are blind, open our eyes for us, and may God give you light in Heaven.

So that was it. He would not be leaving. Rassam was a hostage.

In Queen Victoria's letter, delivered by Rassam in January, a mistranslation had occurred. From the Amharic version, Tewodros had understood that Rassam would grant him his '*feker-kasa*' – a favour or gift in exchange for the prisoners' release.

Tewodros's thoughts were again on technology. What he could not win by diplomacy, he would gain by coercion. He wanted, as always, a gun industry. Only guns, large guns, and the expertise to use them would give him the chance to restore his power. He asked for 'skilful artists . . . workmen' who could help him. They should include two gunsmiths, an artillery officer, an iron founder (able to build a foundry, and to come equipped with necessary tools and instruments), one or two boat-builders, a cart- and wheel-wright. 'Rejoicing in their coming,' Tewodros promised, 'I shall receive them with great honour, and give them good pay.' Acknowledging the question that would naturally concern such a party, he wrote that when they 'wish to return to their country, I shall, through the power of God, give them a splendid pay and with great honour send them back to their country'.

An impressive shopping-list of equipment went with the request for personnel – a small blast steam-engine for a foundry, a lathe, a distilling machine, gun-cap machinery with the necessary copperplate, a good telescope, a gunpowder mill (with rollers), some handsome carpets, silks, guns and pistols, and two good regimental swords.

Rassam also sent a letter from himself to the secretary of state for foreign affairs, a letter which is coloured by his knowledge that Tewodros had asked to read it. So Rassam was forced to speak of the 'magnificent reception' Tewodros had given them, the 'honour' of Tewodros coming to visit him in person, and that Tewodros had 'in every respect been very kind and hospitable'. He made oblique reference to his position: 'Your Lordship will perceive that we are all detained in this country for the present, for friendship's sake.'

The emperor's dilemma was now to deliver the letters. He needed to send one of the Europeans, but he had to be sure that the messenger would return. He selected the missionary Martin Flad. Flad was no more trustworthy than the others, but he did have a wife and children in the country. At four in the afternoon on 21 April 1866, Flad rode out of the camp at Zeghie for the coast and the long journey to London, 'after a heart-turning leave of my dear wife and children, and all my other friends who I had to leave in the hands of the savage Theodore, cruel, inhuman and sly despot'.

The swollen band of hostages, more than thirty with their

servants, now settled down for a long wait. Stern was furious to find himself detained again. 'The camp, which was never a very agreeable home, after the blighted prospects of freedom, became a perfectly loathsome abode.'

'Our cage was gilt,' wrote Dr Blanc, 'but still a cage; and the experience we had had of the King's treachery made us constantly fear a recurrence of it.'

Lieutenant Prideaux was more pragmatic. 'Although we had lost our hope of leaving the country immediately, we anticipated at all events no indignities.'

Skilled diplomacy and patience had ensured Rassam's initial success. Now he had to endure both failure and fear. He doubted that the British would meet Tewodros's request. He himself admitted to no low spirits directly, but others noticed his dejection.

'You can do no good by appearing gloomy,' urged Kentiba Haylu, Tewodros's 'adopted father'.

Yetemegnu, Tewodros's consort, the sharer of his tent, also counselled him:. 'If you take matters cheerily, you have nothing to fear; everything will come right at last, for the king really loves you.'

VIII

Moritz Hall in chains. From a photograph by Henry Aaron Stern

43

Now that the question had been resolved, and he had Rassam where he wanted him, Tewodros settled into a state of eccentric magnanimity. He sent regular greetings to Rassam: *How are you? How did you spend the night? How are your companions?* When he found that Rassam's tent had no groundsheet, he himself went to fetch carpets and spread them on the bare earth. Soldiers and sutlers alike were amazed to see in the dusty alleys of the camp their sovereign walking hand in hand with the 'disgraced' Rassam.

Tewodros dismissed the guard outside Rassam's tent: 'I have nothing to fear from him.' The guard watched the emperor part his lips and jab a royal finger into the shadows of his mouth. 'Not even if he were to put the muzzle of a pistol here!'

He finally presented the golden saddle to Rassam (though the Order of the Cross and Solomon's Seal was still not finished). Decorative shields, swords and spears were awarded to him and the two others. They were each given fine mules and a thoroughbred Oromo horse. Tewodros sent twenty fine *shammas* for the British envoys to use as bedding, as well as three silk and cotton *margafs*. Rassam was reluctant to wear his, but Tewodros said: 'Wear it not for my sake, but for the sake of my queen, from whom I have taken it.'

When he discovered that 24 May was Queen Victoria's birthday, Tewodros cancelled all his official business and gave himself up to 'merry-making for the sake of the regard he entertained towards Her Majesty'. Merry-making for Tewodros involved guns, and he gathered all the Europeans on the beach for a twenty-one-gun salute.

He also invited Rassam, Blanc and Prideaux to the test firing of the latest three-pounder cast by Waldmeier and the missionaries at Gefat. Such was the success of the trial that Tewodros ran up to Moritz Hall – who had arranged the firing – and kissed him on the head. 'My pet son! My pet son!' he cried, in an 'ecstasy of delight'. He then sat, and for some time absorbed everyone with the wonderful things he had done with guns as a youth, how his path to the throne was paved with improvised ordnance, the mines he designed to send the Mussulmen to Gehenna.

On another occasion Tewodros invited the envoys to the launch of two new boats. Traffic on Lake Tana had always been confined to the three-man papyrus *tankwas*, but in the name of progress Tewodros had spent a month or so building two experimental craft 'in imitation of a steamer'. They lay ready in the shallows, sixty feet long and twenty in the beam. Their decks were wooden and their hulls papyrus. A pair of paddle-steamer wheels, hand-turned, had been fixed to propel them. Afraid that they might get wet, Tewodros told the English envoys to watch from the shore. He himself boarded the first boat with about a hundred others. As the hulls settled in the water, it appeared that the wheels were too high for propulsion. They turned without purchase. But as the papyrus soaked up water, so the boats settled lower, and the wheels began to work. The boats picked up speed. Rassam watched as Tewodros became 'almost frantic with joy'. He transferred to the other boat, cleared the peninsula and entered the vast expanse of water beyond. Coming out of the lee of the shore, they found a breeze that drove a light swell against the papyrus sides. The craft began to flex along their length. The wood and the papyrus flexed separately, the lashings loosened, and slowly the boats began to break up. All hands paddled for the shore.

For months afterwards the two ships remained where they were, beached and abandoned.

Tewodros liked to take Rassam shooting along Lake Tana's wooded shores. Sometimes they would go after duck and geese, at others hippo. When once Rassam slipped on the shoreline boulders, Tewodros helped him up. 'Rise, my son; may your enemies die in your stead!'

Rassam was always amazed at Tewodros's agility, his nimble barefooted step, the swiftness with which he covered the steep and rocky ground of his kingdom. Watching him play *gugs* that month, surrounded by hundreds of other warriors in mock combat, Rassam marvelled at him. Dressed the same as all the others, it was still *his* figure that stood out.

'I could not help deploring on this occasion that Theodore, who had so many qualities calculated to make him the idol of his people, and especially of his army, should possess those qualities which neutralised his influence for good, and made him the scourge of his people.'

When Tewodros took to shooting vultures his courtiers always knew it was a bad sign. Then the master of the horse would suggest to Rassam that they left camp to go for a ride. Tewodros did not want his esteemed visitor around. Many high-ranking officers received the *giraf* that month. A woman was whipped to death when her husband defected to the rebels. Tewodros himself killed a peasant with a single blow to the head.

The prisoners were well aware of their own peril. They knew that a single comment could condemn them, that insults might be detected in anything they wrote or received. They had already destroyed many of their papers. They had soaked them in basins, eaten them, slipped them to their cook to throw in the fire. In conversation, they took to referring to the disruptive Bardel as 'Shrimps'. Tewodros was 'Bob'. None of them gave much hope to Flad's mission to England; much more relevant to their future was the hothouse of Tewodros's camp and the vicious insurgency beyond it.

44

In the month of Ginbot, 1866, a visitor arrived unseen at the edge of the Zeghie camp. Stern spoke of him as the 'rider on the pale horse'.

He had been before, ten years ago exactly. Then as now Tewodros had been plundering cattle. Then too the emperor was camping on the shores of Lake Tana. On the Feast of St George, 23 Ginbot, 1856 – with his forces all gathered at the church of St George – 'God sent a catastrophe which made all the soldiers dead.' At once Tewodros had returned all the cattle to their owners.

This time, though, it was too late – the cattle had been eaten. Tewodros eased up on his persecutions and turned to the Book of Psalms. In Ethiopia the 'rider on the pale horse' was called *neftegna fengel* because it struck its victims with the speed of a *neftegna*, a rifle. It was cholera.

Dr Blanc had predicted trouble. 'Living in a confined camp without any sanitary regulations, I fear that our health will suffer.' Now, with the rains coming, the situation was about to become worse. The royal herald wandered the great city of tents announcing a move to the healthier heights of Debre Tabor. Tewodros sent his women back across the lake, and kept only Yetemegnu by his side. The great camp was abandoned. Tens of thousands hurried to gather food and weapons for the journey. They left behind a wasteland, and the mound-graves of the first victims.

The journey soon turned into a hellish trek. Waldmeier, who with the other Gefat artisans was not a prisoner, recalled the sick and dead being carried on litters. Others staggered and dropped to the ground, 'the multitude passing over them, so that the smell became fearful, and the lamentation for the dead was heart-rending'.

By the time they reached the foot of the lake and crossed the Blue Nile, hundreds were dying each day. On the night of 8 June, three hundred of Tewodros's soldiers died; another seven hundred contracted the disease. The emperor sent Kentiba Haylu and one-eyed Aggafari Golem to assist Rassam. Stern recalled the moment when the *aggafari*, 'squatting in an easy attitude near me, was suddenly struck by the invisible shaft'. Within a very short time he was dead. Tewodros gave Ato Samuel provisional instructions for the burial of Rassam. In Qorata, every inch of the church burial ground was full. The corpses were piled in the road outside. As well as cholera there were dysentery, smallpox and typhus.

On 16 June, in the middle of a scalp-bruising hailstorm, the Europeans at last arrived at the small knoll of Gefat. A number of their servants had died. But for Waldmeier and the artisans it was a homecoming. For Rassam, Blanc and Prideaux it was their first sight of Tewodros's nucleic industrial centre. Oblivious to the storm, Tewodros took them on a tour of his cannon factory, the stores, the workshops and mills. While they stood hunched beneath the hail, he spoke of the guns that had already been built there – and those he planned. He had a fire lit in one of the foundries, and sat for three hours on an improvised bench, drinking Rassam's Hennessy brandy and talking to them about his tax-shy citizens.

Rassam told him that the English had taxed horses and male domestics to great effect.

'Mr Rassam,' Tewodros smiled, 'you do not know the Abyssinians. Were I to tax their mules, horses and domestics, not one of them would ride, and every man would become his own servant.'

Tewodros announced that they would spend the next few months there. He gave Rassam a billet, and worried all night that it might be uncomfortable. The next morning he came to Rassam's quarters with carpets. He furnished the main room with his own throne, swept the bare earth floor, bundled up the dust and pitched it out of the window.

Throughout all the movements of the last months, illness had been following the royal camp like a pack of hyenas. Dr Blanc again found his time stretched: 'From morning to night, I was in constant attendance on the sick.' One patient in particular occupied him – Waldmeier's 'dear wife', the half-Ethiopian daughter of John Bell. Now she was suddenly 'seized with a violent attack of cholera, followed by typhus fever'. In her distress, she cried ceaselessly for her daughter – *Rosa! Rosa! Rosa!* Blanc warned the open-hearted Waldmeier that he should not let the three-year-old go near her – and to prepare himself for the worst.

'My heart was breaking,' wrote Waldmeier, 'and it seemed to me that every tree and shrub were mourning.'

For a few days after their arrival, death hung heavy over Waldmeier's Gefat household, over the court, the military camp, and the whole region of Debre Tabor. But following the advice of Dr Blanc, Tewodros dispersed his soldiers, broke up the camp, and the worst of the epidemic passed. Susan Waldmeier began to recover.

Soon after Rassam and the others arrived at Gefat, Tewodros paid a visit. Rassam had asked for the throne to be removed from his small quarters because it took up too much room, so he spread a red cloth over a camp chair for his royal guest.

Tewodros was 'in excellent humour' that morning, and the two had a long and wide-ranging conversation. The emperor asked about Diogenes – 'Was he mad or just eccentric?' Alexander the Great had famously been to see Diogenes and asked, 'What can I do for you?' 'Move out of the sun,' Diogenes told him, 'and stop casting a shadow on me.'

'I am descended from Alexander,' explained Tewodros. He said the Macedonian had once visited the court of the great Ethiopian queen Candace. 'Fetch the book!' he ordered Kentiba Haylu.

Kentiba Haylu was one of the emperor's most loyal courtiers. He had supported Tewodros from the beginning, and even now 'considered him the best man living'. His loyalty was matched only by his profound piety. Delicately he turned the vellum pages. The importance of Alexander to the Ethiopians was enormous – Tewodros told Rassam he was held in the 'highest reverence'. Their own Ge'ez version of his mythical journeys, the *Zena Eskander*, was widely circulated. When Alexander visited Candace he was so amazed by her beauty, 'and her noble stature and her royal bearing', that he wept. She led him to her chamber along a passage of red gold, its walls studded with precious stones. The vast room emitted a brilliant light. When the queen travelled, the entire structure would be placed on beams, and elephants would haul it wherever she wanted to go. The Ethiopian queen was wearing a dress of gold and precious stones, and a scent of musk and ambergris. She took Alexander's hand, led him to the divan and embraced him, and put the royal crown on him; and he lay with her that night until sunrise. Hence Tewodros's claim.

With hushed reverence Kentiba Haylu recounted Alexander's adventures, his wondrous voyages and his wide-eyed wandering through the groves of Paradise. Like most Ethiopians, the *kentiba* 'believed in these legends as he believed in the revelations of the Bible'.

'What do you think of the story?' Tewodros asked Rassam.

Anything more absurd, Rassam had been thinking to himself, could hardly be conceived.

'To tell the truth, Your Majesty, I think Alexander was wise in wishing admittance into Paradise, but I think he was a fool for returning to earth again.'

Tewodros burst out laughing. He almost fell from the chair. 'Do you imagine that I believe in such trash?'

Beside them, Kentiba Haylu was 'speechless'.

45

On 10 July 1866, the Reverend Martin Flad, lay missionary of the London Jewish Society, arrived in London. With him he brought Tewodros's request for gun-making experts and equipment. The diplomatic crisis and the fate of the hostages now hinged on him and this letter.

A German by birth, Flad had been based in Ethiopia for a good twelve years – longer than any of the other Europeans. He had first gone to the country in 1854, despatched by Samuel Gobat when Tewodros was still Dejazmach Kasa, and had watched the tragic arc of his reign. With his wife Pauline and his children still there, he was terrified above all that the British government might use force against the emperor.

'If England would take a hostile position against Abyssinia,' he implored the Foreign Office in his Germanised English, 'a fatalist like [Tewodros] would at once, in a most cruel and barbarous manner, slaughter all our people.' Either that, or he would take them deep into the mountains 'and torture them – what is worse than to be killed at once – in order to force them to write that the troops shall leave his dominions. Therefore it is most desirable to finish with this man in peace.'

Keen to wrap up the Abyssinian difficulty with a minimum of fuss, the Foreign Office agreed. They put Flad on a guinea a day, and told him to go ahead and arrange the artisans and equipment requested.

But poor Flad was flummoxed. He was a stranger in London. He had spent the last twelve years in the wilds of Ethiopia. He had no idea how to go about the task. When, after a few weeks, James Murray at the Foreign Office found out that nothing had been done, he was furious. Flad, he wrote, was 'useless'. Instead he commissioned Colonel Merewether, political agent in Aden, who happened to be in London on leave.

Merewether had soon assembled an impressive cache of machinery with which to excite Tewodros. To each item, for the penny-conscious Foreign Office, was attached an estimate of its cost:

One steam-engine with boiler and fittings complete, 12 horse-power, ready for setting up £300
Cupola and fans. £50
Puddling and smelting apparatus complete with different classes of iron £400
One vertical drill for general use, including fine and common work £100

Merewether also included: one lathe, one saw bench, one threshing machine, a patent churn, drive belts, machinery for screw bolts, two anvils (one 4 cwt, one 3), a vice, carpenter's tools (set of), smith's tools (ditto), gunpowder mill (small size), copper-cap making machine, assorted steel (one ton), filters, paint, hand-lamps. Gifts should include: one ordnance telescope of good power (with tripod), gunpowder, caps, carpets (large, handsome), silks (assorted colours), tumblers (large, ornamented, a dozen), a fowling piece (breech-loading), a Jacob's rifle, a Prussian needle gun, and a Dean & Adams revolver.

Tewodros, he wrote, had heard of a telescope capable of

making out a man's face at ten miles. 'Send a couple of such detectives,' Murray scribbled on the list.

Merewether was also recruiting personnel. He had had some success, and was even having to make choices between various men. The cost of the enterprise, including salaries for the artisans and a contingency for breaking it down for mule transport in the highlands, came to about £3,500.

When the Foreign Office saw all the detail, when they pictured more men going into Ethiopia, they were struck for the first time by a sense of impotence. Until then, the Ethiopian problem had been an inconvenience, a minor difficulty between their consul and an uppity local ruler. Now they realised their dilemma. What was to stop these men from also being detained, and more demands being made? What incentive was there for Tewodros to release the envoys? In those far-off mountains, all the resources of the British Empire counted for nothing.

In the meantime, rumours of Egyptian moves towards Ethiopia had filtered through to London. A British official had seen guns 'suitable for mountain warfare' being loaded onto a train in Egypt, and troops were becoming active in the Ethiopian border region of Bogos.

Sidelined by Merewether, Flad followed all these developments, and his anxiety grew. Knowing the country and knowing Tewodros, he regarded British reluctance and Egyptian hostility as the very worst combination for his family and the other hostages.

46

For a year or more, the Egyptians had been pushing south. They had taken over the governorship of Massawa in April. They had promised the Sublime Porte to expand Ottoman interests in the area, and with Tewodros's power declining there was plenty of opportunity. As Wagshum Gobeze's influence grew in Tigray and the north, he too helped loosen Tewodros's grip in favour of the Egyptians. Flad was right to be anxious.

Until the start of the *keremt* rains of 1866, Tewodros continued to be 'extremely kind and attentive' to the Europeans. 'Oh God!' he cried to Rassam in late June, 'how can we Abyssinians forget the English who have given us so many thousand Bibles?' But then, a priest arrived from Jerusalem and told him some alarming news: a railway had been built, running from the Red Sea coast, across the desert to the border town of Kasala. Tewodros's explosive suspicions were now triggered – clearly the Egyptians' allies the British were behind this railway, which was there to bring troops south to annex Christian Ethiopia for good. Now at last he understood the true motives behind Rassam's journey. For him, the railway represented a deadly trio of the threats that had crippled his reign – foreign invasion, personal betrayal and European duplicity.

Tewodros summoned Rassam's party. They all gathered in a tent of black goat-hair, the one usually used by Yetemegnu. He did not appear himself but sent his *afe-negus* to deliver the charges. Throughout the afternoon, messengers went back and forth from Tewodros's quarters.

Was the railway not a conduit for Egyptian troops to reach his borders? Did it not signal the start of a campaign by the English and French against him? If you, Rassam, my friend, passed through Kasala just six months before, why did you not mention it? Does this not show a breach of the friendship you profess for me? Does it not confirm that the English are not sincere, and want to deceive me?

Rassam denied the charges. He said he had always been honest with Tewodros. He knew of no railway. 'These reports are invented by wicked people for mischievous ends.'

Tewodros had heard that once Rassam had secured the hostages and left the country, British forces would invade and punish him. 'Is this true?'

'This report,' said Rassam, 'is false and villainous.'

The *afe-negus* was kept busy that day, running between the tents. At one point – 'to the terror of all' – the *Fetha Negest* was quoted, and new charges made against Stern and Rosenthal. In the end, the proxy trial did not escalate. Tewodros's anger receded and Rassam's defence kept him just the right side of royal favour.

'Your mouth is sweet,' concluded the emperor, 'and you are a good man, but those above you are bad.'

The cordon became a little tighter. The Europeans were confined to Debre Tabor, their firearms confiscated to prevent suicide. Tewodros reverted to affection in his treatment of Rassam. He was not a prisoner, and Tewodros encouraged him to go out in the town. 'If you stay and mope, you will fall ill, and then what shall I, your friend, do? Shall I not be ill too?'

All the while, Tewodros's own demons were multiplying. He had been planning a great campaign against Wagshum

Gobeze. The *wagshum*'s forces now equalled Tewodros's own, his territory too. As the hereditary ruler of Wag and Lasta, he had in the eyes of many a better claim to the throne than the upstart from Qwara.

Each day Tewodros issued orders to pack up his tents and move against the *wagshum*, and each day the tents stayed put. Indecision now afflicted Tewodros. The commands that had once flowed from him, sweeping his vast army from one end of the country to the other, had now slowed to a dry-season trickle. It became harder to forget the powers gathering against him – the rebels, the Egyptians and the Europeans beyond, harder too to contain the wild range of his moods.

'You are my friend, and I love you,' he wrote to Rassam on the morning of 3 July, adding with mannered deference: 'With your permission, I now go to Gefat, to inspect some work of my children.'

47

That morning Tewodros and his party left Debre Tabor to see the Gefat missionaries, his 'children'. It was a journey of no more than a couple of hours, one that in the past Tewodros had always been glad to make. In contrast to the stifling atmosphere of his court, and his own reactionary people, Gefat felt free from intrigue and hostility. He could sit with Waldmeier outside his two-storey *à l'allemand* house, debating the Bible or technology, or progressive ideas for the country's future, or the science of founding, about which both were so ignorant.

An account of an earlier trip there includes a cameo of Tewodros in better days, late in 1862. Henry Dufton had just arrived in the country when the emperor invited him to visit the missionaries' mortar factory at Gefat. Tewodros bounded down the slope from Debre Tabor, his bare feet swift and unflinching on the rocks. When he reached the bottom of the hill, Dufton watched him mount his horse. 'Agile and supple, he sprang off the ground into the saddle without touching the stirrup.' The emperor then spurred his horse to a gallop, speeding out across the plain in mock pursuit of one of his courtiers, on muleback, and so sustained was the chase and so good that the laughing Tewodros bought the mule on the spot. Seeing the emperor later that day, with his arm around the child of one of the missionaries, chatting, Dufton wrote: 'No, Theodore is not all devil! Else how comes it that those who have known him best and longest have given the most favourable account of him?'

Now Tewodros trotted out towards Gefat in a brooding silence. Debre Tabor rose behind him while in front, glowing in the early-morning sun, was the missionaries' low knoll. Since returning from Zeghie, the emperor had been discussing with Waldmeier and the others the campaign against Wagshum Gobeze. He needed carriages for the guns, and on the knee-breaking roads of Lasta, he needed the carriages sometimes to be borne by mules. If he was dithering about the campaign in Debre Tabor, at Gefat at least it seemed real.

But that morning even Gefat failed to stay his anger. As Tewodros was leaving the foundry, a beggar hobbled up to him. 'My lords the Europeans have always been kind to me,' he pleaded. 'Oh, my *negus*, you too can relieve my distress!'

The emperor rounded on the man. 'How dare you call anyone lord but myself!'

He told his men to beat the vagrant.

'Mercy! Mercy!'

'Beat him! Beat him!'

Under their blows, the man fell to the ground. Within minutes he was dead.

Tewodros then turned on Rosenthal. A lance quivered in his hand. 'Donkey! Why did you call me the son of a poor woman?'

Blanc watched the lance. 'Every minute I expected that he would throw it.' Blanc too was being held tight by the emperor's men. Tewodros's rage seemed uncontrollable. 'Slaves!' he spat at the European workmen. 'Who are you that you dare call yourselves lords?'

Tewodros took Blanc and Rosenthal back to Debre Tabor, and sent Ato Samuel to fetch Rassam, Prideaux, Cameron and Stern. Pulling on their coats, the Europeans hurried out. They found the emperor perched on a rock, with his officers assembled below. Rassam was alarmed to see Blanc and Rosenthal under arrest. Tewodros, he recalled, 'looked as if he had gone mad'. Prideaux thought him in a 'state of great passion – real or feigned, I cannot say'. Dr Blanc was more clinical about Tewodros's anger. In such a state, 'his black face acquires an ashy hue, his eyes bloodshot and fierce, seem to shed fire, his thin lips, compressed, have but a whitish margin round the mouth, his very hair seems to stand erect'.

Tewodros sat alone on his rock, chipping at it with the butt of his spear. He surveyed the familiar group of Europeans below him. To Stern he cried: 'Was it as a Christian, a heathen, or a Jew that you abused me? When you wrote your book, by whose authority did you do it?'

He then turned to Rassam, who only that morning had received a devoted letter from him. 'You also have abused me.'

'I?'

'Yes, you; in four instances.'

First, he had read Stern's book, which insulted Tewodros, and that itself was an insult. Then he had failed to bring the prisoners to him to be reconciled before leaving. Third, Rassam's government accepted the Turkish occupation of Jerusalem – *his* legacy!

'The fourth I have forgotten.'

Suddenly his voice rose. 'I want Europe to restore me to the Holy Land!'

Rassam listened. He tried to explain that the prisoners had left Qorata on 13 April with His Majesty's permission, and that 'with reference to Jerusalem ... the European powers were not given to interfere in such matters'.

'Ato Kokeb, you know history; will you, therefore, tell me whether I have an inheritance in Jerusalem?'

'I know that there are Abyssinians living in a convent at Jerusalem,' offered Stern.

'Are you not aware,' Tewodros cried to all those present, 'that India and half the world belong to me?'

His words echoed off the rocks, bouncing around the hilltop, around the countless staring figures of his soldiers and his courtiers, his ministers and the Europeans. They said nothing. No one dared speak.

Tewodros ordered the Europeans to be held. Fifteen guards, carrying the men's bedding, led them into a poky and odorous room. It had no windows. One or two candles cast a thin, yellowy light into its depths. It was here, said Lieutenant Prideaux, that 'we tasted first the bitterness of real captivity'. Rassam says it was the treasury, Prideaux that it was a store or magazine. Blanc calls it a 'go-down . . . a black house'. It only needed more of them in there, he wrote, to re-enact 'the fearful drama of the Calcutta Black Hole'.

For the three men of the British mission the threshold had at last been crossed. The six-month transition from favour to disgrace was complete, from the 10,000-horse reception in late January, through their lakeside idyll and the season of gifts and honours, the first arrest in April, to total imprisonment. That evening, Rassam sent the emperor a candid message. 'It is our fault for not having believed what we heard before leaving Massawa; but we could not credit what His Majesty's enemies said against him.'

'My foes,' came the reply, 'would spread evil reports against me, even if I were to carry you on my head.'

Tewodros's anger passed, as it always did. Its departure left him frail and regretful. He wanted to visit Rassam. In his private tent, Yetemegnu begged the emperor to stay with her. But he insisted, sending a messenger to Rassam back out into the night: 'How could I go to sleep knowing that you are unhappy, my friend?'

Late that evening, the guards pushed open the door and the emperor stepped into the crowded, windowless room. He clutched candles in his right hand. Over his shoulder hung a horn of *arak*. Behind him an attendant brought a beaker of *tej*. He dismissed the guards, chastising them for their mistrust, and sat down. The flames guttered as the door was pulled to, then stood firm. The light glowed on the chaff-flecked mud of the wall and on the emperor's face. With a smile, he poured a glass of *arak* and handed it to Rassam.

'I know you do not normally drink, but I feel sure you will not refuse to drink with me on this occasion, to make me feel happy.'

They toasted each other, and Tewodros poured more glasses and handed them out to Blanc and Prideaux. Stern and Rosenthal – most persecuted of all the Europeans – remained standing. 'How are you, Ato Kokeb?' the emperor called over his shoulder. 'Why do you look so gloomy?' Tewodros laughed, saying to Rassam: 'Tell him not to moan.'

Becoming serious again, he apologised to Rassam. 'Do not regard my face, but trust to my heart, because I really love you.'

In the isolation of the room, unguarded, plainly dressed, Tewodros looked small and vulnerable.

'My father was mad,' he said quietly, 'and though people often say that I am mad also, I never would believe it; but now I know it is true.'

'Do not say such a thing,' urged Rassam.

Tewodros pushed himself to his feet. His voice was a whisper: 'I am mad.' He turned in the doorway, facing them, the darkness beyond.

'Goodbye.'

Another twenty-one months passed before they saw him again.

IX

View from a Point Near the King's House, Magdala, by Robert Baigrie (1868)

48

In London, it had been a period of mixed news from Ethiopia. First, in April, came word of Rassam's success – the hostages had been released, he was waiting to bring them home. Then reports arrived that they'd all been detained again; and finally, in September, that they'd all been imprisoned.

Martin Flad heard through a letter from his wife, written at Gefat on 7 July: 'My dear Martin, only with a few words I venture to inform you of our last sad experiences, our present situation and our gloomy future.' She went on to describe in rather more than a few words what had happened since he left – the cholera around Lake Tana, the deaths of many of their servants and converts. But it was the trial and arrest of Rassam that was most alarming. Reading about it in the heart of Bloomsbury, Flad had a sudden glimpse of how far Tewodros had fallen.

'Can it be,' ended her letter, 'that we shall meet again or was our sad parting on the shore of the lake for eternity?'

For all those following the crisis from London, Tewodros's violent arrest of the Europeans was a shock. Calls for military action grew louder. Even Flad now realised that sending the artisans would solve nothing. He suggested that a better way to win Tewodros's favour would be to help fight the case of the expelled Ethiopian monks in Jerusalem. 'If, after all this, the King should go on in this way, then, may the consequence be whatever it may, attack him at once with your arms.'

He translated his wife's letter, and within a couple of weeks it was printed up and laid before Lord Derby's cabinet. The cabinet did not agree to use force. They decided on a compromise. Flad would go back to Massawa with the machinery and the artisans and a letter from Queen Victoria. He was to go up alone to Tewodros in the highlands, and let it be known that the equipment and personnel would only be granted when the hostages had left.

In the meantime a new option emerged, picking up, in part, on Flad's suggestion regarding the Ethiopian monks. It came from the Armenians of the Ottoman Empire, and was based on their network of Levantine communities, on the very tenuous linkage of ancient alliances, factions, religious affinities and worldly disputes. But it offered a chance.

His Holiness the Armenian Patriarch of Constantinople approached Lord Lyons, the British ambassador to the Sublime Porte. He proposed intervening with Tewodros. Lord Lyons forwarded the suggestion to the British consul in Jerusalem, who in turn took it to the monastery of Sourp Hagop in the Old City. There His Holiness the Armenian Patriarch of Jerusalem was at once enthusiastic. For years, the Armenians had been helping the Ethiopian monks. Since the expulsion by the Copts, the Armenians were providing the homeless and churchless Ethiopians with their daily bread: twenty-five loaves and two large cauldrons of soup. That, it was thought, should work well with Tewodros (that the Armenians were also complicit in earlier persecutions of the Ethiopians was overlooked).

From Jerusalem, the Armenian patriarch sent an archbishop, a monk and an assistant. 'We did not hesitate,' wrote the monk, 'to take on this difficult mission, out of respect for the government of Great Britain and in humanity's name.' It took them four months to reach Ethiopia. The assistant died fairly soon from disease. The monks carried on, wandering the highlands in their black surplices and their cowls of moiré silk, their boxes of gifts and their letters for the emperor. Tewodros heard of their arrival and wrote saying he'd be delighted to see them. He would send troops to escort them to his camp. But it never happened. Rains, rebels and the rising tide of chaos intervened. The opportunity was lost. For another year and a half the Armenians continued their wandering, before returning to Jerusalem.

49

On 9 July, the foreign prisoners left Debre Tabor. They headed east, around the lower slopes of Mount Guna. They had not been told where they were going, but they knew. Everyone knew. The villagers who stepped aside on the road to let them pass were used to such convoys. 'May God release you!' they cried. The foreigners were bound for Meqdela.

A week or so later, in darkness, the prisoners reached the saddle of Selamge. In the moonlight, they looked up and saw the organ-pipe cliffs of the summit. At the second gate, they waited for some time while their papers were taken in. 'At last, one by one, counted like sheep, we passed the doors,' wrote Blanc. On the mountain's flat top they were taken to a piece of open ground before the emperor's house. Lined up to greet them were the mountain's commandant, Ras Kidane Maryam, and his six-man council.

For the first few days they all slept in the same hut. At 10,000 feet, the nights were cold. Late on the third morning, Ras Kidane Maryam arrived again with his council and a crowd of others. Those who could squeezed into the hut. The greetings continued for some time, and opened up into some general talk among the Ethiopians about religion. The Europeans had no idea why they had come. The officers stood around 'looking pious'. Then at last the kindly and hesitant Ras Kidane Maryam turned to his task. They had to – they didn't want to, of course – they had no unfriendly feelings towards the distinguished *farenjis*, no – no, it was just custom . . . Please, come . . .

Out in the noon sun was a large mound of chains. One by one, the prisoners had them fitted to their legs. The smith knelt to position a ring around each of their calves, an inch or two above the ankle. Placing their foot on a stone, he then stood and swung a heavy hammer to close the ring, until no more than a finger could be slid between fetter and skin.

Dr Blanc watched each blow fall, biting his lip to hide the pain. When it was finished, he stumbled to his feet, raised his cap and, with a smile to the officers and crowd, cried: 'God save the queen!'

Ras Kidane Maryam said with an apologetic smile, 'May God release you.'

The prisoners returned to their hut. They sat around and looked at each other in chains. 'The sight was so ridiculous,' recalled Blanc, 'so absurd, that for all our sorrow we could not help laughing.'

Blanc held out little hope for Flad's mission, but was 'certain' that when news reached Britain of their outrageous treatment, troops would be despatched at once to free them. They had, he estimated, a wait of about six months.

Rassam was less confident. Everything else he had managed to endure – the year-long wait at Massawa, the journey, the crushing disappointment in April. He had always been resolute about the mission. Now for the first time he let his stoical and diplomatic front slip. When asked to send a message to Tewodros, he said with sarcasm:

'Tell the King that my fellow-prisoners and I have reached this jail in safety, and that when this act of his becomes known, it will doubtless serve to increase his fame; especially when people hear that a great Sovereign has imprisoned a man merely because he was his friend.'

Some days later, Ato Samuel freely translated the message to Tewodros: 'Rassam feels highly favoured in having so exalted a locality allotted to him during the rainy season, and one so near the royal enclosure, and that his only regret was being so far from the royal presence.'

Those early days at Meqdela were one of the few times that Rassam showed any form of personal reaction. 'Our lives hung by a thread,' he said, and spoke of 'gloom and low spirits'. He knew how unlikely the British were to use force, and began to think about escape.

Abune Selama, confined to his hut nearby on the mountain, heard of the hostages' arrival and had similar ideas. He sent a message to Rassam with a plan: he would darken his face, pass in disguise out through the gates and join the rebels. His authority would then become a rallying point for those disaffected with Tewodros. The plan, perhaps wisely, was never tried.

Over the coming weeks, Rassam managed to settle down into the rhythm of life on Meqdela, tedious as it was. It was a strange imprisonment. They suffered a great deal from their chains. They learned to shuffle around their compound. As their legs thinned they tied strips of calico around the chains to stop them chafing. But there were comforts too. Rassam and Blanc 'messed' with Prideaux, Cameron and Stern, and in the evening, while a brush-fire crackled in the centre of the hut, they pushed their fettered legs beneath a table spread with a clean tablecloth. They flicked open napkins and waited for their Indian servants to bring the dishes. Rassam listed the meals: Soup – Fish *(when available)* – Two or four entrées – joint of meat – pudding or tart – anchovy toast or cream cheese.

'A millionaire could not have lived better than we did,' said Rassam. He quickly learned the value of having money on the mountain. Money bought favours and kept them out of Meqdela's disease-ridden death cells. He had some of his own, and when his possessions arrived, a stock of gifts to distribute. When the money ran low, Waldmeier sent more over from Gefat. Once when the rebels gained control of the road, Tewodros himself authorised a draft for Rassam to be made on the Meqdela treasury.

Rassam made sure that he always had a quantity of good *tej* and *araq* for Ras Kidane Maryam and his council. His prestige on Meqdela was based also on the 'extraordinary affection' that Tewodros was known to have for him. Curiosity led many high-ranking women to the door of his hut. In the main they were the wives of prisoners. They would always acknowledge his chains with a sigh and a polite 'May God release you!' He found their soft-spoken sympathy an immense comfort, though he wrote coyly that it was 'no pleasure to sit near them': washing was not part of their daily routine.

The women quizzed him about life in Britain. They pored over Rassam's photo album. Sometimes it would be gone for a week or two, circulated among his 'lady-visitors'. In a packet of mail brought from the coast he received a carte-de-visite from a woman in England. When his Ethiopian ladies saw it, they addressed the image.

'Did you not weep when you heard that Mr Rassam was in chains?' They took the card and kissed it. 'May the Lord comfort you!'

50

'On the sixth day of Hidar,' wrote the chronicler, 'the stars in heaven began to fly about as if struck by fear.'

Tewodros took a corps of men to Gondar. He left Debre Tabor and rode westwards, through the night, without halt, for sixteen hours. Dawn revealed the walls of the crumbling palaces, the rounded castellations, the bald towers. Women in white *shammas* rushed to flank the imperial horse, ululating and clapping in celebration; on the other side of the city the last of the rebels slipped into the hills.

The emperor ordered a search for any who remained. None was found. He burnt the churches. Azezo, Lideta and Qusqwam, John the Baptist and Qiha Iyesus – these ones he favoured and spared. The churches of Abora and Be'ata and Adebabay Abune Tekle Haymanot by a miracle refused the flames, but the dozens of others were destroyed. The emperor looted 5,500 holy books and took the sacramental robes and the silver and gold crosses, and the *kebbero*, the sacred drums, and the censers and chalices and pitchers and basins. When the priests complained, he had them thrown into the flames. He asked the wives of the traders to bring gold to him and then set light to their hands and hair. Then he pointed to the women in white *shammas* who had greeted him and commanded that they too should be thrown into the fire. Gondar was destroyed. Only beasts were left to roam in the ruins. Tewodros took the tens of thousands of its people who had survived back to Debre Tabor and announced that henceforth Debre Tabor was the new Gondar.

He was received like a conqueror. Everyone was too afraid to do otherwise. Kentiba Haylu wept in private for the destruction of Gondar, the country's greatest city where he'd been born and where he had been mayor for many years. He wept for the sad decline of his 'son' the great emperor, for the killing, for the terrible sacrilege of the burning churches. The *kentiba* had always been unbendingly loyal to Tewodros, who in turn believed he possessed magical powers. He was a kind, devout man, but his favoured position made him many enemies in the court. One of these reported his private grief to Tewodros, and some time later the *kentiba* and his favourite grandson were arrested. Together they were bound with ropes so tightly that the blood dripped from their fingers.

'My power over you will soon expire,' Haylu cried. 'Your reign will end in the fourteenth year.'

'Well,' said Tewodros, 'if you're wrong, you will pay with your life.' He sent the two to Meqdela. He was in the thirteenth year of his rule.

The community at Gefat also came to greet the returning Tewodros. They clutched burning torches and chanted: 'Your Majesty is like Hezekiah who did right in the sight of the Lord!' Hezekiah, who 'removed the high places, and brake the images and cut down the groves, and brake in pieces the brazen serpent that Moses had made'.

But even Waldmeier had lost faith in Tewodros: 'The anger and hatred of the King towards all the Europeans, and also the natives, increased every day.' Tewodros worked the missionaries of Gefat ever harder; in September they had produced one of the largest of all their cannon.

It was at about this time that Tewodros was handed a letter

from the English queen. Flad had arrived back in Massawa, and with him were artisans and equipment. Tewodros was amazed. He never imagined that Flad's journey to England would produce anything. There were conditions attached, but Tewodros was not deterred.

'Call me a woman if I will not get them in with all the articles!' he boasted to Waldmeier.

Tewodros still believed he could restore his power. He sensed that he had one advantage – British reluctance to send an army into the highlands. And he was right. With help from Queen Victoria and the new artisans and machinery, Gefat's guns would help him bring the rebels to heel. He wrote to Rassam on Meqdela, and asked confidently: 'Please send word and arrange for [the artisans] to come to me. Once this has been done, by the power of God, I shall make you happy and send you back with an escort.'

Yes, he had his difficulties. But had not his predecessors faced difficulties too? 'Even Solomon,' he wrote, 'the son of David, the great king, the creature of God and the slave of God, had great trouble in building the temple. He courted Hiram, King of Tyre, fell at his shoes, besought him and after having brought and received artisans, he built the temple . . . And now, just as Solomon fell at the shoes of Hiram, so have I fallen at the shoes of the queen, all her officers and her friends.'

Rassam, imprisoned on Meqdela, played his hand deftly, but with some risk. He replied to Tewodros with an open letter to the British government asking it to allow Flad and the artisans to leave Massawa for the highlands. At the same time, by his own secret messengers he sent word direct to the artisans at Massawa: *Do not go*. He hardly dared contemplate what would happen if the message failed to reach the coast, even less if it fell into Tewodros's hands.

At Gefat, Pauline Flad heard that her husband was in Massawa, and wrote to him of her ceaseless fears: 'Literally I can say that tears are my food day and night.'

In time she realised that Tewodros did not plan to release the hostages, that his 'intention is to play a very bad trick'. She sent another message to her husband on the coast: 'I tell you, yea even I entreat you, don't trust, don't trust, don't trust! If the workmen come, not one single soul will be able to leave the country.'

Waldmeier had now witnessed too much violence to maintain his rosy view of the world: 'The British should throw all that they have in vain brought to Massawa into the sea . . . [Tewodros] would rather cut all the Europeans into a thousand pieces than hand them over.'

51

In the end Flad did come up, but he came up alone. He had brought from England some gifts from the families of the hostages, as well as a few guns for Tewodros and a small flour mill. He also had the telescope Tewodros had requested through Rassam, but nothing more than a letter from the British government.

On 16 April Tewodros heard that Flad had reached Metemma, but that the artisans and machinery were still in Massawa. It was strange – why had Rassam's request failed? Tewodros had become so suspicious that he failed to spot real subterfuge.

Now he knew there was no way out. The British would not give him what he wanted.

The next day he rode out to Gefat with a force of soldiers, and arrested the entire European community.

'If I am to be killed,' he snarled, 'then you will die first!'

Moritz Hall, who years earlier had fled Tsarist Poland for a footloose life, called out: 'Kill us at once, but do not degrade us in this way.' The emperor told him to shut up.

Over the next few days, Gefat was destroyed. The little leafy hill where Walter Plowden had once lived, that Theophilus Waldmeier had first seen six years earlier, and that had been mission, gun factory and home to him, where he had buried four of his children, was stripped. The cannon were taken to Debre Tabor. The houses were plundered, the foundries wrecked, the mission school emptied. In an upstairs room, Susan Waldmeier looked at the golden saddle given to Theophilus by Tewodros for their wedding, at its gleaming threads and high cantle – then in fury, she pitched it out of the window. It landed on a group of soldiers.

Hagos the lion was killed. His skin was made into a *lemd* by one of Tewodros's generals.

Debtera Sahalu had been appointed by Waldmeier to head the Gefat school. Tewodros's men came for him, dragged him from his home and hacked off his hands and feet. He died a few days later. The European community was moved to Debre Tabor. Tewodros left to scourge the rebels in Dembea.

It was there that Flad found him. He had ridden through regions paralysed by famine. He dismounted on the edge of the camp, and entered the mass of tents on foot. It was strangely silent. The smell of rotting horseflesh choked him; carcasses lay scattered everywhere. Listless from hunger, troops and followers watched him as he passed.

He presented the letter to Tewodros, and told him he had the telescope.

'Let me see it.'

Flad raised the lid of a wooden crate. The brass tubes gleamed in beds of velvet. Flad took them out and began to put them together. Tewodros watched him. He saw him assemble the interlocking barrels, first one way then the other. In the end Flad held out the tapering form in his upturned hands. It was a beautiful object. Tewodros raised it to his eye and could see nothing. Flad adjusted the eye-piece. Still nothing. Flad again twisted the eye-piece – but Tewodros had lost patience.

He shoved it back to the missionary. 'The man who sends me this telescope only wants to annoy me.'

Tewodros dismissed everyone but translators. He turned to Flad. 'Have you seen the queen?' he asked.

'I have, and she gave me a verbal message.'

'What is it?'

Flad did his duty. 'If you do not at once send out of your country all those detained so long against their will, you have no right to expect any further friendship.'

Tewodros heard the message in silence. He asked it to be repeated, two or three times: *you have no right to expect any further friendship* . . .

A stillness settled over Tewodros. Now it was confirmed. 'I have asked from them a sign of friendship, but it is refused to me.'

Flad travelled on to Debre Tabor. In England he had been at liberty. He had travelled to Osborne House and had dinner with Queen Victoria. Now he stepped voluntarily through the gap in a ten-foot hedge into a muddy compound to join a group of fearful, starving prisoners. Among them were his wife Pauline and their three children. 'What a reunion!' he wrote. 'What poverty, what misery!'

52

Every month or two on Meqdela, a man – usually a different one – would slip out through the gatehouse, down the cliff road and into the rebel-held mountains of Lasta. Sewed in patches in his trousers or belt, or folded up and inserted into the amulet that Christians wore around their necks, were letters from the European captives – from Rassam and Blanc and Stern.

The urge to send news from Meqdela had been immediate. 'Every hour lost was a day added to our discomfort and misery,' wrote Blanc shortly after his arrival. He was confident their rescue would not be long coming.

At all stages of the message-sending there were risks. Writing them was hard enough, hidden from the sight of anyone who might tell the nervous guards. Nor was finding a messenger always easy, one who was both trustworthy and willing. First he had to dodge arrest by Tewodros's men, who would beat or even kill him if the letters were discovered. He soon moved out of Tewodros's territory and into that of Wagshum Gobeze, whose men might beat or even kill him if they discovered he had come from Meqdela. Then came numerous little fiefdoms and sheikhdoms where he might be beaten or even killed for any number of reasons – coming from the *wagshum*'s land or Tewodros's, being Amhara or Christian.

Robbery was possible at every stage – often the messenger was carrying a couple of hundred thalers.

Until the chaos of the last few months, they lost only one packet – the first. It was being carried by two men whose quarrelling drew attention to them. They were arrested, bound with ropes and the letters destroyed. It was after that that the prisoners learned to conceal the letters, and to send them by single messenger.

It was reckoned to be a good two-month walk to the coast. The envoys found that often a messenger would do it in less – at least the first time. The twenty thalers he was paid would make the next trip slower. He would stay at inns where Tigrayan women served beakers of yellow *tej* and were themselves easily available for another thaler. In this way the days slipped by more quickly, the miles more slowly. Back on Meqdela the Europeans were constantly on the lookout for fresh recruits.

With the second rainy season approaching, and no rescue in sight, Blanc's early confidence had seeped away. 'We had expected great things, and nothing was effected.'

In March 1867, he smuggled a letter out to the Foreign Office trying to persuade them to act. He chronicled Tewodros's reign, the innate violence disguised in his dizzying rise, and now revealed in his fall, in order to prove that any diplomacy was wasted: 'only one thing remains, *force*'.

Back in London a military option looked unlikely. As the Ethiopian crisis intensified, so the letters page of *The Times* filled with the advice of seasoned army officers, self-appointed experts, charlatans and quacks, warnings of deadly fevers, incurable diseases, flesh-eating worms and rapacious natives. The cuttings found their way by clandestine messenger up to Meqdela, where Blanc and Rassam read them with a mixture of 'despair and disgust'.

A stalemate had been reached. Diplomacy had failed, force was risky. All the prisoners could hope for, like everyone else in Tewodros's narrowing territory, was a swift and bloodless end to his reign. Yet for all the rebels' success, not one of them would attack him. Even if they did, everyone knew that the emperor could simply retreat to the fortress of Meqdela.

Each of the foreign prisoners endured confinement in his own way. 'Wearisome days and restless nights, constant anxiety and everlasting suspense,' wrote Stern, 'were a trial of our faith and patience that required more than an ordinary degree of Divine grace to sustain us without sinking into utter abandonment or miserable idiocy.'

Rassam coped with good Victorian fortitude. He dressed well, kept his whiskers trimmed and washed rigorously. He learned that there was no mood so heavy that it couldn't be lightened by a good spell in the kitchen garden. When he wasn't entertaining his lady visitors, or those in power on the mountain, flattering them, giving them *tej* and generally ensuring good conditions for himself and his fellow hostages, he was tending to his vegetables. He'd been given some tomato seedlings by an Egyptian on the mountain (tomatoes not being part of the highland Ethiopians' diet), and was amazed by their success. Within a short time, trained and trellised, their leaves provided shade for him and his guests. He later asked for more to be sent from the coast. His plants were never dormant, but gave fruit constantly. Soon tomato soup was added to their menu. Peas, French beans, potatoes, beets and turnips all flourished, lettuce too.

Rassam's tending of his vegetables brought another benefit. He learned to love the birds that flitted around his plants. By spreading grain in front of his hut, he brought in a host of red bishop birds and flycatchers. The birds became used to the clank of his chains, and he built a trough so that in the dry season they could drink – although, he was pleased to see, they were just as keen to use the water for bathing. They would appear in shifts all through the day, sweeping down to settle in his plants, in the trough, flying off in a single squeaking gang, to be replaced by another. Then that one too would leave, swooping up over the prison huts to the trees and cliffs and down to the fields far below. 'How I envied their freedom!' he recalled.

He became an expert on their social habits, their courtships, and would delight in the song that filled the hanging branches of his tomato plants. Nothing escaped the ears of Tewodros, who wrote asking after his friend and his avian visitors: 'How are Rassam's children?'

The prisoners had few other distractions. They had accumulated a small and eccentric collection of books and pieces of books: copies of McCulloch's *Commercial and Geographical Dictionary*, Adam Smith's *Wealth of Nations* and a text called Gadby's *Appendix*.

'I had made myself conversant with every known spot in the universe,' wrote Stern. 'And I could argue on supply and demand with a fluency that was perfectly awful.'

Rosenthal used an Italian Bible to teach himself Italian, and a portion of Guizot's *Histoire de la civilisation* to learn French.

Blanc sketched out a typical day: 'Smoke a pipe with Cameron. Lay down and read McCulloch's *Dictionary* ... crawled about for an hour between the huts; lay down, took Gadby's *Appendix*; but as I know it by heart, even his curious descriptions have no more attraction.'

For the two missionaries there was also the Bible. 'With raptures the eye rested on its soul-thrilling pages,' gushed Stern, 'picturing to its view the cross, the emblem of redeeming love and mercy, or wandering, by faith, amidst scenes of glory and bliss, that poured a flood of gladness into the desponding heart.'

Dr Blanc found more empirical sources of solace. Smallpox, cholera and typhus were rife on the mountain. One of his servants had an impressive case of elephantiasis, which swelled his scrotum to such a size that he could hardly walk. From the coast Colonel Merewether sent the doctor tubes of vaccine lymph, and he persuaded parents to bring their children for inoculation. When the lymph ran out, he drew some out of those already vaccinated and produced more. Not once did he fail to take down his 'Thermometrical Observations', his four-times-a-day temperature readings.

Apart from their ailments, Blanc had little time for the Ethiopians: 'I must declare that as far as I am aware, the Abyssinians have not a single good quality.' He couldn't understand the unflagging patience and diplomacy of Rassam, who spent so much time talking and laughing with them. But Rassam found the people to be 'without any caste prejudice, they are observant and shrewd, fond of learning and by no means deficient in intellectual ability'. Blanc stuck to medicine. In a letter written to Colonel Merewether he said: 'My qualifications are in the pills and the black draught line ... Rassam having frequently asserted I would be no good as a political officer. Amen.'

The dry season was drawing to a close. Buckets were lowered ever deeper into the mountain's wells; the splashes sounded more hollow. Money too was running short – for the European prisoners, their dwindling funds were as terrifying as any order from Tewodros; it was only money that kept them out of the mountain's deadly jails. At about this time an epidemic in the prison killed eighty prisoners, and spread to the guards. Tewodros became worried about the ratio of prisoners to guards. Rather than increase the number of guards he sent orders to Meqdela for two hundred prisoners to be taken from the cells and executed.

From Tewodros's camp at Debrē Tabor came news of further butchery. Six hundred soldiers were killed. No one dared go against his word, and they participated in the killing to spare themselves. Those who could were deserting. Sooner or later, the foreign prisoners at Meqdela knew that Tewodros would turn his attention to them.

Stern sent a letter to his wife. He warned her that it might be the last. 'Our separation will only be for a short period and our union in glory for ever and ever ... God bless you, my love, and the darling children.'

217

53

'In the year 7359, the year of Saint Luke, on the fifth day of the first moon, the twenty-fifth of the epact, terror began to reign throughout the world.'

In truth, terror had been in power for some time; but it was coming closer to home. Columns of smoke and the crackle of burning thatch, long the sign of imperial reprisal in the provinces, had become part of everyday life in Debre Tabor. No one could afford to pause as they passed the flames, nor show alarm at the screams of those trapped inside, nor give water or food to those lying in the dust without hands and feet.

'Mother of God,' they muttered, 'have mercy on your soul.'

These ones, still free and unaccused, wanted just to slink away, to be invisible, to be far off in the hidden valleys where the rebels now held sway.

But a stockade had been built around the town. Many who tried to slip through it were captured and killed – and those who were successful were as likely to be slaughtered by the rebels waiting in the forest outside. But everyone knew that the real purpose of that fence was not so much to keep them in, as to keep the insurgents out.

The powerful and the ones who escaped in force were successful. The chiefs of Amara and Saynt deserted, so their men were massacred – five hundred in all. Another five hundred, suspected of plotting desertion, were taken and killed with spears. Three hundred more were yoked and left to die inside a ring of thorns. Their wives could not bear the slow grief and joined them; those still alive after two weeks were shot. When a number of soldiers escaped, their women were stripped and lashed naked to posts along the road; in the evening their bonds were cut and they were shot.

A torpor began to overtake the townspeople, who knew that death would come to them whatever they did. Starvation sapped their remaining vitality, hollowing their cheeks and leaving the eyes of the children covered with a gluey film.

Tewodros alone remained active. Only a year earlier he had been paralysed by indecision. Now a terrible energy had risen in him. It pushed all before it, allowing him no rest, filling his every moment with the need to issue orders, exact revenge, punish betrayal, snuff out every dark and treacherous thought in the minds of his people. He was God's judgement! The candles in his tent glowed all night. Those around him saw him pace up and down, bare to the waist, murmuring prayers and curses. Sometimes in the night he went to stand before the cages of his four lions. He rarely slept.

He raided the lands of Karoda and Jagur and Mahdere Maryam and rounded up all the people in their own huts, and after paying them for their loss, burnt them alive. Whenever he came across anyone on the road he burnt them in their huts. Yet even now, in the savagery of his mass killings, he could be swayed by a single soul. Seeing a five-year-old child and his weeping mother suddenly swamped him with regret. 'Oh my God, my Creator, what kind of man have you made of me? Destroy me soon, so as to give your creatures some rest!'

But God did not destroy him, not yet, and the killing continued. A rhyme was repeated by the people, and spread from mouth to mouth because it told of the moment the emperor's madness began:

God and the emperor fell out one day
St Mikael they made the judge
God on the left, the emperor on the right
I heard the emperor say, Grant me the right
Of universal destruction.

That year's rains alarmed Tewodros even more than the rebels. Supplies were running low. From his first days as a *shifta* leader in the wilds of Qwara, to the height of his reign – when one in ten of the country's entire population was with him in his camp – he had always been able to provide. As his territory shrunk, so he had sacrificed his ideals and fed his people by plunder. But now his reach was so limited that he was reduced to pillaging his loyal heartlands. The region around Debre Tabor had been stripped bare.

One pocket of plenty remained – Belessa, to the east. In the entire region, Belessa alone had kept its grain and stock intact. Tewodros announced that he was setting off on a campaign to the west. Swiftly, secretly, he led his hunger-driven men eastwards to Belessa. But secrets were no longer his to keep. As they neared Belessa, they saw on the horizon the smoke of burning villages. The peasants had taken their grain and fled.

The emperor and his men marched to Lake Tana and attacked the island monastery of Mitiraha. The island had long been a haven, a place of asylum, and the choice of harried chiefs as a repository of valuables. Tewodros stormed it, took its store of grain, and its treasures. He ordered the artisans to turn their cannon on the fleeing monks, but their shot landed harmlessly in the water. Those he caught on the island were burnt in their huts.

On 13 June, a letter reached Tewodros from the British government. It was an ultimatum. It gave him three months to send the prisoners to Massawa. After that there would be no more concessions, no more talking. Tewodros took the letter and, out of respect, placed it on his head.

But he sent its bearer away without replying.

He had known for some time where his detention of the British envoys would lead. One way or another, the British would wrest him and the people of Ethiopia from his cycle of horror. In his darker moments the thought of such a defeat filled him with the perverse pleasure of self-destruction. But at other times, sweeping aside all the hellish damage he was inflicting, his old will burned so strongly that he couldn't help but see the threatened invasion as an opportunity. At these times, he appeared to be working to a plan. He would pull the *farenjis* in, withdraw to Meqdela. His enemies would unite with him against the invader. He would strike a deal with the British – get them to flush out the last resistance to him. Then, magnanimously, he would release the prisoners.

The plan depended on two things: the unassailable fortress of Meqdela and the enduring myth of his invincibility. Tewodros knew that there was one way to bolster them both – to increase his armoury.

54

Debre Tabor's agonies continued. Its people were starving and terrified. Hyenas dragged corpses by the feet from the ash-rings of burnt-out huts. Tewodros called his old friend Waldmeier to him.

'You Europeans are very clever,' he said. 'I want you to make me a gun which will discharge a ball of 1000lb weight.'

In the last year at Gefat, Waldmeier and the artisans had managed to build four large cannon, eight smaller ones and a number of other assorted pieces for Tewodros. But the Gefat foundry was now destroyed, the workforce scattered, and hunger made the slightest task a trial. Waldmeier thought such a large gun would be impossible to forge, even in good conditions.

'If you say you do not know how,' warned Tewodros, 'I shall regard you as liars, and you know what I have done with those who have deceived me.'

'We will try our best.'

They began work. Waldmeier sketched out a plan. Tewodros approved it and the artisans went on to produce a scale model. The weapon was to follow the same design as previous ones – a stub-barrelled mortar, still betraying something of the bell shape of Moritz Hall's original. With a two-foot calibre it was to be about double the size of any they'd made before. Two thousand men were assigned to the Europeans. They were all given food. As the weeks passed, a pair of furnaces began to rise from the ruins of Debre Tabor.

It was at this time that Waldmeier heard a rumour. Word came from the emperor's court that he would use the Europeans, his children, like slaves, and once the job was done, take them out on the plain and have them killed. To Waldmeier the news was 'very discouraging'. But he could not give up.

Every piece of available metal was gathered. Fifty large copper vessels were ordered from Meqdela and melted down. The previous year, when sacking Gondar, Tewodros had found a hollow in the *iḳa-bet* of one of the churches, and in it were 490 silver thalers. Tewodros's gun-lust for now outstripped all fears of starvation. The money too went into the melting pot.

Whenever Tewodros visited the foundry, often several times a day, and stood beside him, Waldmeier could not help trembling: 'he would change so suddenly, and then it seemed he could not rest without shedding blood'.

From the beginning, the size of the mortar gave it a reputation that far exceeded its military potential. The other guns rarely fired, and when they did their shot was rarely fatal. As desertions shrunk his regular forces, the guns' presence propped up the emperor; the supernatural scale of this new one was a reminder of his God-given powers.

Hunger crept back into Debre Tabor. The booty from Mitiraha had been exhausted, the silver thalers melted. A single *qunna* of grain cost a thaler. Tewodros took some of the wealthiest prisoners and stripped them. He bound them with ropes. He tied their genitals with wire until they agreed to send their servants to fetch their money. Their servants came to the Europeans' camp, hissing through the hedge: 'Please, in the name of the Virgin, give us coins!'

One day, Tewodros arrived at the foundry and said: 'I was angry today and was going to execute Staiger and Brandeis – but because of your work, I have spared them.'

Waldmeier did his best to spin out the building of the new foundry. But the time came when he could delay it no longer. Everything was in place. With great nervousness, he told Tewodros that they were ready to cast the gun. The people of Debre Tabor gathered to watch. Tewodros took Waldmeier by the hand and led him to a spot between the furnaces. 'Tell me what is to be done, and I will give orders!'

Waldmeier watched while the metal was heated. The workers stoked the fires. The temperature rose. They could feel the heat on their faces. Still Waldmeier waited. Were it to fail, he thought, we will all be cast into the flames!

At last he said it was ready. Tewodros gave the order, the channel was opened, and from the furnace mouth the molten metal began to flow. It shone 'like a fiery serpent' as it sought out the enormous cast, then flooded into it. Ten minutes passed, and still it was only half-full. Waldmeier watched the molten stream, praying that it would not stop. The level crept up until the mould was full, and then it was closed.

Three days later, the great mould was attacked with hammers. The *chink-chink* sounded out around the town. When at last it fell open, like a shell, the gun inside was found to be intact. Tewodros said it was the happiest day of his life.

Already he pictured the British army landing and marching into his country, while he with his gun and his loyal forces would sit on the Meqdela heights and resist as the Russians had done in the Crimea. Tewodros named the gun 'Sevastopol'.

Again those around the emperor urged him to kill the Europeans, but he said: 'Let them live and make a wagon for the gun.'

When the wagon was completed, one of the chiefs urged: 'Your Majesty, we have what we wanted, and you have made yourself an everlasting name. We are no more in need of those white asses.'

But Tewodros still refused. There was one more thing he needed them for – a road to take the guns to Meqdela.

X

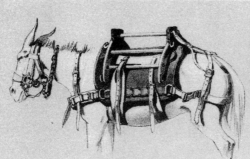

THE Mc MAHON SADDLE.

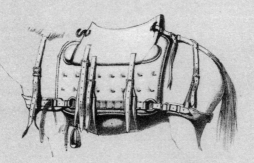

THE OTAGO SADDLE.

THE PERSIAN PAD.

Types of pack saddle used during the Abyssinian campaign. From Holland and Hozier, *Record of the Expedition to Abyssinia*, Vol. II (1870)

55

One hot morning in the middle of August 1867, Lord Derby's cabinet met to discuss the Ethiopian crisis. After forty-four months of shoulder-shrugging, foot-dragging, thumb-twiddling and blind hoping, they now agreed they must use force.

The decision was reached by the persuasion of negatives: no other option remained, no reply had been received to the last ultimatum sent to Tewodros, no one could be seen to treat Her Majesty's representatives in such a way. The British government simply could not afford not to use force. The restive peoples of India and Arabia, and the expansionists of Tsarist Russia, were reading their inaction as weakness. In the early stages of the crisis, a prudent move here, a decision there could have averted it. Now it was too late. Her Majesty's government had been shunted backwards into war.

Fortunately, they didn't have to take total responsibility. It was accepted that any expedition to Ethiopia would best be launched from India. That same August afternoon, a telegram was sent to Bombay appointing Lieutenant-General Sir Robert Napier, military commander-in-chief of India, to lead the expedition. It signalled the end of the political phase. Within hours, four years of dither were swept aside by a martial surge of activity. Observers watched Bombay being sent into a 'flutter of delight', its arsenals and dockyards ringing with 'the din of preparation'. The *Friend of India* was soon reporting far-reaching zeal among the military: 'Harriers, ensigns of marching regiments and engineers serving in the Himalayas ... sprang from the ground, ready armed, and demanded to be led against the enemy. It appeared as though in the desire to reach Abyssinia, India would be depopulated.' Then it became clear that, at least in part, India would be paying. The *Friend of India* observed coolly: 'We see that in monetary matters the English Government do not behave quite properly towards India.'

The politicians pressed Napier for economy: 'You will be careful to avoid any unnecessary expenditure,' wrote the Secretary of State for India. But Napier considered all expense necessary. Keen to avoid the catastrophic muddle of the Crimea, he allowed no cost-saving measure to jeopardise efficiency.

An invasion of Ethiopia presented immense difficulties. In the library of the Bombay Asiatic Society, Napier had every travel account, every historical passage, every passing reference to Ethiopia gathered. After it was all analysed, the conclusion was placed before him: 'There are few countries about which we know less.'

Napier and his staff had no idea where on the Red Sea coast an expeditionary force could land, where there might be fresh water, nor the best route through the highlands, nor the diseases that might attack their men and beasts. They did not know exactly where Tewodros might be. They did not know whether the other rulers in the country would unite with the Anglo-Indian force to try to slaughter Tewodros – or the other way round. Most worrying, they were not sure how to get out.

Critics cast their gloomy predictions over the expedition. They pointed to the Afghan campaign, the Crimean war and Napoleon III's recent, disastrous foray into Mexico. One survivor from a force of 15,000 had limped out of Afghanistan; 50,000 of the British contingent were killed or invalided in the Crimea; only half of the French force returned from Mexico. None of these campaigns could be called a success.

Ethiopia presented greater problems than any of these places, wrote David Urquhart in his much-read *Diplomatic Review*. 'It has chains of mountains rivalling Mount Blanc in height; it has passes where the inhabitants with stones can overwhelm armies; it has heats that scorch, and rains that deluge . . . it has dangers and pestilences of unknown kinds, except among the plagues of Egypt.'

Napier was undaunted. He began to work out the logistics in reverse, back from a projected front-line fighting force of 5,000 through a series of depots and posts and a supply line of several hundred miles, itself protected by another 7,000 combatants, back to a coastal base supplied by two routes – one up the Red Sea to Suez, the other across the Indian Ocean to the bustling port of Bombay.

In the 1860s both British imperial power and technology had reached unprecedented heights. Napier had each at his disposal. From Liverpool to Woolwich, Chatham to Bombay, Aden to Madras, quartermasters and storekeepers, technicians and chemists, coolies and cooks, design clerks, book-keepers and stevedores began to work towards freeing the captives from the grip of the 'gorilla king'. The emperor's stand in Ethiopia was a twisted fulfilment of the world-conquering Tewodros prophecy. If his own conquests had come to nothing, Tewodros at least required Napier to mobilise a fair proportion of global resources to meet him in battle.

The detail was astonishing. Clothing, food and equipment for every man were itemised, budgeted for, ordered and gathered in stores in Bombay and Suez. On board ship, troops would receive as rations: *Mondays and Thursdays* 12 oz of salt beef; *Wednesdays* 12 oz of salt pork; 2 oz sugar (unrefined) each day except Mondays and Thursdays (4 oz); a pound of fresh bread was allowed every other day; on Wednesday ⅔ of a pint of split peas would be issued; while once a week they were given 6 oz of pickle, ⅙ pint of vinegar, ½ an oz of mustard, 2 oz of salt and ⅓ oz of ground pepper. Native troops had separate itemised diets, and were further subdivided into variations for Hindus, Muslims and Sikhs, and those who cooked on board and those who did not. And that was just during passage to the Red Sea coast.

Never had a force been better cared for. Three hospital ships were to be fitted out and stationed on the coast (each supplied with Bibles, prayer books, eighty volumes of 'general literature' and Medical Comforts, including 250 dozen pints of port wine, ten dozen pints of champagne and five dozen pints of Old Tom gin – though there was no mention of medicines).

Stores were assembled in England and assigned for transport, including two hundred Ethiopian vocabularies, 70,000 pounds of Admiralty salt beef, seventy-two bottles of ink, 30,000 gallons of rum (in wooden casks), 350 miles of copper telegraph wire (BG, 85 standard). From India the list was as long (1,210 pickaxes, 6,417 sets of mule shoes, 5,400 pounds of Bombay ordnance powder, and another 30,000 gallons of rum).

The campaign drew on a futuristic range of technology. Seven photographers were assigned, complete with specially adapted blackout tents for processing. Norton's tube wells, Bastier's chain-pumps, a telegraph system and water condensers would all be deployed. It was the first time flag signals had been used. To deal with the possibility of night attacks, sets of Prosser's lime-lights were despatched that could light up an entire camp in an instant.

There were no roads in the country: the wheel was of no more use in the Ethiopian highlands than a cricket bat. Napier needed animal transport; he needed mules. Two thousand were found in the Punjab, and another thousand were bought in Baghdad. But this was a fraction of his estimated requirement. British consuls at Malaga, Alicante, Cádiz, Barcelona, Genoa,

Tripoli, Beirut, Constantinople and Smryna were 'requested to look out at once for mules'. That autumn ten ships, fitted with stalls and forage, a hoist for loading and a ship's vet, constantly criss-crossed the Mediterranean. Tens of thousands of mules were landed at Alexandria.

In London, the campaign's critics highlighted its absurd scale, and the Mediterranean mule-hunt in particular. 'If the expedition should run short of mules,' suggested *Punch*, 'there will always be an abundance of asses in the chief military departments at home, which may be freely drawn upon.'

Napier required 'treasure' with which to buy fresh food and forage, and to keep Ethiopians on side. It was established that the only currency in the country was the 1704 Maria Theresa thaler – a coin that had not been minted for some years. Agents scoured Germany to buy up all they could, and the imperial mint in Vienna agreed to restart production, promising as many as 200,000 a week, as long as the British provided the silver.

The operation swelled. Napier's plans escalated in price. In the next few months, nearly three hundred ships were commissioned to take stores, men and animals to the Red Sea. All around the region could be seen 'impoverished shipowners, and traders of all kinds, luxuriating, after a long drought, in a grateful shower of British gold'. A *Punch* ditty summed up the sense of profligacy: 'But dash the expense/However immense/ We can nothing cheaper than fight'. Even with India bearing a good deal of the cost, Parliament had to add a penny to income tax to pay for the war. Then expenditure rose, and it became known as the twopenny war. By the end of the campaign nearly 64,000 people and 55,000 animals had been transported, equipped, watered and fed. The estimated cost of £2 million now looked like rising to £4 million.

All this was to rescue a handful of people. Among them were a few British citizens – Stern, Mrs Rosenthal and Kerans – but the focus of the efforts was on four British officials, a three-man mission who themselves had gone to rescue the detained Consul Cameron. So the entire enterprise, every detail of Napier's plan, every foray into a Spanish village or Levantine market to buy mules, every thaler gathered and minted, was essentially directed towards the rescue of one man from his remote mountaintop prison.

56

In his hut on Meqdela, Consul Charles Duncan Cameron lay in the half-darkness. Beneath his large frame, the *alga* creaked with the slightest shift in position. A pile of chains lay like a snake at his feet. Sometimes he raised himself to shuffle out into the yard. Blanc said Cameron had let himself go, and become quite 'seedy'.

Ever since he first stooped breathless into Tewodros's tent on 7 October 1862, and asked to sit down, Cameron had been constantly ill. He received little sympathy from his fellows. When Tewodros reconciled himself with the captives in April 1866, everyone except Cameron prostrated themselves before the emperor.

'Cameron,' observed Stern, 'made a mess of it. His spine or knees were evidently out of working order, for he neither toppled down nor rose up in conformity with the prescribed court etiquette. The masters of the ceremony were quite in distress, and they had to do their utmost to get him through the ordeal.'

Cameron had managed to upset all parties. Before even reaching Ethiopia, he had infuriated the Foreign Office by hanging around in London for so long. He offended Tewodros at his first interview, did not leave the country when asked, returned when not asked, visited Ethiopia's enemies and casually disposed of Tewodros's letter to Queen Victoria to a messenger. He could not really be blamed for the crisis – it was too complicated to pick out one culprit – but he had played his part. Now, chained up on Meqdela, he was in despair. In April 1867 he let slip his view of the threat of death which now hung over them all: 'perhaps the sooner the *mauvais quart d'heure* is over the better'.

The rainy season was drawing to a close. For several months the weather had kept Tewodros from reaching Meqdela. Everyone there feared that as soon as the rivers dropped and the roads were passable again, he would leave Debre Tabor and head for the mountain. Then none of them would be safe. Each day the clouds were a little higher, a little thinner, and the rain less intense. Soon it would be the Feast of Mesqel.

One hundred and fifty miles away, behind the protective hedge at Debre Tabor, the horror continued. The rebels pressed closer, the hyenas grew more bold and Tewodros's fury was offset only by the gleaming new hulk of Sevastopol.

'Let us fire the mortar,' he said to Waldmeier. 'I want to hear its voice!'

Waldmeier was not at all sure it would work. He told Tewodros that the gun's tremendous power made it dangerous to use: 'If we fire it now it will cause every woman with child to lose it. The people will become ill and die.'

There was a time when Tewodros would have laughed at such an idea, but his own violence had swollen his conscience. Superstition now surrounded his thoughts like the hedge around his own capital. Just as his rise was marked out with a clear set of signs, now he saw everywhere portents of his collapse.

In six months' time, his reign would enter its fourteenth year – the last, according to Kentiba Haylu. With meat so scarce he was now forced to poison his lions. When he had managed to capture tens of thousands of cattle on a recent raid, he had them all slaughtered. The peasants had begged to have them returned, but someone told him: 'There is a prophecy, Your Majesty – a king will seize a great quantity of cattle and the peasants will plead for their return and the king will return them and then die.' It took his soldiers a whole day to kill them. They lay in a vast forbidden pile beyond the fence, too many even for the hyenas and vultures. Inside, the people continued to starve.

Tewodros looked around at Debre Tabor. He saw the lanes and alleys turned to ravines by the recent rains. He saw the cowed and hungry figures, the carcasses of starved mules. Outside the stockade were the mounds of rotting cattle, and beyond them, from the forest a thousand rebel eyes watched and waited.

On 9 September he wrote a letter to his beloved Yetemegnu on Meqdela. As his reign collapsed, so his thoughts reverted to brighter days some twelve years earlier, with his first queen, Tewabach:

Do not fear; by the power of God, unless I am dead and buried, I will not refrain from seeing you. I left Tewabach in Qwara when I was fighting Dejach Goshu and his men and when I was fighting Birru Aligaz and his men. And now Meqdela is Qwara. It is my home, from which I shall not stay away, unless my body and soul be separated.

Three weeks later he gave the order to torch what remained of Debre Tabor.

57

As Debre Tabor burned, the first contingent of British forces arrived on the Red Sea coast. It was a reconnaissance party – a dozen officers, a battalion of Bombay Marines, some sappers, miners, lascars, forty men of the 3rd Bombay Light Cavalry and 149 mules.

Their task was to find a location for a shore base. Massawa was no good – too little fresh water, too wide a littoral. In the first days of October they steamed east into the desert-rimmed Annesley Bay. The heat stifled them, the approach was hazardous (one of the ships struck a coral reef), there was no town, no forage nearby. From the bay it was hard to see where the water ended and the plain began. The nearest surface water was miles inland, and there was no stone or wood. The bay was shallow and exposed to northerly gales.

They chose it. The coastal plain was narrowest at this point – rising above it, just twenty miles into the haze, was the first great ridge of the Ethiopian plateau.

Preparations began at once. They buoyed the channel, placed navigation lights on Shumma island and Desi, along the shallows to the south and on a nasty little rock in the bay. The Bombay Marines took soundings and landmarks, drew up tidal charts for springs and neaps, located an anchorage with good holding ground and shelter for up to a hundred vessels.

They watched the mules splash ashore, through hundreds of yards of shallows. They needed piers. The commanding engineer sent specifications for three of them, seven hundred feet in length, pile-driving machinery and Zanzibar rafters to come from Aden. Dozens of ships might need unloading at any one time. Four tramway sets were ordered, with rolling stock, also condensers and four-hundred-gallon tanks for fresh water. Wells were sunk, but at thirty feet were still dry.

Within ten days, the first supplies arrived on the stony shore – 650 tons of coal, a shipload of camels and, sealed in twenty-five wooden cases, a total of 50,000 Maria Theresa silver thalers.

A team set off inland to find a route to the highlands. For days they tramped south across the plain, through low hills and along the pebbly beds of dry torrents. They returned to base after ten days. That way, they said, was 'unusually severe'. They looked for another route.

Following a dry bed to the west, they reached the scarp. The slopes on either side began to narrow; they were walking in another waterless riverbed. Here the ground was soft, the alluvial sand fresh from the recent rains. As they climbed, the valley narrowed further and they were suddenly in shadow. On either side the cliffs rose sheer for a thousand feet. In the thin strip of sky the black dots of vultures and kites drifted back and forth. The cliffs, reported the reconnaissance team, leaned 'as if yearning to clasp each other to their craggy bosoms'. The gorge was no more than 250 yards long, but full of vast boulders. They called it the Devil's Staircase. They reached the town of Senafe and agreed that this should be the route into the highlands. When they returned to the coast, Colonel Merewether despatched the 10th Native Infantry and Bombay Sappers to start work clearing a way through the 250-yard Devil's Staircase – a task which in the end took four companies of men three months to complete.

58

Tewodros left behind him the ashes of his capital, the burnt and rotting flesh of his victims, and began the journey to Meqdela. Fifty thousand reluctant people went with him, soldiers, civilians, refugees, prisoners. They were all hostages to some degree, to the madness of their ruler, and the creep of the great gun Sevastopol.

During those months on the road, some of the darkness lifted from Tewodros. He worked all day alongside his men. He dressed like them, did the same jobs, and in the evenings was seen to go out into the fields and pick a handful of barley seeds, roll them on a rock and make a paste with stream water. With a Herculean task before him, the wild brutality of the last days at Debre Tabor receded; something of the old Kasa re-emerged.

'His march was,' wrote Blanc, 'the most wonderful feat he ever accomplished; none but he would have ventured on such an undertaking.' Every mile, from clifftop and forest, the rebels watched them. But no one dared attack. Twenty years of camp-gatherings and market-day gossip had built up the idea of Tewodros's strange powers. The moment you planned to attack him, the moment you thought you were safe – that was the moment he would strike.

'He never shuts his eyes,' it was said. 'He never dreams. Beware of him in the night before the mist vanishes.'

After five weeks they reached Checheho. Until then the road had been more or less level. Now to the north were the depths of a gorge that wound into the Tekeze; to the south a gorge that ran to the Abbai, the Blue Nile. They had reached the natural bridge. A knife-edge of rock ran between them, and on the far side a wall of broken basalt with a zigzag of a road running up it. The missionaries Zander, Bender and Kienzlen had worked at this place, road-building. But their road was too narrow for the axle beneath Sevastopol. For weeks the chink and thud of pick and mattock, the barking of orders and the melodies of work songs echoed from the basalt face. From time to time they came across a rock too large to shift. Then they would hammer holes in it, fill them with 'English powder' and stand to watch it spray its shards high into the air. Even before the pieces dropped to the ground, the crowd of workers would converge to shovel it all flat and stamp it down. Day by day the road inched up the cliff.

It was one afternoon at Checheho that Tewodros said to the Europeans: 'I hear that some donkeys have come to steal my slaves.'

He did not explain what he meant. That night they heard the shuffle and chatter of soldiers approaching their tent. They were taken to see the emperor. A pile of chains lay before him as he hurled charges at the Europeans. Tewodros did not manacle them but said they would now be kept in a small hut near him. They still did not understand why.

Towards the middle of December, the road was completed and the camp at Checheho broken up. As the great crowd climbed, and the gun-carriages crunched up over the new clinkstone, the attacks began. Spears and stones dropped from the cliffs. The dead and wounded fell, the rest panicked. Mrs Rosenthal almost had her new baby dragged from her hands in the stampede.

Witnesses recalled seeing Tewodros standing alone, watching the assault, tearing at his hair and crying: 'Why does God not kill me if I am bad? Justice sleeps in heaven, and until it wakes I will reign, and exact vengeance on earth.'

One day a week or so later, a messenger brought him a sheet of paper from the north, confirming what Tewodros had heard earlier. The slave-stealing donkeys had arrived:

To the Governors, the Chiefs, the Religious Orders, and the People of Abyssinia.

It is known to you that Tewodros, King of Abyssinia detains in captivity the British Consul Cameron, the British envoy Rassam, and many others, in violation of the laws of all civilised nations.

All friendly persuasion having failed to obtain their release, my Sovereign has commanded me to lead an army to liberate them . . .

When the time shall arrive for the march of a British army through your country, bear in mind, people of Abyssinia, that the Queen of England has no unfriendly feeling towards you, and no design against your country or your liberty . . .

The letter was printed and signed by R. Napier. An 'inscrutable smile' was seen to pass across Tewodros's face. He did not tell anyone what the proclamation said. He had it placed in the small tin trunk given to him by Rassam, and returned to his task – dragging his guns to Meqdela.

59

On Meqdela, they received two pieces of news at the same time. Tewodros and a great horde had left Debre Tabor, and Menelik and his army had left Shoa. Each was heading for the mountain. Those in power on Meqdela looked north, hoping that Tewodros would reach them first; the rest prayed for Menelik.

A few months earlier, another rumour of liberation had set the mountain ablaze with expectation. Wagshum Gobeze secretly sent a message to Abune Selama, explaining that he was ready to attack Meqdela, if the *abun* could organise a revolt. Plotters were recruited. Stern noted that on the mountain there was suddenly 'a wonderful taste for battle and slaughter among all classes'. They waited and waited – but the *wagshum* never appeared. Soon a new message reached them. Wagshum Gobeze was going after Tewodros directly: 'My soldiers will frown at me, my wife will spit at me, if I do not destroy the monster!' But he never even tried.

The promise of Menelik seemed more solid. On Meqdela, wrote the chronicler, 'there was no one who did not love Menelik. When he was staying at Meqdela, there was no one like him at the sports on horseback, or in the festivities on the days of St John.' Since fleeing two years earlier, young Menelik had become king of Shoa. He was looking to pick up the pieces of Tewodros's broken rule, and now headed a force of some 30,000 men. If he could take Meqdela, he would be united with his old friend Abune Selama and together they could reunite the entire country.

Both the *wagshum* and Menelik identified Abune Selama as a figurehead, not only on Meqdela but in the country as a whole. In truth he was now a broken man. Nothing remained of the great alliance forged between him and Tewodros, between Church and state, in the glorious days of 1854. Tewodros had never really accommodated the power of the priests; they had never really accepted him. Abune Selama's driving ambitions for unity soon came into conflict with Tewodros's own. It was a conflict which had helped destroy both men. Most of the Christian highlanders who once believed in Tewodros had returned to a more traditional faith, the muttered Ge'ez of the clergy, the parade of the *tabot* and the whispered spells of the *debteras*. The *abun* had been confined to his hut on Meqdela since 1865, a prisoner in all but name.

Though for over a year he lived only four hundred yards away from them, Abune Selama never met the *farenji* prisoners. But common cause and a regular traffic of hidden notes between him and Rassam and Blanc made them friends. Dr Blanc sensed a man 'disappointed in his ambition, deprived of his property, insulted, degraded, without power, without liberty'. The *abun*'s health was ruined. He had, according to Blanc, 'succumbed to the too common temptation of men who suffer'. He drank, he ate too much, and exercised too little. He had also developed a taste for opiates. He blotted out his woes and his corporeal needs with the homemade tablets of Stern, who likened the *abun*'s obsessive interest in them to 'a drunkard in his bottle, or the miser in his gold'.

For a while, Blanc persuaded the prelate to moderate his habits. He ate well and cut his drinking. His health improved. But it wasn't long before Blanc received the old requests from his proxy patient. Could he have a little *arak*? Perhaps some opium? Surely one of his favourite dishes would do no harm?

In early October, rumours reached Meqdela of Menelik's advance, and the hopes of the *abun* rose. If Menelik was thinking of uniting with him for political ends, the sickly bishop had other plans – he wanted to return to Egypt. At about the same time, his condition worsened. He applied to the prison *ras* to see Dr Blanc in person. He was refused. Tewodros would not tolerate any contact between his enemy and the Europeans, and anyway would be far from sorry if the *abun* died. The mountain's cow-doctor was sent instead.

Just two weeks after Tewodros left Debre Tabor, on the afternoon of the fifteenth day of Tekemt, Abune Selama died. On Meqdela there was great and heartfelt mourning. The priests and *debteras* sat for a twenty-four-hour vigil. The body, according to the chronicle, was covered in a gold-threaded velvet cloth and placed in a coffin hung with crimson silk: 'The ceremonies and ordinances that were carried out were too lengthy for description here; let this suffice.'

Some weeks later, on 29 November, in the thick orange light of evening, a cloud of dust appeared to the south. Those on the mountain woke the next morning to find that in the night a vast camp had appeared below – mounted troops, baggage animals, foot-soldiers and the black and red tents of the Shoans.

'It's Menelik!' cried the people of Meqdela. 'He has brought every creature in his kingdom! Nothing is beyond the scope of God!'

Tewodros's estranged queen, Tirunesh, tried to arrange the mountain's defence. She laid on a breakfast feast for forces loyal to her disloyal husband. She scratched together enough money to buy *tej* and food, and the mountaintop rang with cries of defiance. That morning, they all watched while a small force left the camp below and advanced a short way towards the cliffs. Blooms of musket-fire appeared before them, and several larger clouds from a number of small cannon. But they advanced no further. The group was then seen returning to camp.

The following day was Sunday, so no movement was made. Stern saw this as a true sign of the 'beneficial influence of the Gospel' in Ethiopia, and went straight to tell some Muslims he was trying to convert. Then cavalry were seen to leave the camp below, and Stern forgot the Sabbath and the Muslims and hobbled over to watch. But it came to nothing. They returned to their tents.

The next day, the same, and the next. On Wednesday, at daybreak, again the people of Meqdela scrutinised the camp for any sign of movement. And this time, among the tents they could see the mustering of a much larger force. Of course! It was the feast of the great Shoan hermit-saint, Tekle Haymanot. They all realised that Menelik had been waiting for this day to free the mountain.

'Now they are coming!' gushed Stern. 'Now the prey will be wrenched out of the clutches of the destroyer! Now our shackles will drop! Now our prison doors will burst!'

But as they watched, Menelik's force wheeled away and headed back towards Shoa. The defenders of Meqdela puffed themselves up with an imagined victory. The imprisoned Ethiopians sunk further into their fatalistic slough. Dr Blanc and Stern felt 'disappointment beyond description'. They nicknamed Menelik the 'fat boy', and spread the rumour that such was his weight that he managed to exhaust six mules a day.

Menelik sent word to Rassam that fear of low supplies for his army had driven him back. But another reason was also mooted. It was said that on the Tuesday evening, he spotted a distant column of smoke from the valleys to the north-west. Menelik knew that, according to Blanc, 'His large army would be scattered like chaff before the wind at the cry "Theodore is coming!"'

60

But Tewodros was still a long way off.

For the European prisoners, there had been no messengers from the coast for months. After hope in the rebels had come to nothing, they found it harder and harder to keep their own dark thoughts at bay. Stern described the mood with Gothic flair: 'Shadows, gloomy and dismal, danced on our prison walls, and floated before our eyes.'

Then at noon on Friday, 13 December, a road-weary man stepped in through the gatehouse. He had passed through the warring territories of Tewodros, the *wagshum*, Ras Kasa, tramped the mountain paths of Wag and Lasta and Tigray. A whispered message reached the *farenjis* that he had letters for them. He would bring them later. That evening they all gathered in Dr Blanc's hut.

Stern remembered the evening of the letters well. 'There were, as usual, none for me. A kind of fatality hung over my letters. My friends wrote, but of the scores which they forwarded not a tithe ever reached me.'

He skulked off. In his own hut he flopped down and reread for the hundredth time the random pages of Guizot's *Histoire de la civilisation*, drawing some comfort from the passage describing the damage inflicted on Europe by the aberration of monasticism.

'Stern! Stern!' Blanc was calling from the other hut. Stern hobbled back across the yard. 'Troops are coming! Colonel Merewether has landed!'

Stern's relief was instant. 'Our chains were light, our hearts merry; we were in a transport of delirious joy – a sensation to which the majority, for more than four years, had been perfect strangers.'

Blanc too was ecstatic. He read the news several times to make sure. 'No lover,' he wrote, 'ever read with more joy and happiness the long-expected note from the beloved one.' He had suffered from a sense of abandonment, the impression that those they were serving could do something about their plight, but hadn't – until now.

'It was,' he said, 'one of those exciting moments in a man's life that few can realise who have not passed through months of mental agony, and then been suddenly overcome with joy.'

The news brought from the usually unsentimental doctor a burst of patriotism. Whatever happened to them, 'at least England's prestige would be restored, her children's blood not left unrevenged'.

Yet they were still prisoners. When the evening had passed and the news been digested, they were still in chains, still trapped on their mountaintop. How well had Napier prepared? Did he have any idea of the difficulties of this impossible country? Why would he succeed in overthrowing Tewodros when so many others, better informed, and closer to home, had failed? If Tewodros did reach Meqdela, how would an alien force ever manage to take it?

Two great hopes of liberation – by Wagshum Gobeze and by King Menelik – had come to nothing. Now a new period of tense expectation began. 'Will our expected liberators fore-stall our dreaded captor,' wrote Stern as if puffing the plot of a penny thriller, 'or will they allow him to inundate the Amba with blood ere they make their appearance? Never were the chances of freedom and death so equally balanced; never were the steps of friend and foe so eagerly watched.'

61

Down at Annesley Bay, British preparations had not been going well. By the new year, a great number of supplies had already been landed (986,085 pounds of beans, 16,832 pounds of onions, 11,384 gallons of rum, more than 2½ million pounds of hay, etc.). The road through the Devil's Staircase was progressing, the piers had been erected swiftly, the condensers were pumping, wooden buildings had gone up. The Indian camp-followers had begun a busy market on land that, just weeks earlier, had been baked desert.

But there were problems. Henry Morton Stanley, still a little-known war correspondent for the *New York Herald*, arrived at Zula at this time to cover the campaign, and was at once critical: 'The English army had rusted so long in their barracks in Bombay and Chatham, that very many things appertaining most essentially to campaigning had been forgotten.'

Eight thousand mules had arrived, but no pack-saddles, and none were available locally. So an order for others was rushed back to Woolwich. But the model ordered was from the Crimean campaign and was, according to one report, 'probably the very worst that could possibly be invented'. These were sent back and the Suez saddle ordered. They were just as bad.

The Otago saddle was adopted in the end, which was far from perfect. It weighed a full forty-three pounds, and was ill suited to large loads.

Then the Persian muleteers demanded double pay, in advance, and went on strike when refused. The Egyptians, according to the official report, were even worse. They also struck, and learned from the Persians the habit of riding the mules themselves – thus reducing the carrying capacity of the corps by about a third. In fact most of them were not muleteers at all. Clements Markham called them 'the vilest sweepings of Eastern cities'. Colonel Warden of the Bombay Staff Corps identified the Indian contingent as 'the off-scouring of the Bombay streets, consisting of broken down native tradesmen, discharged Europeans and Eurasians and the class named "loafers"'. Many were opportunists. One man from Persia, a baker, had come simply to slip away and do the *haj*. One day a large proportion of the muleteers simply disappeared, fleeing *en masse* to Massawa.

Nor were the officers blameless. They generally had no language in common with those they commanded. When one of them found himself surrounded by 150 'jabbering mulemen', he reported a mutiny. Nearly half of them were given fifty lashes. It turned out that they had been given no rations for three days, and were only asking for food.

Many of the mules were abandoned. They wandered through the camp, confused by their alien surroundings, nosing for forage in the thorny scrub, gathering around rapidly empty-ing wells. At the troughs in camp, when the chutes opened from the just-installed condensers, sometimes a thousand mules would surge forward. They jostled and shoved and bit each other in their desperate thirst. The men too elbowed their way through to drink beside the mules' muzzles, which were dripping with the infectious mucus of glanders.

Soon the animals started dying. Their bodies littered the camp and the shore, and joined those of dozens and dozens of camels. Those animals still working had to work twice as hard. Many collapsed from exhaustion.

Men were ordered to gather the roaming beasts in batches of twenty or thirty. But the only halters they had were of rope, not chain, and within an hour the tethered mules had chewed through them.

'Suddenly there appeared a new and fatal disease,' recorded the official report, 'unknown in character, insidious in its approach, and appallingly swift in its course.'

The air around the camp became unbreathable. Mule bodies lay thick on the ground. The sanitary officer could not bury them quickly enough. To issue an order, he had first to address his Hindu servant, who translated it into Arabic to another, who translated it into Shoho for the local workers. But the Shoho still did not understand. They were not familiar with spades, nor the idea of burying mules, nor burial pits, nor anything on such a scale as this sudden, chaotic city on their empty shore.

In the end the veterinary officer managed to identify the disease as equine typhus fever of the epizootic class. He recommended treatment with mustard embrocations, cantharides, quinine and brandy – and no exercise.

'Can the ordinary man conceive,' fumed the *Hindoo Patriot*, 'how it was that thousands of valuable mules, each animal averaging about £25, were thrown day after day without attendants, without even tethering gear, food or water, on this arid coast?'

Eleven thousand souls needed more than a gallon of water each per day. Animals and machinery needed water too. Producing it was costing £28,000 every week. The threat of water shortage was constant, and two emergency tanks were brought out from Britain, filled at Suez and brought down the Red Sea in a ship.

To push a fighting force hundreds of miles up into Ethiopia, to keep it fed, watered, supplied and defended, looked a tall order. Precedent was not encouraging. The Crimean expedition had begun with Lord Raglan's disastrous massing of troops at Varna. Nine hundred men had died there, far from the enemy. The current shambles in the extreme heat of the Red Sea coast was alarming enough, but beyond it, campaigning in the hostile and mysterious highlands was a prospect that made even the mildest military man in London and Bombay predict catastrophe.

62

Tewodros was making better progress. He had hauled Sevastopol up to the Zebit plateau; he had survived the rebel attacks. Now the great wagon creaked across a flat expanse of grassland, scattered with grazing cattle. The villagers had never imagined that Tewodros would be able to reach their tableland, so his men were able to plunder with ease. For the first time since leaving Debre Tabor, they fed well.

After ten days, on 25 December, it all changed. When the ground began to slope downwards, Sevastopol was given a brake team, and for a while the two ends worked in tandem. Then the land ahead dropped away entirely, and they jammed rocks under the wheels and gathered at the edge of a vast gorge. Three and a half thousand feet below was the Jidda river. Through the haze they could see across to the bluffs rising from it, which levelled out a little to a shelf and terraced fields and scattered huts, then rose again, some seven miles from where they stood, to a rim of shadowy cliffs and the edge of the Delanta plateau.

Tewodros called for Theophilus Waldmeier.

Since leaving Debre Tabor over two months earlier, Waldmeier had been ill. Dysentery had weakened him to such an extent that he had to be carried. One night, a few weeks earlier, Tewodros had him hauled from his bed and brought before him.

He jabbed a finger at the sagging missionary. 'You are ill just to spite me. You are planning to escape! You and the others.'

'Your Majesty,' Waldmeier wheezed, 'I could not do so even if I wished.'

Chains and shackles were brought into the tent, but the guards looked at Waldmeier and said: 'We can keep this one without chains.'

They took him outside and dumped him on the grass. Tewodros spotted him a few hours later and sent him back to his wife and family. But the next evening he ordered him taken again. This time they dragged him to the edge of the camp and left him there. He lay cheek down on the icy ground. At sunrise, paralysed by cold, he watched the sparkle of frost on the grass-blades.

Waldmeier's eight years in Ethiopia had come to this. During that time he had married, had children, opened a school, spread as he was able the clear light of the Gospels, and won Tewodros's friendship. Everything was now destroyed. What had happened to bring about such evil, to lead him here, discarded, face down in the frost, close to death? 'I wished and asked the Lord that He would end my great sufferings.'

He remained on the edge of camp for several weeks. His wife found an expert in the use of herbal medicine and sent her to him. A course of linseed and cress seed saw a little of his strength return.

When they reached the edge of the Jidda gorge, Tewodros summoned him back. Waldmeier, still weak, looked out across the gorge to the 'stupendous wall of rock' on the other side, and knew what he was required to do. Over the coming weeks, the two of them worked together to choose a way down the slope, across the river, and up the other side. They ran out traces before the crowd of workers followed, thousands of men chipping and digging and blasting.

On the other side of the gorge, between Tewodros and Meqdela, were the twin plateaux of Delanta and Daunt. The people there were famously stubborn. All it needed was their resistance and Tewodros would have found it near impossible to reach Meqdela. For months the chiefs of Delanta had been waiting for Wagshum Gobeze to attack Tewodros's ragged convoy, and rid the country forever of the fallen emperor. Like the prisoners on Meqdela, they had been disappointed. The *wagshum* had not attacked.

Tewodros needed them not just to be friendly, but to supply him with their food and manpower. He called their chiefs and gave them his word that he would not plunder them. 'By the death of Christ,' he promised. Shortly afterwards, trains of grain-mules began to arrive in camp from Delanta; thousands came down to join the workforce.

It had taken them about three months to reach here from Debre Tabor. Meqdela was twenty miles away – but across two vast gorges. In terms of time, they were now something like halfway.

Railway bridge over the Kumayli. From Holland and Hozier, *Record of the Expedition to Abyssinia*, Vol. I (1870)

63

The arrival at Zula of Sir Robert Napier, commander-in-chief of the expeditionary force, was a spectacular piece of military theatre. He had remained in Bombay to ensure the campaign's supplies. Now, on 7 January 1868, in his cabin on the SS *Octavia*, he dressed in full uniform, a swag of medals clanking at his chest, and climbed up into the full glare and heat on deck. High in the rigging, sailors stood in immaculate tiers, their legs wide apart on the yards, their white uniforms brilliant against the pale blue sky. As Napier transferred to the tender to go ashore, the *Octavia*'s guns fired.

From the two-month-old port, the Armstrongs of the mountain battery boomed back.

The first pier now projected three hundred yards into the hot and shallow water. Beyond it, Napier saw the white ensign flying from a pole in the naval ground. He saw the carpenters' sheds, the commissariat store, the office of the harbourmaster and, scattered over the flat littoral, the tents of 10,000 people. A guard of honour presented arms, the officers dipped their swords and a military band played. Napier stepped ashore.

He was fifty-seven. In his oak-like bearing was the full sturdiness of imperial authority. His strength was softly spoken, his gaze assured and unshakeable. For forty-two years he had served in the Indian Army, first as an engineer then as a combatant. He had commanded the defence of Lucknow in the Mutiny, then in 1860 led the British expeditionary force into China. He had just married an eighteen-year-old English girl, his first wife having died, and he had left her back in Bombay. The time had come for him to take to the field.

The débâcle with the mules had troubled him. His entire plan depended on transport, and it was already unravelling. He set to work at once. An early advance was impossible. Forty miles inland, the forward force and its 2,000 followers had 1,300 sabres and bayonets, and only four guns. The supplies that were reaching them barely kept them alive. There was a log-jam at the coast. A single accident could lead to calamity. Napier despatched an officer inland, along the supply line to Senafe, to report on the road gangs and storemasters, the mule trains, on every man and beast that he encountered, what they were doing and what condition they were in. He began to reorganise the epidemic-hit transport train. The original muleteers, those who had not deserted, were to be replaced by 5,000 good Punjabis. Napier spoke to the commissariat, collated information and wrote to Bombay with an order: 15,000 pairs of boots (the Indian boots were wearing through; the mountains required the stout English ammunition boot), 15,000 extra blankets, 15,000 pairs of woollen socks (the existing socks, he noticed, had a prominent, footsore-causing seam), 500,000 pounds of biscuit, 100,000 pounds of salt meat and another 30,000 gallons of rum.

Napier's meticulous planning, his dependence on a vast supply corps, had its critics. Tewodros was known to be labouring towards Meqdela, slowed to a crawl by his cannon. Why not send a swift, self-contained force to cut him off, to attack him before he reached Meqdela?

Napier was not swayed. On hearing of a British approach,

he believed, Tewodros would abandon Sevastopol and the other guns and be in Meqdela within days, long before any force 'short of the speed of wings' could cut him off.

64

Napier was wrong. Tewodros was unable to leave his guns. The scouts of Wagshum Gobeze watched his every move from the cliffs, and every yard the swarms of road-builders made down towards the Jidda. Thirty thousand men were poised to attack. All that prevented them was the guns. Stern wrote of their reputation among the Ethiopian rebels: 'Those marvellous engines, it was rumoured, mowed down, as the ripe harvest before the reapers, whole lines of hostile troops.' Tewodros feared that if he made a dash for Meqdela, as soon as he was separated from his artillery the *wagshum* would strike. He was wedded to Sevastopol and her train of smaller-calibre attendants.

At this point, in early January, the emperor appeared to be in high spirits. His agreement with the plateau-dwellers of Delanta had opened up the road to Meqdela for messengers. He was also able to write to his people on the mountain and, for the first time in a year, to his 'friend' Hormuzd Rassam. Rassam had heard of nothing but the savagery of Tewodros in recent months. He was concerned that now a large British force was on its way, he would be regarded with hostility. The first message he received was verbal. As Rassam faced the courier Yashalakah Lih, he knew that even coolness of tone might presage the prisoners' deaths:

How are you? How are you, my friend? Thank God, I am well. I have now reached Bet-hor, and hope to be with you soon. The nearer I approach towards you the happier I feel, knowing that the pleasure of meeting you is at hand . . . I have had a large mortar cast, which has detained me on the road; but when I reach Meqdela, and you see and admire it, I shall forget all the trouble it has given me. Ask your brothers how they are from me . . .

Rassam wrote back in similar vein:

I have had the honour of receiving your Majesty's kind message by Yasalakah Lih, and I was delighted to hear of your safe arrival at Beitahor.

I was not a little pleased to learn that your Majesty was in perfect health.

May the Lord give your Majesty health and prosperity, and show us the light of your countenance soon; and may you enjoy a happy Christmas.

Dr Blanc and Mr Prideaux, Mr Cameron and his party, and Mr Stern and his party, send your majesty their respectful compliments.

Which was nonsense. Blanc found this obsequious exchange 'ludicrous'. It reminded him of the 'sunny days of Qorata' two years earlier, waiting for the prisoners to come from Meqdela, when Tewodros sent boat after boat across Lake Tana with gifts and friendly messages. And that had ended in their all being seized.

Stern too found the correspondence absurd. 'The letters that passed between [Rassam and Tewodros] were unique speci-mens of diplomacy on the one side and of craft and duplicity on the other. The king was all courtesy, devotion, and love; Mr. Rassam all deference, regard, and esteem . . . Mr. Rassam's task was not easy. He had to flatter, to praise, and to admire the man whom I believe he cordially hated and despised.'

The relationship between Rassam and Tewodros was indeed bizarre. The careful path that Rassam had trodden for three and a half years, and his own personality, had helped maintain Tewodros's esteem for him, and had probably saved the European prisoners from harsher treatment.

Yet Stern, for one, thought Rassam was wrong to be so trusting: 'Like all his diplomatic predecessors, [Rassam] misunderstood Theodore.' Stern saw Tewodros as consistently scheming: 'His apparent purity of life, his pretended religious impressions, and the perpetual brag that the weal of his people, though unappreciated by the ingrates, were the objects for which he lived.'

But perhaps Rassam understood Tewodros only too well. Of all the Europeans he was able to separate the dual, unreconciled sides of the emperor. He found it possible to ignore the demons in order to address the man. And it was Rassam, not Tewodros, who was being duplicitous. At the time, using every one of his cleverly developed lines of messengers, he was writing to Wagshum Gobeze, to King Menelik, to the Galla queen Metsawat; each of these, each one of Tewodros's enemies, he was urging to attack.

At this time, Tewodros also sent some of his prisoners on to Meqdela. Most feared of all was Wagshum Teferra. If he escaped and fell in with the men of Gobeze, they might well be encouraged to attack. Tewodros sent a large armed escort with Teferra. When they reached Meqdela, the guards fired their muskets as a signal. Tewodros was now close enough to hear.

With Ethiopian Christmas coming, and the seasonal fast over, Tewodros sent word to his 'queen' Yetemegnu to cook some of his most cherished dishes, and send them back by return. It was probably at this time that Tewodros sent some at least of a series of five undated letters to Yetemegnu. They are a touching glimpse of the private Tewodros. On Meqdela she shared a hut with Tirunesh, Tewodros's wife and their son, Alemayehu. All the letters begin with the usual invocation of the Trinity. There then follows the address: *King of Kings Tewodros. May this letter reach Itege Yetemegnu.* In each letter there is also the greeting:

How have you been? I am well, thank God. Say to your mother, and to Weyzero Senayit and to her people, and all the people of my household on my behalf, 'How have you been?'

The core of each letter is a brief entreaty to Yetemegnu, similar in each case:

. . . Do not be afraid. Now I shall be coming to you . . . We shall meet on the day God permits . . . Whatever you need, by the power of God, until God brings us together, send to me saying, 'This I lack.' . . . Do not be afraid, my sister, my mother's daughter. Unless my body and soul are separated, by the power of God, it shall not happen that I shall not see you.

65

When Merewether's reconnaissance team first stepped onto the western shore of Annesley Bay in October 1867, their boots pressed onto a firm biscuity crust. It stretched flat for twenty miles towards the distant scarp of the Ethiopian highlands. They would build a railway. On 8 November they put in an order to the chief engineer in Bombay for 8,500 twenty-four-foot rails, 35,500 sleepers, sixty trucks, twenty complete sets of points and crossings, thousands of fish-plates and dog-spikes, picks and shovels and barrows and crowbars, hammers and wedges and explosives, signal flags, one hundred yards of water hose, twelve guards' bells and four station clocks. A thousand labourers were recruited, and budgets drawn up for a railway staff.

It did not, at first, go according to plan. Five separate types of track were sent to Zula, with four different fittings; many rails were bent and worn. The heat of the plain only allowed five or six hours of work per man day, and the men were soldiers of the Army Works Corps, not railway engineers, so the work was utterly new to them.

Any doubting Briton – and there were plenty back home, forecasting doom for Napier's force – would have found much at Zula in January 1868 to confirm their fears. The mule train was crippled, the railway stalled. The locomotives, unable to use sea water as thought, would need 1,200 gallons of precious drinking water a day. No real progress had been made towards the interior.

After Napier's arrival, morale rose. What the railway workers lacked in experience they made up for in spirit. 'The cheerfulness and willingness of the men of these corps,' went the report, 'inspired by the spirit and tone of their officers, have been most conspicuous.' By late January 1868 several miles of track glinted amidst the baubul scrub. A girder bridge of three twenty-foot spans was erected over a branch of the Hadas river. The first station had been built, largely out of empty biscuit tins, and on 19 January a locomotive, one of two, inched forward on its steel track. Within weeks the railway was working fifteen hours every day.

Twelve thousand men and animals now lived at the base, entirely dependent on technology. American condensers supplied them with water; steamships with food.

A field telegraph system was to link Zula with the advance party. By late January 5,000 bamboos had been delivered from Bombay, and 350 miles of no. 16 copper wire from Messrs Bolton of Birmingham. A flying line stretched from the coast up as far as Suru. Where possible the line was attached to trees; in the Devil's Staircase it was fixed to the bare rock. As the line pushed further south, poles were bought locally, and many Tigrayan *godjos* collapsed as the beams were ripped out of them.

The service proved invaluable to the British force – communicating messages in minutes that would otherwise have taken days. But it suffered frequent interruptions. 'Carts and camels, elephants and camp-followers, apes and Abyssinians' all damaged the line in their own way. The copper was stolen, and mules, once free of their loads, liked to back their rumps against the poles and rub vigorously.

Such an expedition into unexplored territory provided good cover for scientific exploration. Clements Markham was sent from the Royal Geographical Society, a zoologist from the Bombay Zoological Society, a geologist from Calcutta and a meteorologist from the Indian Army. The promise of antiquities, in a country known to have ancient associations, prompted the trustees of the British Museum to send the archaeologist Richard Holmes with a generous purchasing allowance.

On 25 January, three weeks after landing, Napier was satisfied that everything at Zula was running effectively. He set off inland. More than three hundred miles now lay between his advance force and the prisoners at Meqdela. He would have to pass through territory controlled first by Ras Kasa, then by the *wagshum* – enemies not just of Tewodros but of each other. Winning them both over would not be easy.

Tewodros himself had less than fifteen miles to go.

66

As Tewodros drew closer to Meqdela, and received more reports of the British advance, his moods again grew wilder. He became obsessed by Napier's force, both fascinated by their approach and full of pique at their presence. To Martin Flad, he could not even say their name: 'The people of whom you brought me a letter, and of whom you said will come, have arrived.' At the same time he regretted the route they were taking, as if they were invited guests. 'Why did they not choose a better road? That road by the salt plain is very unhealthy.'

He longed to see their technological prowess. 'We are making roads, and what will it be to them but playing to make roads everywhere?'

To him a peaceful outcome was still possible. 'With love and friendship they will overcome me,' he told Waldmeier. 'But if they come with other intentions I know they will not spare me, and I will make a great bloodbath, and afterwards die.'

The unbearable tension of those weeks found relief only in a divine fatalism. 'It seems to me the *will of God* that they come,' Tewodros told Flad. 'If He who is above does not kill me, none can kill me; and if He says: you must die, no one can save me.'

He referred more and more to his own biblical precedents. Sometimes they pointed towards victory. 'Remember the history of Hezekiah and Sennacherib,' he told Flad. As God destroyed the Assyrian army to protect Hezekiah and Jerusalem, so He would help Tewodros destroy the British.

At one point, to Waldmeier, he announced: 'I am like Simeon.' Just as Simeon waited to hold the young Jesus in his arms before dying, so Tewodros was waiting for just one glimpse of the future, of the steely new weapons of a European army.

And at another time: 'We have a prophecy that the time will come when a European king will meet with an Ethiopian king in this country; and the Europeans will then take their mouthful and speak the truth before the people of this country; and after this time a *great* king will come.' Shyly he confessed to Waldmeier: 'But I don't know whether I shall be that great king, or someone else.'

With the support of the Delanta people, Tewodros crossed the Jidda gorge. He was now in a better position than he had been for months. The British were still hundreds of miles away, and there were signs that their advance was working in Tewodros's favour. Local areas were beginning to offer him their support. Even a delegation from the Yejju Oromo, the kin of his old enemy Ras Ali, was said to be on its way to make an alliance. The Wadela district was preparing to do likewise. With the approach of an alien force, Tewodros was given the chance for the unity which had been denied him for years.

Once again, the emperor defeated himself. Blanc had said that 'he seems to have been possessed with an evil spirit urging him to his own destruction'. Now the spirit whispered to him. Having struggled up from the Delanta gorge, up through Avercot and over the final, almost sheer section of outcrop and cliff, Tewodros turned on the Delanta chiefs and plundered them.

A few days later, he struck out across the high Delanta plain on a sortie. Waldmeier went with him.

'We saw some beautiful fields of wheat,' wrote Waldmeier. 'The ripe ears of corn were quickly cut down by his soldiers.' What they couldn't take, they burned.

That day, Tewodros was in expansive mood. Standing outside a church, he quizzed Waldmeier about European churches.

'It is particularly important to have light in our churches,' said the missionary. 'In Ethiopia, it seems darkness is loved above all else.'

Tewodros made no comment; he probably agreed. Back in camp, at about this time, Waldmeier suggested to the emperor that he make peace with Napier. It was a suggestion that followed logically from some of Tewodros's own pronouncements, his admiration for the army, his surviving ambitions. But it was also one, Waldmeier wrote later, that 'brought me into the greatest danger of my life'.

Tewodros rounded on his old friend, his eyes flashing with rage. 'Ass! Beggar! Spy! You want me to sell my country! Did you not eat my bread? Wouldn't you rather die with me? You want me to make peace?' He pulled a pistol from his belt.

Waldmeier stood shaking, watching the pistol. He remained silent.

'You think I should reconcile myself with those white asses? Do you?'

Tewodros did not shoot. He took his spear and hurled it at Waldmeier. It 'flew against me, and missing my body, entered deeply into the ground'.

The fury then turned itself inwards. Waldmeier was astonished to see Tewodros's fists close around his own *shamma*. He tore it off, then collapsed to the ground and lay there as if 'in a fit'.

67

In the north of the country Ras Kasa, the young ruler of Tigray, was shown a copy of Napier's proclamation:

> To the Governors, the Chiefs, the Religious Orders, and the People of Abyssinia.
>
> It is known to you that Tewodros, King of Abyssinia detains in captivity etc. . . . .
>
> When the time shall arrive for the march of a British army through your country, bear in mind, People of Abyssinia, that the Queen of England has no unfriendly feelings towards you, and no design against your country or your liberty.

That time had now arrived; the British had entered his territory. Ras Kasa agreed to a meeting with Napier.

For each man, the encounter was to prove decisive. The outcome of the British conflict with Tewodros would, in years to come, help propel Kasa to the very top – to become emperor himself. For the British general its importance was more immediate: Kasa controlled more than a third of the road to Meqdela.

Napier brought up a force of some 850 men towards the

appointed place. He waited a day, then another. No sign of Kasa. For a man like Napier, with the machinery of his expedition so delicately tuned, a two-day wait was hard to endure. There was now little chance of cutting off Tewodros from Meqdela, but every day lost was still a bonus to his enemy. In the end he waited six days for Ras Kasa. On 25 January, near Hawzien, the *ras* arrived with 4,000 armed men. The two groups approached each other on opposite banks of a small stream.

The morning was bright and hot. The thousand-foot cliff of Korkor rose to the north-west. The Tigrayans, in their brilliant *shammas*, approached in a line. The 'boom-boom' of *negarits* sounded before them. Red and yellow pennants flickered in their midst to mark the *ras*'s position. As the Tigrayans neared the stream, their line opened and there was Kasa on a white mule, his fine-featured face and bare plaited head shaded by a red velvet umbrella.

For Napier it was the first sight of an Ethiopian military corps; for Kasa it was the first sight of a European army. Napier received the *ras* formally in a *durbar* tent. He presented him with a double-barrelled rifle, some nice Bohemian glass-ware and an Arab charger. He refused to help him in his bitter fight with Wagshum Gobeze (knowing that another third of his route south was controlled by the *wagshum*). He asked Kasa for supplies, and guaranteed payment for every sack of grain. His queen, he promised, would reward the *ras*. A decision was deferred. They drank port pilfered from the expedition's 'medical comforts'. Kasa reviewed the British forces, watched the scarlet-coated, turbaned manoeuvres of the Sikh infantry, the blue-and-silver-coated charging of the Light Cavalry. The Armstrong guns interested him most – he spent a long time looking over them, weighing the shells, peering down the barrels. The Tigrayans believed the British would be unbeat-able in open country, but that in the mountains they stood no chance. These Armstrongs looked so small, much smaller than Tewodros's guns.

Napier and his staff then crossed the stream to the Tigrayan camp. At once the mood changed. Crowds pressed around the British officers. The *negarits* began to sound again. Inside Kasa's red silk tent, the light cast each man in his own blood-coloured glow. Lines of serving girls brought *mesobs* and *injera* and steaming dishes of *wat*. More girls bore hollowed-out bullock horns and filled them with *tej*, and as they were emptied, so they were filled again. The music began with a great lowing pipe, clapping and ululations, and an *azmari* stepped up to the general and sang his own satirical tribute. Napier left with a silver armlet and a shield of gold filigree. Kasa took off his lion-skin *lemd* and put it around Napier's shoulders. 'You are a great general and a great man,' he told him.

In the morning Kasa came to say farewell to Napier. He would severely punish any man interfering with the British, and deliver every week 3,000 madrigals of wheat, about 60,000 pounds. Half each would go to the British bases at Antalo and Adigrat.

Sure of his supplies, Napier continued his southward advance.

68

By the end of February, Tewodros's hordes could be seen from the Meqdela massif. Standing on Selassie cliff, the elders of the council trained telescopes on the slow train edging down the southern face of the Delanta plateau – soldiers, captives, civilians, and the elephantine bulk of the guns. When Tewodros reached the banks of the Beshilo, he was again able to send messengers. It took them four hours to reach Meqdela; it would take Tewodros and Sevastopol another three weeks.

'I am so near you now,' he wrote to Rassam, 'that I must not ask you, how have you passed the time, but must bid you "Good morning."'

On 16 March, Rassam responded in his oleaginous style, 'to impress upon His Majesty the fervent friendship he felt for him, and the sincere admiration and deep devotion which time had only strengthened'.

Tewodros wrote back with friendly greetings for all – even Cameron and 'Kokeb'. He sent Rassam 2,000 thalers, one hundred sheep and fifty heifers. 'By the power of God, if He grants me to arrive safely, we shall see each other face to face and talk together. Do not worry!' He also ordered Rassam's chains to be removed.

On 25 March, in a heavy rainstorm, Tewodros reached

Meqdela. He hauled the guns up to the cliffs below Selamge and, while the final section of road was built, climbed up onto the saddle below the prison *amba*. The journey had occupied him for five and a half months. His seething thoughts had been distracted, his rage in large part absorbed by the task of rock-breaking, road-planning and gun-heaving. The success of his journey now brought a new set of dilemmas. He had factions to deal with, feuds and betrayals to root out, traitors to try, desertions to avenge; he had his loyal friends, his family, his prisoners.

He summoned the men of the Meqdela council and listened to their reports. He sent for his estranged wife, Itege Tirunesh, and his lover Yetemegnu. On further reflection, he sent another message telling Tirunesh not to come.

The next day he issued a summons to all the clergy. A great robed host of monks and priests and *debteras*, confident in their numbers and in their faith, clutching prayer-sticks and glittering hand-crosses, assembled on open ground before the prison. They all bowed and waited for the emperor to speak.

Seeing them before him, beneath the rush of mountain clouds, Tewodros felt his fury grow. The Church's obduracy had crippled his reign as surely as any of the rebels. In 1860, one of the missionaries wrote of Tewodros's frustrations towards 'the spiritual class which holds the greatest part of the land, and from which the King can neither draw taxes nor upon which he can even quarter his troops'.

Now he gave vent to his rage: 'Those who call themselves *echage* and *abun* have oppressed the people and the whole country!'

The *echage* – the head monk – stepped forward. '*Jan Hoi!* Your Majesty! What have I said, whom have I injured? If any one among your soldiers can say a word against me, let me bear my punishment.'

The monk placed a stone on the back of his neck and dropped at the emperor's feet.

Tewodros looked down at him with contempt.

Then a Tigrayan, a priest named Abba Gabre Mikael, challenged the emperor to confirm his faith in the creed of Alexandria.

'What faith should I profess other than that of Alexandria?'

'They say you have adopted the faith of the *farenjis*.'

In his own eyes, Tewodros had struggled harder than many of the priests before him to maintain the indigenous elements of Ethiopian faith. The clergy themselves had proved quite capable of turning to Rome if it suited them, or of adopting the worldly corruptions of the Third-Birthers. Priests and traitors like Niguse had conspired to sell the country to *farenjis*. Now they were charging him with the same crime!

He told them to sit. He turned to the well-known figure of Aleqa Gabre Iyesus, a judge.

'Why,' he asked calmly, 'did Saul put Ahimelech and the priests to death?'

Suddenly the priests were nervous. They listened to the *aleqa* tell the story of David fleeing from Saul's anger, and taking shelter with Ahimelech the priest. They knew what was coming. When Saul discovered that Ahimelech had given David hallowed bread and the sword of Goliath, and had prayed for him, he demanded: 'Why have you conspired against me?' Then Saul ordered Ahimelech to be killed, and all those who were with him, because they too had helped David. That day were slaughtered fourscore priests.

Tewodros asked: 'Was this done legally or not?'

The *aleqa* was a wise man 'who, along with knowledge of books, was deeply versed in the great subtleties of the Amharic language'. He saw at once the dilemma. If he said it was done with justice, Tewodros would take it as a precedent for killing all of them. If he said it was not, claimed the chronicler, Tewodros would take it as a personal attack on his habit of extra-judicial killing.

The *aleqa* said: 'I do not know if it was done justly or not.'

Having asked him, having invoked the unarguable precedent of David, Tewodros was bound by the *aleqa*'s equivocal words. The priests were spared.

But Tewodros did not forget their accusation of him. The next day, he climbed the rock-cut steps to the summit of Meqdela and headed for Medhane Alem church. All those with him could sense his coiled-up anger. At the entrance to the church, he grabbed a priest by the beard.

'You say that I want to change my religion,' he cried. 'Before anyone could force me to do so, I would cut my throat!'

The very sight of the clergy now drove the emperor to a frenzy – but he held back from bloodshed. Some shred of sacerdotal respect remained. He diverted his anger by screaming curses at the late *abun*. He then took a spear and plunged it through a carpet, crying: 'That is what I will do to those foreigners who have abused me!'

He left the church for the prison hut. After nearly two years, he was due to see the European prisoners.

69

For months the *farenji* prisoners had hoped that Tewodros would never reach Meqdela. In January, wrote Dr Blanc, with news of his advance alternating with that of the British, began 'a period of great mental excitement'. Now, with the emperor here, the excitement had gone. They felt only dread.

On reaching Meqdela, Tewodros had ordered an increase in the number of the *farenjis'* guards; many of the new ones were known xenophobes. The hostages took that as a bad sign. One of those suddenly tried by the emperor had been the mountain's 'unimpeachable' commandant (who was found guilty and stripped of his post). Tewodros's apparent devotion to Rassam was no guarantee of clemency.

Waiting to see him again for the first time, wrote Blanc, 'we slept but little, expecting that the morning would bring some change for the worse'. At 2 p.m. on 28 March the hostages received word that Tewodros had left his camp just below the cliffs. He was on his way to see them. In their huts there was a hurried hiding of papers. Rassam himself had letters from a perilous range of Tewodros's enemies – Wagshum Gobeze, Imam Ahmed, the Oromo chief, and one delivered just an hour before from King Menelik. He pushed them into the cracks and cobwebs of his thatched ceiling. His servants shook their heads: that would be the first place the soldiers would look. He threw them all into the fire.

Tewodros climbed the rough-cut stairway to the *amba*. He passed the huts of the hostages and headed for the church. He sent a message to Rassam: 'I am going to visit the church of my country. I have been called a *farenj* by some of my priests . . . Prepare yourself to meet me.'

Blanc's servants told him the emperor 'appeared to be a *little* drunk'.

In the end, Rassam alone was called. Late in the afternoon he changed into his blue official uniform and left the thicket enclosure. It was the first time in all those months he had done so. Dizzy in the sudden space of the mountaintop, he crossed the open ground below their compound. A red tent had been erected. He recognised it as the same one in which he had first met Tewodros in January 1866. An area around it of hundreds of square yards was spread with a sea of carpets. The summit's gentle undulations rolled beneath them. Five hundred of Tewodros's officers were already there. They were as confused as everyone about their sovereign's attitude to this *farenj*. Was he friend or enemy? Was this a trial or a reception?

As Rassam approached the tent, Tewodros stepped out towards him. He shook him by the hand and said that, on this day, 'we must all be English'. He was smiling.

Inside the tent, Rassam was placed on Tewodros's right, Waldmeier and the road-weary artisans on his left. Tewodros looked at the British envoy and said, 'Why, Mr Rassam, I had heard that you had become quite grey; but I do not see one grey hair on your head. Look at me, and see how grey I have become!'

It was true. Tewodros's hair was now largely white. He also, to Rassam, looked about 'ten years older'. But the envoy was able to deliver one of his timely platitudes.

'It is not to be wondered that Your Majesty has turned grey considering that you have been enjoying the happiness of wedded life, whereas I am still unencumbered with the trouble and care of a wife.'

Tewodros was estranged from his wife; he had a mistress. Both of them had been at Meqdela. But the two men understood the game-playing behind such banter. 'There you hit me hard, my friend Rassam!' And the emperor covered his face in his hands.

They drank *tej*. Tewodros showed 'excessive condescension', flouting the usual protocol. He dispensed with his throne and allowed Rassam to command the others to be seated. He agreed to remove the shackles from Blanc and Prideaux, and the order was carried out at once. Only mention of the familiar figures of hate – the late *abun*, Cameron and Stern – exposed the glare of Tewodros's anger. Rassam managed to deflect it.

Tewodros's dangerous instability was obvious now even in his lighter moments. He flitted from subject to subject, mood to mood. He was suddenly angry or fearful or lucid, before wallowing in moments of strange calm. He was never far from the one topic that filled the thoughts of everyone on the mountain: the approach of the British. How would their weapons compare? Tewodros had heard that the enemy had rifles that could both shoot and stab, and that his own armoury was known to be 'rubbish'. He compared himself to a pregnant woman – not knowing whether he would have a girl, a boy, or would miscarry.

'I hope,' he told Rassam, 'you will assist me in giving birth to a boy.'

Tewodros asked Rassam about his quarters, whether there were carpets and whether he was comfortable. Ignoring the fact of eighteen months of chained imprisonment, Rassam assured him they had everything they needed. 'Your Majesty would be pleased if he saw the nice home I have.'

Tewodros glanced upwards to the sky. 'My friend, believe me, my heart loves you; ask me for whatever you like, even for my own flesh, and I will give it to you.'

The meaningless exchanges continued, before settling once again on the presiding anxiety. Leaning close, Tewodros suddenly dropped his voice. 'I hope that when your people arrive they will not despise me because I am black.'

Later he was even more candid: 'One day, you may see me dead; and while you stand by my corpse, it may be that you curse me for my bad conduct towards you.'

That evening, back down at his camp on Selamge, Tewodros showed his officers a more dangerous face: 'Rassam has made asses of us, and a fool of me.' The envoy had professed friendship, but all the time was encouraging his government to send a force to 'slaughter' the emperor's men, 'ravish their wives, and reduce his people to bondage'.

Then again next morning, talking to Martin Flad about Rassam, Tewodros confessed: 'I thought of him all last night, and I had sweet dreams in consequence. I wish I lived next to him, as you do.'

70

A few days later, Tewodros threw the edge of his *shamma* around his shoulders and left his camp early. He sent a messenger up the path to Meqdela itself and crossed the flat, broken ground of Selamge to the cliffs.

The messenger reached the *farenji* prisoners and told Rassam, Blanc and Prideaux that they must go down and join His Majesty. They had no idea, wrote Henry Blanc, what the summons meant: 'a polite reception, imprisonment or something worse'. They dressed in their uniforms – Rassam in his blue diplomatic uniform, the other two in the scarlet of their respective corps – then climbed down the rock-cut steps to the gates and guardhouse. They 'were astonished to find [the *amba*] much larger than we expected'.

They found Tewodros just below the lip of Selamge cliff. From his belt curved the stocks of two pistols; he clutched a spear in his right hand. The early-morning sun shone on the side of his face. He greeted the three men 'most graciously' and invited them to take a seat on a rock. He himself sat in front of them. After all those months, Blanc was amazed to be staring at the neck of his hated captor. 'We had only to give him a sudden push and he would have rolled down the precipice below.'

Some hundred feet down, at the foot of the cliff, the first of Tewodros's arsenal of big guns were gathered for the final ascent, the last stage of the journey from Debre Tabor. In silence, the emperor watched his men haul them one by one up the slope. Then around the corner with its vast team of human haulers came the 'monster mortar' – Sevastopol.

Tewodros turned to Rassam. 'What do you think of it?'

'A splendid piece of artillery!' Rassam exclaimed. Then he pushed his luck. 'I hope that before long the British forces will be viewing it with the same amicable feelings as I have.'

The translator said nothing. He went 'quite pale'.

'What does he say?' demanded Tewodros.

When he heard it, Tewodros just laughed. 'I hope so too.'

Below them, hundreds of men fell into place before Sevastopol. They formed teams, spaced along the length of a number of leather straps. Tewodros now stood. Together the party went a little way down the slope, and stood on either side of the makeshift road. Rassam estimated the incline at forty-five degrees.

As the men below, well-practised after months of such slopes, pressed their feet into the ground, kicking aside loose stones to secure a good grip, as they took the straps and placed them over their shoulders and the mortar – huge, open-mouthed – squatted on its tumbril, the task looked impossible. The thin silhouette of Tewodros and his spear was at the top, the fat gun at the bottom.

The men leaned into the slope. The straps tightened, the leather creaked. There were shouts, the groan of timber, more shouting. Very slowly the wheels began to edge upwards, and the gun was seen to climb. After each yard gained, officers rushed forward to jam rocks in behind the wheels. They all knew what would happen if the gun rolled back and broke free. *Cra-ack!* One line of men dropped as if shot. In went the rocks and the much-used strap was repaired and the team again began to haul. *Ayzore! Ayzore!* A chorus of encouragement, grunts and orders surrounded the silent gun. The clamour would rise and rise until, from the very top of the slope, Tewodros would quietly raise his hand. The hundreds of men below fell silent.

'No one but Theodore, I believe,' wrote Blanc, 'could have directed that difficult operation.'

When Sevastopol was up on level ground, Tewodros urged his hostages to inspect it. 'We all three jumped on the gun-carriage,' wrote Blanc, 'greatly admired it, and loudly expressed our astonishment and delight.'

Tewodros asked them again to sit with him, and for several hours they all perched on the clifftop 'in quiet and friendly talk'. Below them the hauling of the guns continued. But now that Sevastopol was at the top, Tewodros allowed others to oversee the climb.

He spoke of the journey. He told the envoys how the rebels had tracked them all the way. None mounted an outright attack, but they picked off those who strayed.

'Whenever I caught any of them,' said Tewodros, 'I caused them to be burnt; while they on their side did not spare any of my subjects who fell into their hands.'

'This,' recalled Blanc, 'he told us in the quietest way possible, just as if he had done the right thing.'

As the sun grew hotter, Tewodros suggested the three men put on their hats; then he called for an umbrella.

In measured tones he discussed the approach of the British force. In all his years of fighting, he had only ever once encountered a foreign army – twenty years ago at Debarki, when the Egyptians had sliced down his men with their guns. He had never met Europeans on the battlefield. What, he now asked Rassam, are the words of command? What is the range of the rifles? How many soldiers are coming? How is peace made?

The British envoy answered the questions as best he could, but said he had no military experience.

'I know,' Tewodros smiled. 'You are a man of tongue.'

The only time he flinched was when he was told that only 5,000 men made up the fighting force of the British.

'Were I as powerful as I once was, I should certainly have gone to meet your people, and asked them what they came into my country for. But how can I?' He pointed above, to the shadowy cliffs of Meqdela. 'I have lost all Abyssinia but this rock.'

He became thoughtful; the lines of his face softened. 'I am ready to meet them here, and resign myself to the protection of my Creator.'

The sun was high. He watched his men below, struggling to raise the last of the guns. He shook his head. 'How can I show those ragged soldiers of mine to your well-dressed troops?'

Tents had been erected some distance away. In church, the Lenten prayers had been said and food could now be eaten. Tewodros rose to his feet.

'Now, Mr Rassam,' he asked as they walked like old friends towards the tents, 'what do you think the proper charge would be for a large mortar like that?'

That afternoon, Tewodros sent Rassam a message. He said that the day Sevastopol was forged and today, when he spoke with Rassam, 'were the happiest he had experienced' in nearly two years.

Rassam viewed things rather differently. Although he had not seen the emperor 'so calm as on that day', he was aware too of a great sadness. The furies were catching up with Tewodros. Rassam had been watching him closely that morning, as the teams of men heaved at their straps and Sevastopol inched its way up the slope.

'I shall never forget,' he wrote, 'the melancholy expression of his countenance.'

XII

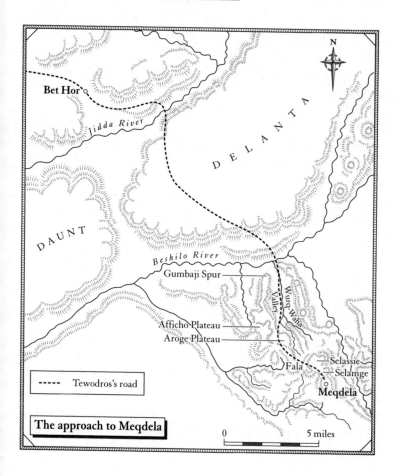

The approach to Meqdela

The approach to Meqdela

71

A few days later, at the beginning of April, Napier and the forward British force reached Bet Hor. There, on the edge of the Jidda gorge, they encountered Tewodros's road. It was the first real sign of the enemy, who until now had been merely an abstract, demonised figure. That this barbarian was capable of such a feat of engineering was a surprise, and made them more anxious about the battles to come.

They made their own camp beside the ruins of his, abandoned just weeks earlier. The stick frames of the huts lay scattered over the ground, along with a flotsam of sheep and cattle bones, cooking pots, quern-stones, torn leather aprons, broken horn, spoons and cups. Stanley said he saw 'a human arm in the last stages of corruption', and at the very centre of the camp a skull broken with a heavy instrument.

From Bet Hor, Tewodros had blasted his road down the cliffs and into the Jidda gorge. It had taken him seven weeks to reach the Delanta plateau on the far side. Using the road, Napier and his men crossed the gorge in a single day. The first troops left camp at five in the morning; many didn't reach the Delanta plateau before dark. Here they found another of Tewodros's abandoned camps and, according to one officer, more 'skulls of wretches he has beheaded'.

At this time, the British in Ethiopia numbered roughly 12,000 fighting men – 5,000 forward and 7,000 defending the supply lines. They were stretched along a course of three or four hundred miles. The carriage of artillery caused them some of their greatest problems, just as it had for Tewodros. Back in Woolwich, experiments had been made in breaking up the Armstrong guns of the standard mountain battery into mule-sized loads – but the one-piece barrels still weighed a thousand pounds. Six-strong teams of horses had tried to haul them, but there had been accidents.

'It would have been impossible,' stated the campaign report, 'to take the heavy guns and mortars to Magdala' were it not for one essential part of the expedition. In Bombay, forty-four Indian elephants had been hoisted from the wharves, their fat feet waving in the air, and lowered into the holds of two specially adapted transports. There they were escorted into strengthened stalls. Detailed instructions were issued for the journey and the hostile conditions expected in the field:

An elephant in good health is constantly in motion, swinging the well-stretched trunk and flapping the ears; a listless state, with the trunk more or less gathered up, denotes ill health.

Elephants when troubled by worms eat mud – and when troubled by it should go 'Naga' or without rations . . .

Disease was more likely to develop under extreme heat or cold; or in excessive rain and wind; from want of sleep (owing to inattention to the importance of giving them their food in the early part of the evening); from violence in the use of the *guzboy*; or from exposure to the sun (the effect of which on the brain renders them liable to 'Surzah', 'a tremor which comes suddenly over the animal, and it falls down and dies').

Each morning, before dawn, by means of a specifically designed pulley and trolley apparatus, eight men would haul the Armstrong guns up onto the backs of the kneeling beasts. While the troops filed out of camp, deeper into the mountainous heart of Ethiopia, and the thump and blast of a military band echoed off the cliffs, the elephants would knee themselves up and lumber along behind. On the flat they were a match for any man or mule in the force, but on the slope they wheezed and struggled. And the slopes, approaching Meqdela, were becoming steeper.

On the afternoon of 6 April, the gun-laden elephants began the long climb up from the Jidda river to Delanta. Twice they were caught by hailstorms, and refused to budge until these had passed. It was after midnight when the first beast struggled up the last muddy yards of the cliff road, up onto the Delanta plateau. As she did so, her feet shifted, the guns on her back tilted her back, and very slowly she began to slide. Gathering pace, she tobogganed on her pads along the muddy road, thirty, forty, fifty, sixty yards or so, back down Tewodros's wide slope, scattering her peers and their *mahouts* and coming to a halt just as she was about to plunge into the abyss.

After that, none of the other elephants would move. Only when the sun had risen, the road had dried and they had been relieved of the great gun-barrels on their backs, did they dare tread the last steps up to Delanta.

Up on the plateau, signs of Tewodros's destruction were everywhere. The wind rattled through charred stubble; clouds of grey ash drifted through burnt-out villages. Sir Robert Napier had several thousand men with him, and more were on their way. They were now in barren land, isolated, far ahead of the supply line. At that moment, the commissariat announced that they had only a day's flour left. Sir Robert Napier was now in exactly the position he had most dreaded.

In a state of some concern, Napier called for Captain Speedy.

72

Captain Charles Tristram Sawyer Speedy, six foot six, strode across camp to see the commander-in-chief. He wore dark damask trousers and *shamma*; but for his red beard and hair, and his always-worn spectacles, he might have been an Ethiopian.

Speedy was one of the more colourful members of the British expeditionary force. He was not a regular, but a member of the intelligence corps. He was a lover of native costume, a maverick, a giant quite capable of slicing a sheep in two with a single swipe of his sword. Napier had him on his staff because he knew Ethiopia, he knew Amharic and he knew Tewodros.

The commander-in-chief was not given to shows of emotion, or shows of any kind. But now he explained the supply problem to Speedy 'with distressed countenance and alarmed voice'.

Speedy told him not to worry. They were in 'what is regarded as the very garden of Abyssinia'. The emperor might have destroyed every plant on Delanta, but Speedy happened to know the chief of neighbouring Daunt, and would pop over and ask him for grain.

'But,' he insisted, 'I must have the largest elephant.'

Seven years earlier – twenty-four, without ties, his commission in the Indian Army resigned – Speedy had been sitting in a Jeddah café drinking a cup of bitter Mocha coffee. He was about to turban his red hair, pull a pilgrim's *jellabiyeh* over his head and march like his hero Richard Burton to the forbidden city of Mecca. He saw a beggar sloping towards his table. 'In the name of the Father, Son and Holy Ghost! Give me alms.' Speedy was surprised that a Muslim beggar should invoke the name of the Trinity. But the man looked around, before whispering: 'I am an Ethiopian priest. I am returning from pilgrimage to Jerusalem. I do not have the funds to reach my country. Please, sir . . .'

Speedy took the man back to his lodgings. There the priest could talk freely, and as Speedy listened to tales of the man's longed-for homeland, he felt himself stirred in a way that would alter the course of his entire life. 'A great desire awoke within me to go to the country,' he wrote. He abandoned his plans to visit Mecca, took a dhow to Massawa and with the priest as his guide crossed the desert plain towards the highlands. They carried water in goatskin flasks. The blue ripples of the scarp shimmered before them. The temperature rose to 150 degrees Fahrenheit. But soon they were climbing. They walked in the shadow of high cliffs. The heat eased.

In the town of Adwa, a messenger arrived. Hundreds of miles to the south, Tewodros had heard of the Englishman's arrival. He must come at once to Debre Tabor; the *negus* wanted to meet him.

This '*negus*' was a month's journey away. Speedy refused. He was going hunting. But the messenger knew his job well. He made it clear that Speedy was in no position to turn the emperor down.

Tewodros was reclining on a blue couch when Speedy first saw him. Above his head the silk of his tent porch billowed and flapped in the wind. Speedy noted his palpable presence, his powerful frame, the five plaited lines of hair that ran over his head. Above all he noted his strange mesmeric gaze. He put his age at 'about fifty'; in fact he was little more than forty.

'All Europeans I like,' Tewodros told him. 'But the English

I love. My two best friends in this world were Plowden and Bell. I shall love you too.'

Tewodros asked his name. He found the '*sp-*' hard to pronounce. 'What does it mean?'

The interpreter explained – and as he did so, the sun bounced off Speedy's glasses and Tewodros said: '*Felika*' – meaning in Amharic both 'flashing' and 'speedy'. 'I shall call you Basha Felika.'

The rains were coming. Tewodros told Speedy to spend the season at Gefat, to live among his 'children' the missionaries, and learn Amharic. He himself was going south to Gojjam to do battle with the rebels; they would talk again when he was back. It was clear to Speedy that he was now unable to leave the country.

When they met again, months later, the two at once began talking of a subject cherished by both: military tactics. Speedy claimed that foot-soldiers, if properly armed and trained, could always defeat an equivalent force of cavalry. And he could prove it. He asked for a hundred men.

After a month he told Tewodros he was ready. The emperor assembled his cavalry and watched from a small hill. He saw Speedy's men sitting around in casual groups. As soon as Tewodros gave the order for the horsemen to charge, Speedy's foot-soldiers rushed to their stations. Basha Felika himself stood beside them, holding a red handkerchief. The riders had *zings*, long spears, with their blunted tips dipped in wet clay. Speedy gave the signal, and a volley of blanks thundered around the valley. The smoke cleared to show the horsemen scattered, some dumped into the dirt, some clinging to the necks of their bolting mounts.

Speedy gave the order to reload. But there was no second charge. He had proved his point. Tewodros was furious. To be upstaged in military matters by a *farenj* was galling enough, but what really infuriated him was the thought of what Speedy's drill might do in the hands of his enemies.

Tewodros summoned him, and asked when he would like to leave the country.

'Tomorrow,' said Speedy, taking his chance.

'Go now,' urged Tewodros. 'Tomorrow Satan may change my heart.'

That was some six years ago. On his way out of the country in 1862, Captain Speedy had met Welde Giyorgis, the ruler of Daunt. They had talked about India, and Speedy told Welde Giyorgis of two very strange things: the telegraph system, and working elephants. The Indian elephant, Speedy explained, unlike the African, could be trained. Two days later Welde Giyorgis took Speedy to church. Kneeling before the *mekdes*, he prayed for forgiveness for this *farenj* and the dreadful fantasies that filled his head.

Now, in April 1868, Welde Giyorgis looked down from the edge of his plateau. A valley separated it from Delanta and he had managed to protect his grain from Tewodros's recent plundering. He saw an elephant padding up the path towards him – and on the elephant's shoulders sat a man. When he saw who the man was, Welde Giyorgis rode down the slope, shouting, 'Felika, Felika, Basha Felika! My son, my son!'

Speedy climbed down from the elephant and the ruler 'literally fell on my neck, and kissed me again and again'. He persuaded Welde Giyorgis up on top of the elephant. They rode to the British camp. It was certainly a strange day for Welde Giyorgis. There in the camp Speedy showed him the telegraph apparatus. Earlier he had telegraphed a message to Welde Giyorgis's sister, who lived far to the north: she must come to the telegraph station and wait there. Now he asked Welde Giyorgis to send her a message. 'Which finger did I lose as a child?' The answer came back almost at once. Welde Giyorgis stared in silence at the machine.

'Abandon this work,' he hissed. 'It is of the devil.'

But later that day, filing down from Daunt appeared a line of one hundred mules. Ten thousand pounds of grain arrived in the British camp. Over the coming days, the mules brought from Welde Giyorgis's stores 40,000 pounds of wheat, 30,000 pounds of flour and 100,000 pounds of barley. Napier had sufficient supplies to support his forces for eleven days.

He was now ready for the final leg of the march.

During the course of their four-hundred-mile march, the British had passed any number of impossible cliffs and natural fortresses. The thought had become common currency in the ranks: 'If Tewodros has not chosen these, what must Meqdela itself be like?'

On 6 April, a group of officers had ridden to the edge of the Delanta cliffs and looked south. They had seen Tewodros's road pushing four thousand feet down into the Beshilo gorge. They had seen the dry cliffs and swollen bluffs that rose from the river. They had seen the land build in courses of bare rock and scrubby slopes, to roofs of flat land covered in fields, and up further still to the summit of Meqdela itself. 'Such an extraordinary set of hills I never saw,' wrote a journalist with these men. 'It was magnificent, and stretched away east and west as far as the eye could reach. Above all this Magdala rose like a great ship out of the surrounding billows.'

From then on, each day, Napier rode out to the cliffs and with a telescope surveyed the vast arena of broken land ahead. With the eye of a military man, aware of how close he was to his enemy, he took in every crease and spur of topography between them.

'It is difficult to give by description alone,' he wrote dryly, 'a sufficient idea of the formidable position which we were about to assail.'

73

Tewodros too was watching.

It was Easter Week. On Palm Sunday, he mounted his mule, rode up the stony path to Selassie peak and pointed his telescope to the north. On the following days he did the same. Rassam wrote: 'Theodore has done scarcely anything but ascend the height of Selassie scanning with his telescope the country towards Delanta.'

For a couple of days he saw nothing. Then on Tuesday, in the shivering blue-grey circle of his glass, he spotted a flash of red. It was the first of the British pushing down the side of the Beshilo gorge. They were using the road he himself had built.

'Hurrah!' he cried. 'There go the donkeys!'

Waldmeier was with him. Tewodros handed him the telescope and pointed towards the Beshilo. 'There you will see your brethren, who have come from England to kill me.'

Tewodros grew subdued. Waldmeier watched as he 'became gloomy and dark as night, restless and angry as Saul, and I trembled with fear'.

In the coming days, as the British drew nearer, Tewodros's temper flitted to and fro. Defiance gave way to conciliation, piety to drunkenness, boasting to fatalism, cruelty to remorse, self-pity to anger, and in turn back to defiance. The confrontation was imminent, and everyone trapped on that mountain, prisoner and priest, soldier and minister, knew that their survival would be decided as much in the emperor's troubled soul as on the battlefield.

The next day, the Wednesday of Holy Week, Tewodros rose before dawn and dressed with unusual flamboyance.

The simplicity of his clothes, usually a plain white *shamma* with red border, had always been a part of his style, in keeping with his loathing of luxury. But that day, in a perverse imitation of the British, he pulled on a costume made of Lyons silk fringed with gold thread, and pantaloons of white tinsel. Rassam thought 'he looked more like a harlequin than a sovereign'.

He addressed his troops. Those they would face in battle, he said, would outnumber them. They would be better armed. 'Their very dress,' he cried, 'is bedecked with gold, to say nothing of their treasures, which can only be borne by elephants.' He called on his men to fight for him, to 'enrich themselves with the spoils of the white slaves'.

One of Tewodros's oldest supporters stepped forward – Afe-negus Bahru. He had been the *afe-negus* under Ras Ali. He had known Plowden and Bell and had witnessed the rise of the young Kasa, from small-time bandit to rebel, to the great Tewodros II.

'Only wait, Your Majesty,' he cried, echoing the spirit of his emperor's words, 'until those asses make their appearance, and we will tear them to pieces!'

Tewodros looked down at him. 'What say you, old fool? Have you ever seen an English soldier to know what he is like, and what weapons he carries? Be assured that before you know where you are, your belly will be filled with bullets.'

Earlier that morning, Tewodros had summoned all the prisoners down from Meqdela. The Europeans mingled with the five hundred Ethiopians – Amhara, Tigrayan, Oromo, one-time allies of Tewodros, high-born chiefs, robbers, soldiers captured in battle, families of defectors, the unlucky, the forgotten, the sick and the innocent. Many had been crammed into the lice-ridden prison huts for years, and had somehow survived the random killings of epidemic, starvation and execution. Some were still shackled, and could do no more than crawl.

'Their appearance,' wrote Dr Blanc, now free of his chains, 'was enough to inspire pity in the most callous heart; many had no other covering than a small piece of rag round the loins, and were living skeletons, covered with some loathsome skin disease.'

Not one of them believed that Tewodros had summoned them 'for any good purpose'.

But lately he had been doing what was least expected. That morning he released seventy-five. Then he took his telescope and rode up to Selassie peak to watch the British. He saw nothing.

The next day he ordered the release of the remaining Ethiopian prisoners. Up on Selassie, he extended his telescope and pointed it towards the Beshilo gorge. This time he spied a line of baggage descending towards the river. He also spotted four elephants and a number of white creatures with black heads.

'Probably Berbera sheep,' suggested Rassam when they met later.

'I am tired from looking out so long,' Tewodros told the envoy. 'I am going to rest awhile. Why are your people so slow?'

The emperor retired to his tent. In the afternoons now he was drinking *arak*. Those around him had learnt to divide the days into benign mornings and furious afternoons. That afternoon was no different.

Tewodros was woken from his sleep by the released prisoners. The prising off of their chains was not easy, and by four o'clock only ninety-five had been freed. The others became impatient, and began calling for food and water.

In the heat of his tent, Tewodros jumped to his feet – 'like a raging lion', wrote the chronicler. He grabbed his sword. He ran from his tent and called for the prisoners. The first two he himself slashed to death. One by one the others came before him and gave their name, region of origin and charge. Each time, Tewodros ordered them to be dragged to the western edge of Selamge cliff and thrown over. He sent his soldiers to the bottom of the cliff to check for survivors; any still alive were shot.

Rassam said he believed that this time Tewodros was driven by more than just rage. A true insanity was taking hold, and he cited one case to illustrate it. One of the prisoners had been accused of trying to force himself on a concubine of Tewodros's. The man's two sons, aged between about twelve and fifteen, had been imprisoned simply through filial connection. These two boys were hurled over the cliff. But when their father appeared, and his crime was read out, Tewodros waved him away: 'Open his chains and let him go.'

More than three hundred died that afternoon. Later Tewodros slept for a few hours before being thrust back into the horrors of his waking world. His valet, Welde Gabre, said he spent the rest of the night in tortured prayer. He heard him 'confess that he was drunk when he ordered the massacre, and he prayed that it would not be laid to his charge'.

It was Good Friday.

'The tyrant,' wrote Stern, 'though a perfect fiend and coarse blasphemer, repaired, from a superstitious impulse, at a very early hour to church.'

Tewodros knew the British were capable of reaching the foot of the mountain that day. He ordered the final deployment of his big guns. Most were placed on Fala, covering the small plain of Aroge far below and the long approach road up its slopes to Meqdela. Several others were dragged to the western edge of Selassie. Among these was Sevastopol itself.

74

Early on that Good Friday morning, across the Beshilo gorge, reveille sounded out around the British camp. The fighting force assembled in the dewy grass of Delanta. They marched to the cliff-edge and began their descent. Within a couple of hours, a long line of figures could be seen snaking down from the plateau, across the shelf and on down to the narrow shingle bed of the river.

Napier had spent days in reconnaissance and discussion. He had briefed his senior officers. He had issued the General Order for the assault in all its detail:

> . . . each officer to carry two pounds of biscuit and two pounds of cooked meat . . . every foot soldier will cross the Beshilo bare-footed, and fill his canteen as he crossed . . . every Staff Officer and officer will provide himself with a certain number of slips of paper of convenient size, as also a lead pencil . . . no one belonging to the attacking force must be allowed to fall out for the purpose of assisting a wounded man . . . a corps of stretcher bearers to be made up of spare drummers and Punjab muleteers . . .

The normal approach to Meqdela was to follow the dry riverbed of the Wurq-Waha valley. This was the way taken by Tewodros and his guns. The valley cut far in towards the mountain, providing a steady climb. There was then a short ascent to the Aroge plateau. From there the road pushed on up to the Fala saddle.

Such a route was not open to Napier. Wurq-Waha could be attacked from either of its steep sides, and the climb up to Aroge was exposed both to ground attack and Tewodros's artillery. Napier needed height before Aroge. He settled on pushing a way up out of the Beshilo, up the Gumbaji spur. The climb was very arduous, and largely conducted in the gorge's stifling depths. The troops, recorded the official report, 'suffered severely from the difficult nature of the path, great heat, and want of water, and many fell out of the ranks exhausted'.

The path was too severe for pack animals, so the baggage and weaponry would move up Wurq-Waha. Those who had climbed the spur were to advance some four miles and cover the point where the mules would emerge. Napier himself rode up the spur and along towards the Aroge plateau. He could now see at close quarters the great heights of Fala and Selassie. Dark clouds had gathered above them. It was just before 4 p.m.

At once Napier spotted a problem. He saw that at the agreed point above Wurq-Waha, there were no forces. At that moment, the first mules with their dipping heads pushed up from the valley. They were unprotected. Napier at once gave orders for the Punjab Pioneers to move forward.

Among those who had come up from Wurq-Waha was Henry Morton Stanley. He spoke of a great silence around the hills above, 'a suspicious silence'. It made them uneasy. As they reached the Aroge plateau and looked up at the slopes of Fala above they saw the slate-grey thickening of storm clouds. They noticed too a slight movement at the top of the slope. Within seconds, the whole mountainside was shifting.

At that moment too, from high above on the Fala ridge, a

tiny crown of white appeared. A round shot screamed over the heads of the officers, and over Napier, and thumped into the ground behind them.

'As if by a preconcerted signal, the steep path and the mountain sides of Fala were instantaneously covered by masses of warriors.' Several thousand men – many mounted, many armed with guns – surged down the slope towards the British.

75

At six o'clock that morning, two messengers arrived at Waldmeier's tent. He was to come and see Tewodros at once. The slaughter of the prisoners was known to everyone by then, and Waldmeier looked at the faces of the messengers. He felt they knew why he had been called. He was very nervous.

When Waldmeier approached Tewodros, the emperor was 'moodily looking at the ground'. He seemed to have forgotten why he had summoned him. Waldmeier remained with him, witnessing the day's first decisions.

Tewodros's first orders were to send Rassam and the other Europeans back to their prison on Meqdela. Waldmeier saw this as 'a very threatening sign, and I feared that all was working together to bring about a horrible end to the Europeans'.

Stern however was delighted. He thought it 'perfect bliss to quit the royal charnel-house, and to breathe once more, if even for a few hours, an atmosphere not impregnated with blood and death'.

Before they left for the short climb back to the *amba*, Rassam urged Tewodros once more to write to Napier for terms.

'I will do no such thing,' growled the emperor, 'as he has been sent by a woman.'

Just as the Europeans started out, Rassam received word

that a messenger had come from Napier with a letter for Tewodros. But again Tewodros was defiant. He said he would see neither messenger nor message, and warned Rassam not to try to communicate with the British: 'The blood of the messenger who carries your missive will be on your head. Beware!'

With the European prisoners gone, Tewodros continued with his battle plans. He ordered the guns to be taken to Fala. Waldmeier, who had conceived and created many of the guns, was now charged with helping to use them in battle.

'Take leave of your family,' Tewodros told him, 'because today you will have the honour to die with a king.'

Waldmeier went to his tent with a heavy heart. He said goodbye to Susan, his 'dear wife', and to young Rosa, who only a few years earlier was happily riding on the back of Hagos the lion. He embraced them both, kissed them for the last time, then followed Tewodros round Selamge, along the rocky path to the Fala saddle. His feet were bare, and as he walked, tears ran down his cheeks. 'It was not a long distance from Magdala to Fala,' he wrote of that Good Friday's walk, 'but it was a Via Dolorosa.'

Tewodros's plan was to remain on Fala directing the artillery. He called his most loyal general to him. Like him, Fitawrari Gabriye was from Qwara and, according to Welde Gabre, he had been 'his constant friend for thirty years'. Tewodros put him in charge of the ground force.

In the early afternoon, as clouds began to build around the mountain, Tewodros mounted his battle horse and addressed his men. This time there was no ambivalence. The enemy was in sight now, just half a mile below them, and Tewodros drew on his biblical twin, the figure whose example had shaped the glories of his youth.

'My children, be not afraid of these English soldiers, because they are like the Philistines who made war against David; but, remember David smote them and in the name of God I shall conquer.' His horse high-paced back and forth before the lines.

'Am I not a son of David and Solomon? Has not God anointed me King of Ethiopia? Am I not the old hero in the battle, the pillar of fire to those who are afraid?'

Tewodros took on not only the mantle of Old Testament warrior, but of priest too.

'As our Abune Selama is dead,' he cried with glittering eyes, 'I absolve in the name of God the Father, the Son, and the Holy Ghost, every soldier who may lose his battle against the Europeans.'

Down below, the first mules had appeared from Wurq-Waha. The British forces on the Aroge plateau were thin.

'Look at those slaves! They are women! Look at them – they bring you clothes and riches and pay! Go down and help yourselves!'

The baggage train was as tempting a prize for his troops as a combat victory. Cheers rose from the massed group of fighters. They drowned out the voice of their leader.

Suddenly, Tewodros hesitated. 'Should I send them down?' he asked, first his staff, then Waldmeier. Perhaps it was too soon to fight . . . he had seen more forces advancing across the Afficho plateau . . . He should wait to see their tactics.

He called his forces back – but it was too late. The men were already on the move, and the officers were unable to stop them.

'So be it – I will cover you with my cannon.'

Tewodros asked Waldmeier to measure out the charges for the guns, and the first shot fired high into the space above the plateau.

76

Tewodros was mistaken. The line of mules coming up his own road, out of Wurq-Waha and onto the Aroge plateau, were not just baggage mules. There was baggage with them, but the mules also carried the rocket tubes of the Naval Brigade and the guns of Colonel Penn's A mountain battery.

As they emerged with the pack animals, the unprepared Naval Brigade did not find the armed support they'd expected. They were on their own. They were alarmed too to see some 4,000 Ethiopians dashing down the slope towards them, through the scrub, sure-footed among the rocks, a great whooping force of nature.

The Naval Brigade hurried to remember what they'd done as drill a thousand times before. The Ethiopian cries grew louder. They set up the tubes, fumbled the rockets – then fired. The Ethiopians faltered.

Tewodros's men outnumbered the British advance by about two to one. Three thousand were armed – with old matchlocks, but armed all the same. They split in half, one group rushing the rockets, the others taking on those trying to assemble for battle on the plateau. The sky had darkened. Thunder cracked and tumbled around the peaks. Twelve hundred feet above the converging forces, the emperor's cannon began to lob their great shells down onto the plateau.

Tewodros had been waiting for months for this, for years. His forces were a fraction of what they once were. He was surrounded by enemies. But for the first time he had the chance to use his complete artillery in battle. And Meqdela's natural defences were worth thousands of men. He watched the surge of his forces and the hurried grouping of the British. He saw his mounted officers in their finest crimson shirts (put on to match the British, though the British had largely shed their colour for battle khaki). After the first salvo of rockets, his men had rallied. At one point he saw a group of them push round the flank of the enemy. They began to close on their rear. The British were going to be encircled! A cry of excitement went up from those on Fala, and a messenger ran back to Meqdela with the good news.

Waldmeier had helped with the initial charges for the guns, but their fire was now being directed by a Copt on Tewodros's staff. It was not effective. From such a height the trajectory was more or less vertical by the time it reached the ground below. Many of the rounds also drove into the soil far beyond the British troops. One of the largest guns on Fala was named 'Tewodros', a forty-pounder. Waldmeier was standing just a few yards from it when suddenly it exploded. It had been double-charged.

'The King,' he saw with alarm, 'became furious, and trembled with rage.'

And now, from down on the battlefield there rose a new sound. The 446 men of the King's Own had arrived on the plateau. Their first shots stopped the Ethiopians, but only for a moment. The Ethiopians surged forward again. They knew what to do against gunfire. If you survived the first volley, you closed on the enemy while they shoved the new charges down the barrels and levelled their weapons again. Thirty seconds was the minimum time it took to reload and fire. That was how it had been since the Portuguese brought the first matchlocks; guns had changed little since then.

Until now. For the British, this was the first battle in which they'd used breech-loading Sniders.

There was no dropping of the stock, no pause. A few seconds was all it took for the men of the King's Own to press the new cartridges in and fire again – and again, and again. There were no volleys. The firing was continuous – thirty or forty rounds per second. The mounted Ethiopian officers in their coloured shirts were the first to fall. Still the warriors pressed on. The lines began to thin. They retreated, then pushed forward. The Sniders were relentless. In the end the Ethiopians fell back. Some made it to the euphorbia of the Muslim cemetery at the foot of Fala, and to the rocks of the lower slope. They continued to fire on the British from there.

From the heights, Tewodros looked down on the battle. He saw his men surge forward and falter; he saw the numbers of fallen as they dropped back. He saw them regroup, and fight on. The British lines remained untouched. Tewodros watched and could do nothing; he sensed the chill of defeat. The Naval Brigade now directed their rockets up at Fala.

When one dropped just a few feet from Tewodros, he cried: 'Would that it had gone through my head!'

XIII

The captives. Left to right: Kerans, Rassam, Stern (standing), Prideaux, Mrs Rosenthal and child, Rosenthal, Blanc, Pietro, Cameron.

77

It was almost dark. For a couple of hours during the battle, heavy rain had fallen, but now it had thinned and stopped. The low sun dropped through a raft of broken cloud. As the darkness hid them, the families of the missing made their way down to the soggy soil of Aroge. For hours their shouts mingled with the cries of the wounded.

At the same time, walking survivors made their way up to the Fala saddle. In the darkness, Tewodros called out to them for news. What of his commander, Fitawrari Gabriye? The general was dead. What of the others? One by one Tewodros shouted the names of his chiefs. They were all dead. They remained where they had dropped from their mounts on the battlefield, picked out in their brightly-coloured silks, picked out and toppled by the Sniders.

Of the British forces, twenty had been wounded, two fatally. Seven hundred Ethiopians had died, while some fifteen hundred were wounded.

Tewodros went back to his tent. Light rain pattered on the roof. A silent rage consumed him. He did not sleep. He was used to settling matters in battle, to concluding disputes with swift force. This time his weapons had settled nothing. His army was defeated, and his options were closing. He could fight on, or he could give in. He could kill the hostages, or he could hand them over. All he had left were the hostages, the mountain and a few loyal supporters. He called them to him to discuss what to do.

Waldmeier, who had been with him all day, had an intimation what decision they would reach. 'His anger had made him almost insane,' he said, 'and he allowed his chiefs to strengthen him in the horrible plan he had for our execution.'

Later that evening, the summons came. Flad and Waldmeier made their way to the emperor's tent. They 'trembled with fear'. Once again, Tewodros surprised them. He was not only friendly to the missionaries, but now appeared calm.

Go up to Meqdela, he told them, take this message for Rassam:

How have you passed the day? Thank God, I am well. I, being a King, could not allow people to come and fight me without attacking them first. I have done so, and my troops have been beaten. I thought your people were women, but I find they are men. They fought very bravely. Seeing that I am unable to cope with them, I must ask you to reconcile me with them.

Rassam thought carefully about what to do. He suggested that Tewodros send Lieutenant Prideaux and Flad down to the British camp in the morning with a representative of his own.

When Waldmeier and Flad took this proposal back to Tewodros, they found his mood 'totally changed'. At this stage, he appeared not so much indecisive as counter-decisive. Every decision he made, every position he put himself in, angered him into reversing it. Thirty-six hours earlier he had freed hundreds of prisoners, then slaughtered them. That morning he had ordered his men to attack the British, then tried to call them back. Now he told Waldmeier and Flad that there was no urgency about making peace with the British.

'Let God do what he pleases. Now go to sleep.'

The Germans were woken a few hours later, at 4 a.m., and summoned to the emperor again. In the quiet chill of the night, the sounds of grief came from all directions.

'Do you hear this wailing?' asked Tewodros. 'There is not a soldier who has not lost a friend or brother. What will it be when the whole army comes? What shall I do? Counsel me.'

'Your Majesty,' urged Waldmeier, 'peace is best.'

Flad said the same. Tewodros then buried himself in thought. A couple of minutes passed in silence before he said, '*Isshi*. Very well.'

So Flad went back to Meqdela to fetch Prideaux. To accompany them to the British camp Tewodros appointed Dejazmach Alemi, who was married to the daughter of Yetemegnu. At first light Flad, Prideaux and Alemi walked together down the mountain. The British camp could be seen spread around the point where Tewodros's road came up out of the Wurq-Waha valley – the point where the battle had begun.

Tewodros, dressed once again in his simple fashion, took his telescope up to the Selassie peak.

78

The previous day the advance brigades of the British had descended the Beshilo gorge, waded the river, climbed the Gumbaji spur, crossed the Afficho plateau, and late in the afternoon, in a thunderstorm, managed to defeat Tewodros's army. They then lay down on the damp ground and went to sleep.

In the night, they were joined by the 2nd Brigade, and with the 2nd Brigade came the elephants and the Armstrong guns.

The men woke to a sunny dawn. 'The clock bird loudly sang in the groves,' recalled Stanley, 'the swallow chirped merrily in the gladsome light, and the lark soared high in the diaphanous air.' They congratulated themselves on their victory, and with such few casualties. Stanley then went with a Captain Sweeny and a detachment to the battlefield. 'It was a frightful scene.' The wounded were scattered everywhere in the mud. The hyenas had already disfigured many of them. Others lay groaning. The British took these back to the camp for treatment.

At about the same time, shouts went up from the camp. All eyes turned to the slope above. A small party of men was coming down from the Fala saddle. Above their heads flopped a white flag; the uniform of a British officer was seen among them. The party came closer. As they rode in through the guards, the soldiers thronged to their side with 'loud cheers and rapturous greetings'.

Lieutenant Prideaux, Martin Flad and Dejazmach Alemi stood before Napier and delivered Tewodros's verbal message. Napier dictated a reply:

Your Majesty has fought like a brave man, and has been overcome by the superior force of the British army.

It is my desire that no more blood may be shed. If, therefore, your Majesty will submit to the Queen of England, and bring all the Europeans now in your Majesty's hands, and deliver them safely this day in the hands of the British camp, I guarantee honourable treatment for yourself and for all the members of your Majesty's family.

Napier chose his words carefully. He had achieved an emphatic victory over Tewodros, and proved the supremacy of the Sniders. Those were, however, 'mere playthings', Alemi was told, as he was shown both the Armstrongs and the elephants which carried them. Yet Napier still did not have the hostages, and no calibre of weaponry could guarantee their release.

When the delegation returned from the British camp, Tewodros was sitting on a rock on Selassie, dictating to his secretary Aleqa Ingida. He paused to have Napier's letter read out to him. He asked for it to be translated twice by Flad and Waldmeier. Its implications were contained within Napier's euphemistic 'honourable treatment'.

'Do they mean to treat me honourably as a prisoner, or do they intend to assist me in recovering my country from the rebels?'

Tewodros had somehow retained the hope that the British could become his allies. But he also understood how little he had left. In response to the offer of 'honourable treatment' for his family, he struck a sardonic note of self-deprecation:

'Have they taken account of my numerous family, for I have as many wives and children almost as the hairs on my head. It would involve immense expense in England.'

He then recalled Ingida, and carried on dictating. All of Tewodros is in this Easter Saturday letter – all the boasting, the scorn, the courage and nobility, the arrogance, the candour. He is both despot and paternalist, conquering Tewodros of prophecy and mortal, defeated Kasa. For all its confusion it reads like a confession, like a final testament.

In the name of the Father, and the Son, and the Holy Ghost, One God: Kasa, he who believes in the Three and in the One, in Christ.

Well then, people of my country, will you not abandon your flight unless I, by the power of God, descend for you? As it seemed to me that I had sway over all Christians, I brought them into the land of the heathens. [*It was probably at this point that the delegates returned – Tewodros redirects his message from his own people to Napier.*] There are young women who have no men, and there are young women who had no men, and tomorrow there will be those whose men have died on them. Old men who have no children, old women who have no children, there are many in my town for whom I provide. Grant them out of what God has given you, for it is a land of heathens. When they said that I had said to the people of my country that they should submit to the discipline of taxes, they refused and quarrelled with me. But you people, who are governed by discipline, you conquered me. The men who loved me and followed me, fearing a single bullet, abandoned me and fled. When you attacked them, I was not with those men who ran away. As it seemed to me that I was master, when I strove with inadequate artillery, alas for me! The people of my country would give me ten reasons, saying that I had adopted the faith of the Franks and had become a Muslim. May God give them good out of what I have done wrong to them! May it be as He wills. I had the thought, if God granted it me, to rule all. If God removed it from me, I should die; this was my thought. From when I was born until now, no man has ever seized hold of my hand. Whenever my men fled, I had the habit of reassuring them. Darkness prevented me. You men who dealt in happiness yesterday, may God not make you like me. Let alone my Ethiopian enemies, it had seemed to me that I should march to Jerusalem and drive out the Turks. A man who has held other men, in his turn cannot be held.

79

Tewodros finished dictating his letter. He sent it off to the British camp, enclosing with it Napier's original. A serenity appeared to settle over him. He told those around him to leave. He remained sitting alone on a rock, as so often during the decisive moments of his reign. The great void of the Beshilo gorge stretched beyond him. Suddenly he stood, drank some water and began to pray. He was seen to bow three times. He then pulled a double-barrelled pistol from his belt, put it in his mouth and pulled the trigger.

Click.

When they saw what he was doing, his officers rushed at him. They grabbed his arm as the second trigger was pulled. This time it fired. The bullet grazed his ear. They all fell to the ground. Tewodros fought for several moments, but soon his movements slowed. He pulled his *shamma* over his head and lay still.

The signs leading to Tewodros's suicide attempt look so obvious with hindsight that those around him appear almost complicit. (Their grappling with him, and the insistence of Ras Ingida that he give them his weapons, show in fact how much they still had to lose by it.) The dismissal, the letter to Napier, the defeat at Aroge, the impossibility of surrender for one who'd lived his life under the star of divine destiny, all pointed to Tewodros's last act of will. Five years earlier Henry Dufton had predicted he would end up 'blowing out his brains'.

But he survived. He stood and dusted himself down, convinced now that God still had plans for him. For two months his fortunes had been mirrored by the drama of Easter. Through the Lenten fast he had hauled his guns through the wilderness. On the afternoon of Good Friday, the battle of Aroge had destroyed his army and his worldly hopes. Now he had been resurrected.

He was decisive again. He called Tirunesh to him, his estranged queen, and they spent some hours alone – for the first time in years.

Something else had been happening as Tewodros dictated what he imagined to be his last words. The survivors of his army had begun to reassemble around him. The losses of the previous day appeared not as devastating as before. The will to fight among his followers had not been extinguished. 'The English are fond of sleeping,' they were heard to say. 'We must attack them in the night.'

Tewodros summoned his council, and asked their advice. Ras Ingida was there, Dejazmach Abiye, Dejazmach Werk, Ingida Werk and a number of others. Waldmeier, hiding behind a boulder, overheard this meeting, and wished he had not.

'. . . these Europeans, who are the cause of this war, they must be massacred now, *now*, NOW'. He heard one suggest burning them in a wooden house. 'Let's cut off their hands and feet,' said another, 'and let the English come and take them away.'

When he called Waldmeier and the European artisans to him later that afternoon, Tewodros gazed at them in silence for some minutes.

'It seemed,' wrote Waldmeier, 'as if the last moment must have come.' The desire for vengeance of the Ethiopians all around the mountain was palpable; the losses suffered the previous day had pushed the hostages further out into the cold.

'I was advised to kill you and all the Europeans,' announced Tewodros. The entire council, except one, had advocated it, 'but you have not done anything against me, and I shall not kill you.'

Instead Tewodros ordered the release of all the foreign prisoners. He sent two of his senior officers to Meqdela to announce the news to Rassam and the others.

No one trusted the decision, no one really believed it. When they reached him, Rassam noticed the 'dejected countenances' of the high-ranking envoys. Among all the Ethiopians, he observed, 'the general opinion was that the King meant to have us massacred on the road'.

Still anxious, still uncertain, they left Meqdela – this group of men, women, children and servants who had lived so long in the shadow of their own death. Again they made their way down towards the flat shelf of Selamge. It was late afternoon. Low clouds hung overhead. The skull-like cliffs of Meqdela darkened behind them. They saw a man approaching them. Breathlessly, he delivered his royal message: Rassam, if he so wanted, should see Tewodros before leaving. Rassam, in full diplomatic uniform, his boots polished, separated from the main party. He did not regard it as a hopeful sign. A sense of *déjà vu* gripped him. The events of that afternoon were beginning to resemble the dreadful sequence of commands that had led to their first arrest at Zeghie two years earlier.

80

Rassam made his way alone to Tewodros. He found him standing among rocks on the edge of Selassie cliff. With him were
some twenty musketeers, and the artisans – Waldmeier, Flad
and the others. He beckoned Rassam towards him, and greeted
him. He glanced out over the cliff towards the setting sun.
'Would you rather go at once or spend the night with me?'

'Whatever pleases Your Majesty.'

Tewodros appeared relieved at the answer. 'Good; you had
better go now.' He was resigned to losing Rassam. A genuine
sadness infused their last meeting.

'Let me have a few words with you before you depart.' He
gestured to him to sit down.

'You know, Mr Rassam, that you and I have always been
on good terms. God knows your heart, but as far as I'm
concerned I've always had a high regard for you. It is true that
I have behaved badly towards you, but that was through the
conduct of bad men.'

Waldmeier, witnessing the meeting, believed that Tewodros
always supposed Rassam to be more powerful than he actually
was. Now the emperor hoped that Rassam's support in the
British camp could reconcile him with Napier. 'I want you to
bear this in mind – that unless you befriend me, I shall either

kill myself or become a monk. Now goodbye,' said Tewodros. 'It is getting late; try and come to see me tomorrow, if you can.'

Rassam said he would try.

Tewodros looked at his old friend, and asked: 'Will you come again tomorrow?'

'It all depends on the orders of the Commander-in-Chief.'

The two men rose to their feet. They shook hands. Tears filled Tewodros's eyes. 'Farewell; be quick, it is getting late.'

Rassam left him. When he looked back, he saw Tewodros standing on a rock, with the musketeers behind him. Go on, he gestured.

Rassam could hardly place one foot in front of the other. He could not match Tewodros's emotional farewell. At this point he felt only fear, a paralysing anxiety that just as he was released, the others would be killed.

They had taken a different path. They had been advised, by Tewodros himself among others, that the emperor must on no account see Stern. The path was narrow, cut into the steep and plunging face of Selassie. From the skyline above, crowds of Ethiopians watched their progress. Blanc was in front, some way ahead of the others. As he rounded a small bluff, he suddenly found himself just yards from Tewodros. The emperor's head was turned, but Blanc could see that he was 'in a fearful passion'. The twenty musketeers stood on the path beyond him. A report confirmed later that, as soon as he had said his farewell to Rassam, Tewodros had taken a gun and in fury hurried with his musketeers to meet the European party. But when he saw the doctor, Tewodros let his arm drop.

'In a low sad voice,' reported Blanc, 'he asked how I was, and bade me good-bye.'

According to Stern's own account, Tewodros also saw him. His words were very similar to those to Blanc: 'How are you? Good-bye.'

'It was,' Stern wrote later, 'the sweetest Amharic to which

I had ever listened – the most rapturous sentence that ever greeted my ears.'

They met up with Rassam some way further on. They descended in the spreading darkness, and by the time they passed the pickets of the British camp, it was night.

Rassam went straight to the tent of Napier, then with Blanc and Prideaux to that of Merewether.

It was over three years since Rassam had left Aden, where he worked under Merewether. No one else had lobbied for the mission's interests so tirelessly as Merewether. It was he who from Massawa had sent the packages of money that saved their lives, he who had found reliable messengers for their personal letters. He had managed to smuggle them newspaper cuttings from London. He had also sent Rassam tomato seeds.

Merewether greeted them. Despite Napier's strict baggage allowances, he had made sure he included something for this moment. From the corner of the tent Colonel Merewether produced six bottles of champagne.

81

The next day was Easter Sunday, and Tewodros dictated a letter to be taken to the British camp. He apologised to Napier for his unfriendly letter of the day before, confessing that 'Satan placed in me the thought that I should die by my own gun.' He now believed that peace was possible. The two sides had settled what needed to be settled in battle, and Tewodros had released the hostages – he would release the European artisans and their families today.

'As it is Easter,' he added, 'permit me to send heifers.'

Tewodros gathered together a total of one thousand head of cattle and five hundred sheep, and sent them down to Napier with the letter. He watched through his telescope as the precious meat wound down his road, down the mountain. As the animals approached the British camp, it appeared that they were refused. Tewodros was baffled. But then a verbal message came back up the mountain, saying they would be accepted. Convinced that negotiations would now take place, he played his final card. He sent word to the remaining Europeans: you are free to go.

Waldmeier came to say goodbye. As with Rassam the day before, Tewodros appeared overwhelmed. Again tears filled his eyes. The better part of his reign, and of his own personality, were embodied in his friendship with Waldmeier. The quiet German had always appealed to him. It was Tewodros who encouraged his marriage to Susan Bell, daughter of his minister John Bell. That was ten years ago. Since then, at least until his arrest, Waldmeier had obeyed the mercurial demands of the emperor. Faith had first called him to Ethiopia, fresh from missionary college, and faith had driven him on. He had believed in all he did, in building a foundry and forging guns, and he had believed in Tewodros, long after mere reason would have allowed it. But for a year now he had been living in doubt.

Tewodros now stood before him. 'Farewell my dear friend. I loved you as I loved John Bell.'

They shook hands. Waldmeier was dazed by his unfolding release. The prospect of 'liberty and peace was almost too much for our hearts to realize'. He quoted from the Psalms – 'When the Lord turned again the captivity of Zion, we were like them that dream . . .'

All the Europeans had left. For the first time since before his coronation, since the day John Bell joined him from the camp of Ras Ali, Tewodros was alone with his own people.

He watched them struggle between the boulders, down towards the Fala saddle. They formed quite a party. Pauline Flad, ill at the time, was borne shoulder-high on a stretcher. More than two hundred people, the missionaries, their families, their servants, and their three hundred animals, climbed down the mountainside. With them went every moveable object, every trunk, every tent, every crate which belonged either to them or to those released the day before.

Tewodros turned to his remaining officers. 'Surely, it is peace now; they have taken my power from me. Surely it is peace.'

But it wasn't peace. As the sun went down on that Easter Sunday, a message came back up from outside the British camp. His gift to Napier, of all the livestock remaining to him, a gesture to mark the end of the *hudaddie* fast, and an end to hostilities, had been refused. Tewodros had been deceived. He was led to believe they had been accepted and had given up the last of the hostages. His valet Welde Gabre watched his lips tighten and heard him say: 'These people having got what they wanted, they now want to kill me.'

His thoughts turned to his native Qwara. He would escape. He told his officers to gather the remaining troops. They would leave that night, cross the Jejaho, reach Lake Tana. They would travel swiftly, as they always had. No one in those regions could touch them! But there was no carriage for the families of his followers, and the men would not abandon them. It was clear that no one would follow Tewodros to Qwara.

He climbed up to Meqdela itself, and urged his men there to leave with him. But they told him to make peace with the British, to surrender. Cowards, he called them. They in turn blamed him for giving up the hostages. Better to have killed them, they said, than squander the chance they had given him to negotiate.

'We are Your Majesty's children until death, if you will only listen to our advice and come to terms with the *farenjis*.'

Tewodros went off into the darkness. He sat alone on the cliffs below the outer gate.

82

With the very minimum of losses, Napier had broken the back of Tewodros's forces, and secured the release of all the hostages.

There were good reasons why he should leave now, return as swiftly as he could to the coast. His supply line was vulnerable, and was already under attack in several places. The rivers were rising. Above his camp, the shadowy hulk of Selassie was a reminder of the natural fortress Tewodros had chosen. The strategic difficulties of the mountain, he wrote to the Secretary of State for India, 'exceeded anything which we could possibly have imagined'.

Over the previous few days, there had also been a subtle shift in morale among Napier's fighting force. They were exhausted. They had marched for weeks through the mountains, driven by the righteousness of their mission: they were coming to rescue innocent Europeans from the torturous attentions of a barbarian. But in the last few weeks that clarity had been muddied. At Bet Hor, they had admired Tewodros's road. At Aroge they had halted the massing enemy, pushed them back, thinned their lines with the Sniders, but still the Ethiopians turned and charged. The Anglo-Indian troops were astonished at their courage, and horrified at the carnage.

Then came the poor hostages themselves. The soldiers and

marines had imagined the people they were rescuing to be skeletal wretches, stumbling and half-crazed denizens of rat-squeaking cells. But here they were, whole families, happily sauntering into camp. One hundred and eighty-seven servants came with them – about a third, the soldiers noticed, being women. As the great crowd passed the pickets the soldiers' cheers died down. Nor were they all British. There were two Irishmen, and Cameron, but most of the rest were German. Why should they pursue the jailors and their leader?

But Napier could not turn and leave. He had forged alliances with both Ras Kasa of Tigray and Wagshum Gobeze on the tacit understanding that the British would do what they themselves had failed to do: end the reign of Tewodros. If he did not, Napier and his men would have to fight their way out.

83

That night the Ethiopians who remained on Meqdela and Selassie looked down from the heights. In the blackness they could see the pinprick lights of enemy fires – a few to the north were British, the rest were Oromo waiting like hyenas for the mountain to fall. That night the moon rose above the plateau drenched a strange blood-red hue. The people of Tewodros took that as a bad sign. They retired to their huts with a feeling of dread for the coming day.

Tewodros himself did not sleep. He wandered the paths of Selamge and Selassie, alone, pacing the last slab of broken rock left to him. He too glanced at the fires of his enemies. He too saw the bloody moon and took it as an ill omen. The rest of the sky was the familiar star-flecked canopy, the same speckled sky that stretched out over the regions he had once ruled, over Begemder and Simien, Tigray and Lasta, and on out over Europe, England, India, and the Ottoman walls of Jerusalem. In his five decades, Tewodros had never even seen the sea. Years ago, when he had first felt the stirrings of the outside world, he sensed that the future lay with that world, or at least with Christian Europe and the powers it was learning to harness. But he was a warrior at heart, and never a statesman, and when Plowden offered him the chance of an alliance, he would give up nothing that might weaken him. When other men brought the things he longed for he found concealed insults, slights and schemes. Then suddenly he would be gripped by rage, by jealousy, by a blind brutality that filled his prisons with loyal followers, that broke the trust of those who believed in him and led to the slaughter of thousands of those he aimed to rule, including the prisoners whose bodies lay rotting below the cliffs where he now walked.

Sleep at last came to Tewodros. He lay for a few hours on the lower slopes of Meqdela beneath a *shamma* draped over two spears.

At dawn he rose and climbed up to the gatehouse of Kokit Ber. He crossed the small shelf of land between the outer and inner gates. Smoke seeped through the thatch of the guard's huts. He climbed the narrow steps to the *amba* itself. From where they sat around makeshift fires, from the entrances of the empty prison huts, his remaining men watched him in silence. He gathered them around him. He spoke in the firm voice so familiar to them: 'Warriors who love me, gird yourselves; leave all behind, take nothing but arms, and follow me; the time has come to seek another home!'

With four senior officers, he led about 2,000 across the *amba*, past the prison and the church of Medhane Alem, and out through the Kafir-Ber gate of the *amba*. They left on a path so narrow, with such plunging cliffs beneath, that it was only possible to follow it on foot. They had not gone far when a number of the troops began to hesitate. It was them, and not their leader, who felt reservations about fleeing. 'We would rather seek death in Meqdela,' they told him.

Tewodros considered it for a while. In the half-light, they could hear the cries of the Oromo, whose hatred of Tewodros had been sharpened in recent days: Napier had offered a 10,000-thaler reward for his capture.

'*Isshi*, very well.' They turned and went back.

Tewodros again crossed the *amba* and climbed down to

Selamge. There he released all those with him from their oath of allegiance. In small groups, in ones or twos, wishing they were invisible, they began to slip away from their emperor. He was left with only a few loyal chiefs and followers. With them he began to move his guns back from Selamge towards the approach to Meqdela. He intended to defend the *amba*. As he did so, dozens of his soldiers made their way past him, out towards Selassie to wait for the British.

It was nine o'clock in the morning – three o'clock Ethiopian time. Tewodros looked up at the sky and saw a dark ring around the sun.

Towards midday he spotted on Selassie, amidst the crowds of his own disbanded soldiers, the first detachment of British cavalry. The sight of enemy horsemen on his mountain ignited his fighting spirit. He called for his war horse, a bay called Hamra. He called for the gun he had named the 'elephant rifle', a gift many years ago from Plowden's assistant in Massawa, Senor Barroni. He swung up into the saddle, and galloped out across the flat rock. He was again dressed in his *kinkob*, his white, gold-threaded tunic. He shouted, he waved his gun, he challenged. 'Send out a champion!' Riding back and forth, firing his rifle, he boasted of his battle prowess, his God-given victories. 'One man, one man!' He called for one man to take him on in single combat.

Among the British vanguard was a candidate. Basha Felika, the giant Captain Speedy. He offered to accept the challenge, but was refused by a senior officer.

Meanwhile, behind their strutting leader, Tewodros's remaining men continued to manoeuvre a few of his artillery pieces back across the short piece of plateau towards Meqdela. The guns they'd left behind were now turned on them by the British. Infantry appeared, from the 33rd Regiment. They began to open fire with their Sniders. When the first Ethiopian was killed, the rest abandoned the big guns and retreated up to the slopes of Meqdela. Tewodros went with them.

Two sets of gates led up to the sanctuary of the *amba*. Between them was a small shelf of rock, fortified with a wall and a fence of thorn and approached only through a roofed gatehouse. Tewodros and his men retreated behind the outer gates, pushed them closed and, with Tewodros and his prime minister, Ras Ingida, leading the work, assembled a great plug of boulders against them. From Selassie, the British gunners kept the shelf and the two sets of gates under shellfire. An advance force began to move up the slope towards the outer gates. It was four in the afternoon, and the clouds that had collected over the *amba* now began to pulse with lightning. The British storming force were the first to tread the slopes of Meqdela itself. They were from the 33rd Regiment, the 10th Company of Engineers, and the Madras Sappers. They reached the outer wall, but had to wait: someone had left behind the gunpowder and axes.

On the other side of the wall, cowering under the shells, were the survivors of Tewodros's regime. One or two soldiers remained, but the majority were ministers and senior commanders – Ras Ingida; Ingida Wurq, son of Aba Mirza who had led Tewodros's artillery; Ras Barak of Tewodros's own Qwara region; old Dejazmach Abiye (insulted by Tewodros a few days earlier when he suggested taking on the English army); his ennobled executioner Aggafari Meshesha (escort for Easter Sunday's spurned cattle); Amanyi (royal gun-bearer); and Welde Gabre (former gun-bearer, now valet). When the shelling began, a number of them fled through the inner gate and onto the safety of the *amba*. About a dozen remained with Tewodros.

He was seated on a rock. A telescope was pressed to his eye. He was watching the guns fire from Selassie. When a shell landed nearby and killed two cows, he flinched.

Ras Ingida, Tewodros's prime minister, was still with him, along with his brother. The *ras* was so loyal to Tewodros that Rassam once said 'he would have swallowed a draught of deadly poison at his bidding'. As he had retreated he sent his three young sons, aged between twelve and fourteen, away from Meqdela. The boys now stood on the slopes of Selassie, watching the bombardment in tears, trying to bribe the British gunners with *tej* to stop their firing.

But it did no good. A shell dropped between the gates, killing both their father and his brother. Amanyi and one other were also killed. With the fire intensifying, Tewodros ordered the removal of the bodies to the shelter of the gatehouse. He also shed his *kinkob*.

The British, still waiting for their powder-bags, had been working at the gates with crowbars. They had finally managed to prise them open. Now they met the boulders, and it took some time to clear them. A number were injured by rifle fire as they did so. Welde Gabre loaded Tewodros's rifle and handed it to him to fire at the assailants. Another group of British had made their way along beneath the fortifications, and managed to climb up. They fired as they entered. Several of the few remaining Ethiopians fell, wounded or dead. The rest – just five – hurried up the stone steps to the inner gate. Tewodros himself took up the rear. Once inside, he cried out to the others:

'Flee! I release you from your allegiance. As for me, I shall never fall into the hands of an enemy.'

He pulled a pistol from his belt, thrust it into his mouth and pulled the trigger. This time it fired. As the first soldier came up onto the *amba* of Meqdela, Tewodros slumped to the ground.

EPILOGUE

I

Tewodros lay in the dirt where he had fallen. He was dressed in loose shirt and trousers; his feet were bare. From one side of his upper lip a black puff of powder-burn spread up his cheek. Within fifteen minutes, a crowd had gathered around his body. Rassam and Waldmeier pushed through to stand over him, the man who had wept a day or so earlier when he wished them goodbye for the last time. Waldmeier turned to Rassam and reminded him what the emperor had said just two weeks ago: *'While you stand by my corpse, it may be that you will curse me for my bad conduct towards you. You may say then, "This wicked man ought not to be buried; let his remains rot above the ground."'*

Rassam did not curse Tewodros. He was appointed by Napier to oversee the emperor's burial. He wanted to show the Ethiopians that 'their late Sovereign had not vainly styled me his "friend"'. The body was buried with 'affecting' respect by the same clergy whom Tewodros had raged against so recently. It was wrapped first in cotton, then in a *kinkob* of silk and gold, then in a rough shroud. Finally it was laid in a trench outside the church of Medhane Alem, rocks were gently placed over it, and straw over them.

In his death, Tewodros had gained a certain redemption. Dr Blanc had helped carry out a post-mortem, and as the body was examined, he forgot some of his blind hatred of his captor. Death gave 'an air of calm grandeur to the features of one whose career had been so remarkable, whose cruelties are almost unparalleled in history; but who at the last hour seemed to have recalled the days of his youth, fought like a brave man, and killed himself rather than surrender'. A probe was passed through the mouth and up out of the back of the head, following the line of the bullet. Suicide was confirmed. As he inspected the body, examining the cheek for bruising, Blanc became aware of a very faint smile on the emperor's face – 'that happy smile he so seldom wore of late'.

When British forces burst up onto the summit of Meqdela, past the body of Tewodros and out onto the flat of the *amba*, they met no resistance. The nerves of battle gave way to greed. Some of the troops squatted in the dust to suck at raw hen's eggs. Others rushed to the grain stores, to the treasury, to the royal quarters, to the abandoned huts of the council. It was not easy moving about, said one witness, as the ground was covered in abandoned matchlocks, 'all charged and their fuses lit, popping off right and left'. While everyone else was grabbing whatever they could, the band of the 33rd selflessly stood in a courtyard playing 'God Save the Queen'.

One of the first to reach the body of Tewodros was Captain Frank James, who later wrote to his mother: 'I send home to the girls a *real* lock of Theodore's hair! which I cut off myself, and to you dear mother, a little coin.'

Tewodros had spent his reign accumulating treasures on Meqdela. His plundering made the British plundering a much simpler task. Dusty store-huts revealed the former wealth of thousand-year-old monasteries, the shimmer of silver crosses from around the country, filigree crowns, vellum manuscripts sewn into heavy wooden bindings, appliqué robes, holy *tabots*, vestments and ornamental umbrellas. Gifts from overseas lay unopened. The troops splintered the casing of wooden crates to reveal hoards of toy soldiers and cameras, musical instruments, tools of English steel. Trunks of papers were likewise prised open and scattered. Tax accounts mingled with official orders and correspondence, and the documents recording Tewodros's fourteen years of rule soon fluttered around the huts, a snowstorm of political record blowing out across the mountaintop and over the cliffs.

A few days afterwards, back on Delanta, a drum-roll sounded out through the British camp. A crowd of officers and troops gathered before a pile of booty so extensive that fifteen elephants and almost two hundred mules were used to carry it from Meqdela. The treasures were auctioned. The money was distributed among the troops. There was interest in all objects, as exotic souvenirs from a victory which many had thought impossible. One enthusiastic bidder was an officer adding to the mess collection of the 11th Hussars, but most avid of all was Richard Holmes, sent out by the British Museum to gather antiquities. He bought 350 manuscripts.

On the day of Tewodros's death, Holmes had sat by the body and sketched the emperor's bullet-pierced head. In those first hours he also acquired, but did not declare to his masters at the museum, a small painting discovered behind Tewodros's *alga*. In a curious parallel with his own sketch, it was a sacred image of the head of Christ bowed and bloody beneath a crown of thorns. Holmes saw that it was not Ethiopian but Renaissance in style. What he had stumbled upon was the *Kwer'ata Re'usu*, a painting that in Ethiopia was believed to have supernatural powers. It was brought to the country by the first of all European missions in 1520, when Emperor Lebne Dengel had shown such a keen interest in the Portuguese flintlocks. Over the years it been used for sacred oaths, carried into battle by Ethiopian rulers and even given its own campaign tent. After Tewodros's death it left the country forever, remaining secretly in the private collection of Holmes until his death, and ending up in a Portuguese bank vault.

The British prepared to leave Delanta for the long journey back to the coast. The day after the auction, Colonel Fred Thesiger addressed the entire force with a General Order from their Commander-in-Chief:

Soldiers and sailors of the Army of Abyssinia! The queen and the people of England entrusted to you a very arduous and difficult Expedition – to release our countrymen from a long and painful captivity, and to vindicate the honour of our country, which had been outraged by Theodore, King of Abyssinia . . .

Never did an army enter on a war with more honourable feelings than yours. This it is that has carried you through so many fatigues and difficulties; your sole anxiety has been for the moment to arrive when you could close with your enemy.

The remembrance of your privations will pass away quickly; your gallant exploit will live in history . . .

I shall watch over your safety to the moment of your re-embarkation, and shall, to the end of my life, remember with pride that I have commanded you.

The forces returned to the coast. They scattered to India, to Britain and other outposts of the British Empire. In London, the victory brought widespread jubilation. Even newspapers once critical of the campaign acknowledged its success. The anti-establishment *Reynolds' Newspaper* described it as 'one of the most brilliant and complete triumphs ever achieved by a British army'. *The Jewish Chronicle*, also sceptical in previous months, now declared: 'We rejoice that the honour of the British flag and the dignity of the British name have been vindicated.'

To many in Britain, wounded prestige was the principal cause of the war, and recovered prestige the principal benefit – especially for imperial interests in the East. The *Christian World* reflected that 'Asiatics will ponder and talk over the fate of a man who imprisoned British subjects' and henceforth think twice about challenging 'the power that triumphed over the Indian Mutiny and the Black King'.

As bills came in and were collated, the full cost of the campaign became apparent. The original budget of £2 million was known to have been exceeded. No one expected it to reach

£9 million. A parliamentary select committee took a year to examine the runaway expenses. In his statement to the committee, Sir Robert Napier admitted that 'he never thought of the cost'. As a result the entire enterprise became a wonderful wagon of public largesse, scattering its funds to every Middle Eastern merchant, every stock-dealer and middleman lucky enough to come near it. The urgent search for mules had inflated their price. As three-quarters of them were left behind in Ethiopia, both dead and alive, little of this was recouped. Some stores were supplied twice, others were wasted – of 35,000 tons of feed shipped to Ethiopia, only 7,000 were landed. Shipping agents named their own prices. Over a third of the total cost of the expedition, £3.5 million, went on ships and coal.

Napier was not blamed. The failures were in the system. With assurances of next-times and lessons-learned, the question of cost slipped quietly into the shadow of a shining military success.

Sir Robert Napier was made a hereditary peer, Lord Napier of Magdala. He was awarded an annual pension of £2,000, to be continued after his death and paid to his heir. Captain Cameron was not so lucky. When the Foreign Office had examined all the reports of his conduct and made their judgements, they withdrew his consular status and left him on a basic pension of £350 a year. They didn't have to pay it for long. He died in Geneva within two years of returning to Europe. The three envoys sent out to rescue him were well rewarded. Blanc and Prideaux were given £2,000 each, Rassam £5,000.

A year after his release, Hormuzd Rassam married the eldest daughter of an English officer. He became a British citizen. Some years later, the British Museum sent him back to the Near East to gather antiquities. He rediscovered his luck as an archaeologist, displaying an uncanny knack, wrote *The Times*, 'for striking the right mounds'. At Sippar, he dug up some 70,000 stone tablets and fragments, and in all added 134,000 items to the British Museum's collections. Those like Blanc and Waldmeier who saw what he did in Ethiopia were amazed by his diplomatic skill, the love he earned from Tewodros, the constant drawing on his wits. Flad felt that 'the Government could not have intrusted a man better fit for the mission of Mr Rassam than himself. In all his business with the king he was calm, prudent, cautious and sincere.' In England though, watching the gradual inflation of the crisis, observers could not help wondering whether it was wise 'to send an Alien of mean station and equivocal character to settle such an affair'. Rassam ended his life in disappointment, his reputation clouded by prejudice against him as a wily Eastern Christian. The formidable Sir E.A. Wallis Budge, who was busy translating many of the plundered manuscripts from Meqdela, accused Rassam and his Chaldean relations of 'stealing' finds. He failed to find a publisher for his autobiography, and although he won his libel case against Budge, he died more or less forgotten in 1910. One of the few public figures who knew him personally was his old mentor Sir Austen Henry Layard. He recalled him as 'one of the honestest and most straight forward fellows I ever knew, and whose great services have never been acknowledged'.

When Theophilus Waldmeier left Ethiopia, he went first to Jerusalem and Bishop Gobat, then to Basel. He recalled his homecoming in typically biblical manner: 'I am returned from a far-off land,' he said on meeting the aunt and uncle who had brought him up.

They said: 'We have a son, away as a missionary in Abyssinia, but we do not know where he is now.'

'I am that son.'

They wept. His aunt peered into his eyes and said: 'Yes, they are the eyes of Theophilus, but where is thy fair hair?'

He told her that because he had to stand hatless in the sun before Tewodros, 'my head became so swelled and painful that in a few days the hair fell off'.

Waldmeier returned to mission work. He found a site at Brummana on the slopes of Mount Lebanon whose people, he'd been told, were 'the greatest liars and thieves in the world'. Twelve years later, funded and run by Protestants and Quakers, Brummana had two schools and a hospital. Seven hundred children had been taught and 30,000 patients treated. Waldmeier had managed to banish some of the 'horrible darkness and superstition' from this corner of the Levant and had done so, this time, without compromising himself in the burning heat of the foundry or having to witness the brutal extremes of man's cruelty to man. In 1886, he felt his own mission drawing to a close and wrote that he would 'have soon to lay down our pilgrim's staff, and go to the better land'. He died in 1893.

Waldmeier was always grateful to the military force that freed him and the other missionaries from Tewodros's grip: 'heartfelt were their thanks and gratitude, first to Almighty God, who was the overruling power, and then to the English expedition, and its noble leader, Lord Napier of Magdala'. It was not in his nature to pass judgement, but in his expression of regret for the affair, he gestured towards British arrogance in the initial stages. He was there at the time, at the court of Tewodros. He witnessed it. His assessment bypasses all the wordy editorials, the back-and-forth correspondence, the re-criminations and reports that followed the return of Napier's expedition. It was Waldmeier, innocent and naïve as Parsifal, who concluded simply: 'I am fully convinced that this Anglo–Abyssinian war, with all its bloodshed and enormous expense, might have been spared by a nobler way of dealing with King Theodore.'

II

With the British force as it marched north towards the coast in 1868 came Tewodros's 'two queens', Tirunesh and Yetemegnu. The women, his wife and his lover, had for some time shared quarters on Meqdela. They offered a striking contrast now, as they rode among the invaders – the Oromo Yetemegnu, full-bodied, hearty and popular; and Tirunesh, anxious, taciturn and bird-like. In mid-May, Yetemegnu waved goodbye to the British at Wadela and returned to her region of Yejju.

Tirunesh continued north with her seven-year-old son, Alemayehu. Tewodros had entrusted Alemayehu to the care of the British. Tirunesh, believing he would not survive if he stayed in Ethiopia, had complied. With reluctance she chose to accompany him on the journey to England. She had nothing left but her son. 'Mine has been a miserable existence since childhood,' she told Rassam, 'and now I am looking forward to that happiness promised me by our saviour.' Within days, it came. Weakened by consumptive coughing, she died at Chelicut on 15 May. She was twenty-five.

Young Alemayehu Tewodros landed at Plymouth in the summer of 1868. He had all the attributes to win over Victorian hearts. As the orphaned son of an emperor neatly despatched by British forces, he was both noble and innocent, exotic and dependent. He soon became a favourite of Queen Victoria, joining other similar children in her affections, like Duleep Singh and Princess Gouramma, offspring of toppled Indian rulers.

When his mother died, Alemayehu was put under the care of Captain Speedy. From Plymouth, Speedy took him to the Isle of Wight to meet the queen for the first time. 'Little Alemayehu,' she wrote, 'is a very pretty, slight graceful boy of seven, with beautiful eyes.' She was amazed to see the frail boy in the arms of the giant Speedy, but she recognised the bond that was growing between them. 'Nothing could be kinder than he has been to the child, quite like a mother. I have written strongly against Alamayu being removed from Captain Speedy's care.'

Alemayehu began his English education, soon picking up the boyish enthusiasms of the time. He wrote to a friend: 'You got plenty butterfly at school? No got any here! Too much cold. Me ride one pony: Oh so very nice! One day me go to hounds, fox run an dogs kill him.'

The following year Speedy was posted to India, and he and his new wife Cornelia took Alemayehu with them. The couple had no children themselves, and Alemayehu soon 'entwined himself around our hearts'. He was, thought Speedy, 'the best boy in the universe'.

When the question of education re-emerged, it became clear that Alemayehu was not Speedy's charge but that of the British government. Nor was his future the concern of some minor branch of the civil service: Robert Lowe, Chancellor of the Exchequer, wrote to the Prime Minister, Lord Gladstone about the matter. He wanted the Ethiopian boy sent to an English public school: 'We are in loco parentis and ought to look after his welfare as if he were our own child. What parents would voluntarily bring up a child in Indian Cantonments where he is sure to become an accomplished liar, and would probably be contaminated with those physical and mental vices which arrest the physical and mental development of boys?'

When she heard about this, Queen Victoria was furious. She offered to pay for a tutor herself, so the boy could stay with Speedy. Cornelia Speedy wrote: 'He is a child of a most affectionate disposition, peculiarly sensitive and reserved, and we greatly fear that were he separated from all home ties and placed amongst strangers the consequences might be to him very serious, possibly injurious to his health.'

For a while Alemayehu continued in the Speedys' care. They obtained a posting to Singapore, where the climate was better for him, and Alemayehu was sent to a good school. 'I am bringing up Alemayehu as my own child,' wrote Speedy. But in the end the British government ordered him back. Speedy visited both Gladstone and Queen Victoria to try to recover the boy. But it did no good. Alemayehu was sent to boarding school, first to Cheltenham, then to Rugby.

Over the coming years his good spirits faltered. He became withdrawn and unhappy. He enjoyed games and riding, but could not apply himself to anything in the classroom. For long periods he lay on his bed, gazing at a football cap given to him by Mrs Speedy. Like his father, his thoughts turned sour with suspicion.

Sometimes a letter would filter through to England from Ethiopia. 'My dear child, my beloved,' wrote his grandmother, Tirunesh's mother. 'How are you from the day we separated until now? Why do you not write to me? The Ethiopian people are looking and longing for you. Try to become wiser and cleverer so that you may be enabled to enlighten them.'

She sent a note too to Queen Victoria. 'I humbly kiss your Majesty's hand. Three of my children I have lost to death, the fourth was Queen Tirunesh. Now only Dejazmach Alemayehu is left to me. I implore you look well after him.'

It was thought best not to show the letters to Alemayehu.

Back in Malaya, on the island of Penang, the Speedys had not forgotten Alemayehu and Ethiopia. In the evening Captain Speedy would pace up and down the road in his cherished Ethiopian costume, playing the bagpipes.

At sixteen, Alemayehu was taken away from Rugby and sent to Sandhurst. But two years later, in 1879, he belatedly felt the need for academic study. He asked to return to the care of Cyril Ransome, who had tutored him some years earlier. He lodged with Ransome in Leeds, worked on his written language and began to study French. One night, according to Ransome, Alemayehu committed a 'foolish act (he went to sleep in the WC in the middle of a cold night)'. He developed pneumonia. He resisted medical treatment and food, and weakened quickly. 'Prince' Alemayehu Tewodros died on 14 November, aged eighteen, and was buried near the entrance to St George's Chapel at Windsor. Queen Victoria had a brass plaque put up inside, which read: 'I was a stranger and ye took me in.'

Beneath it, in Amharic, the name 'Alemayehu Tewodros' was added in 1924 during the official visit of Ras Teferi Mekonnen, who six years later was crowned Emperor Haile Selassie. His visit was the first high-level Ethiopian delegation to London. Had it been achieved when Plowden first suggested it sixty years earlier, the Meqdela crisis would never have occurred.

After Alemayehu's death, Cornelia Speedy asked for his football cap as a memento, while Captain Speedy swore he would never again cut his beard. In later years, to support himself and Cornelia, he toured the country performing a one-man 'Abyssinian entertainment'. He appeared and reappeared dressed as an Ethiopian priest, a velvet-cloaked noble or a spear-carrying warrior. He would act out scenes of looting, or of solemn marriages or funerals, reliving his first journey in 1861. 'His voice imitating Ethiopian drums,' wrote one reviewer, 'is simply astounding.' Later his lecture notes include the prompt: *ask audience permission to sit down because of bad foot*. On 5 August 1910 he performed for the last time, at a vicarage garden party. He 'held the crowded tent for a good half-hour' with tales and acts from Tewodros's Ethiopia. Four days later he was dead.

III

Just two days after Tewodros's suicide, a very old man rode down into the British camp below Meqdela. So much was happening at the time that few noticed the mule and the man's bright silk shirt. The 'true' Solomonic Emperor, King of Kings Yohannis III, Yohannis the Fool, was received, according to Markham, 'with scant ceremony'.

During the years of Tewodros's bloody and drawn-out decline, a number of possible successors had circled him. After the emperor's death it was Wagshum Gobeze who adopted his title. 'In the interests of Christianity', Sir Robert Napier offered him Meqdela, but the *wagshum* said he would be unable to hold it against the Oromo, unless of course Napier could see his way to giving him Tewodros's guns. But the guns had been destroyed (except the unbreakable, and unusable, Sevastopol).

At the time, among the Muslim Oromo were two rival queens. Each laid a claim for control of the mountain. First, on the evening of 16 April, Queen Wurqit entered the British camp. 'We fought with Tewodros as long as we could,' she told Napier. 'When his power was too great, my son submitted to him on receiving a promise of good treatment.' Tewodros had killed her son. He had him thrown over the cliff in July 1865 after Menelik escaped, having watched him cross the ground below Meqdela to defect to her camp. With the death of her only son, Queen Wurqit had lost much of her power to her rival; she could not realistically keep Meqdela.

'Now,' she said sadly, 'I have come to see the grave of my enemy Tewodros, and the place where my son fell.'

The next day Queen Wurqit showed 'symptoms of much distress'. Hearing that her rival Queen Mestawat was approaching, she gathered her people and hurried away. Mestawat swept into the camp, wrapped to the eyes in a cloud of veils. As her meeting with Napier carried on, so more of her face became visible, and she revealed herself as a hearty woman – 'fair, fat and forty', according to Stanley. Asked about the likeness of a sketch made of Tewodros just after his death, she scoffed, 'How should I know? Who ever saw him and lived?'

Queen Mestawat greatly impressed the battle-weary corps

of the British camp. She ate and drank with gusto – 'disposing of what came before her, without regard to the horrified looks of the Political Secretary – pudding before beef, blancmange with potatoes, drinking coffee before finishing her fricandeau, emitting labial smacks like pistol cracks'.

Napier did not award her Meqdela – or not directly. He said he would abandon it, but first he would destroy it. The arrangements for blowing the gates and the magazine, for firing the huts so as not to damage the church, were issued in intricate detail. But the sappers were more obedient than the flames, and the church, like every other structure on the *amba*, was burnt to the ground. Queen Mestawat and her forces stepped over the ashes and occupied it some days later. But then King Menelik of Shoa ousted her. He awarded the mountain, with his support, to the frail Queen Wurqit.

In Shoa, when they heard of the death of Tewodros the joy was so great that they simply added the event to the end of Easter and continued to celebrate. Their own sovereign, King Menelik, did not join in. He went away and grieved in private – not for the brutal enemy Tewodros had become in the last few years, but for the man who had once figured as a father to him, and whose daughter he had married. He grieved for a military commander of genius, who saved the country from the threats of the *Mesafint*, whose ambitions proved too high – or too early – for the country. Most of all he grieved for a martyr who, rather than surrender to his enemy, took his own life.

In the coming decades, after Wagshum Gobeze had been killed in battle with Kasa of Tigray and after Kasa had himself become King of Kings, and then been killed in battle with the Mahdists, it was Menelik who rose to power. Menelik's path to the throne was long and measured. It had begun on the night in July 1865 when he escaped Meqdela and returned to Shoa. Of the three great rivals of Tewodros in his later years – each of whom became King of Kings – it was Menelik who best fulfilled Tewodros's ambitions. He managed to unite Ethiopia's warring provinces, and although he never reached the Red Sea coast, he swelled the country's borders far to the south and east. He embraced the technology and gadgetry of the Europeans, and in 1896, when the Italians came with ideas of conquest, he defeated them at the Battle of Adwa, the decisive moment in modern Ethiopian history.

As the decades passed, and new generations grew to hear of Tewodros, it was not so much his victims who were spoken of, nor the defeat at Meqdela, but his death. Only chance prevented him from being killed by a rifle or a shell in the last hours, and allowed him his dramatic and defiant suicide. But it was good fortune – or divine grace – that helped propel his early success, so perhaps it was only appropriate that it should return at the climax of his life, to give him power over his own death and enshrine his legacy.

When the Italians avenged Adwa and invaded Ethiopia in 1935, Emperor Haile Selassie fled. Many of those who stayed behind to fight a guerrilla war never forgave him for not staying, for not following the example of Tewodros and dying at the feet of the conquerors.

After a failed coup against Haile Selassie in 1960, one of its leaders, Lieutenant-Colonel Wurqneh, was cornered in Addis Ababa. 'Tewodros taught me something,' he shouted to those surrounding him. He thrust the barrel of his pistol between his lips, and shot himself.

At the end of the Eritrean war in 1990, the Ethiopians were fighting to keep Massawa. Walter Plowden had believed that the taking of Massawa was the one strategic act that would release the troubled kingdom from its stagnant antiquity. He thought it was inevitable under Tewodros, but the emperor never even drew close to the port. Highland Ethiopia finally gained the coast by treaty in 1952. But they struggled for years with Eritrean rebels to keep it. As Massawa fell, and the last of the Ethiopian forces were driven back towards the sea,

General Teshome Tesema addressed his men: 'To be captured and see the eyes of the rebel leaders would be a double death for me. Emperor Tewodros chose to commit suicide rather than fall into the hands of the English.' He walked rapidly to the edge of the quay, thrust a Colt revolver into his open mouth, and shot himself. He toppled backwards into the Red Sea.

In central London, at the top of Queensgate, a large mounted statue of Lord Napier of Magdala gazes out across the flat and marshalled green of Hyde Park. In central Addis Ababa, there is no statue to Tewodros. The failures of his reign and his violence make the man himself too ambiguous for a true bronze hero. Instead, it is the Volkswagen-sized Sevastopol that commemorates the emperor. Sevastopol never did anything. In the middle of the traffic island, with wooden wheels stuck firm on an imaginary section of Tewodros's road, its open mouth still speaks of possibilities.

NOTES

The rich body of first-hand accounts has been the principal source for this book. Many of the Europeans involved left extensive versions of the drama as they saw it – Plowden, Rassam, Blanc, Prideaux (a chapter in Clements Markham's *A History of the Abyssinian Expedition*), Lejean, the d'Abbadie brothers, Stern, Waldmeier and Flad. They also wrote letters, many of which survive in the Public Record Office, Kew, London. Others like Dufton and Speedy reached Tewodros's camp and managed to leave. On the British expedition, Markham, Hozier, Henty and Stanley as well as a number of combatants wrote of their experiences. Ethiopian sources are thinner, but I have used them as much as possible. A number of chronicles of the time survive. Zeneb's *Ye-Tewodros Tarik* is published in Amharic (Enno Littmann, Princeton 1902); Hiluf Berhe translated this text for me (as this was a private translation, I have not put page numbers to references). Welde Maryam's chronicle is translated by C. Mondon-Vidailhet as *Chronique de Théodros II, roi des rois d'Éthiopie* (the page numbers are for this translation, unless otherwise stated). Professor Sven Rubenson has edited two invaluable volumes of documents, *Correspondence and Treaties 1800–1854* and *Tewodros and his Contemporaries 1855–1868, Acta Aethiopica* Vols I & II (Vol. I – North Western University Press & Addis Ababa University Press, 1987; Vol. II – Addis Ababa University Press & Lund University Press 1994). These include a number of revealing letters by Tewodros himself. Rubenson was the pioneer of Tewodros scholarship and anyone who tackles the subject owes him an enormous debt. During the 1960s he was professor of history at Addis Ababa University (formerly Haile Selassie I University), and before that had spent more than thirteen years teaching and studying in the country. His short, definitive and well-sourced *King of Kings: Tewodros of Ethiopia* (Haile Selassie I University, Addis Ababa 1966) is a first stop for all Tewodros studies. His longer *The*

Survival of Ethiopian Independence (Heinemann in association with Esselte Studium & Addis Ababa University Press, London 1976) covers a wider period but offers a typically comprehensive overview of Tewodros's reign. The articles and books of Richard Caulk, Donald Crummey and Richard Pankhurst have also contributed a great deal towards an understanding of Tewodros and his time.

Prologue

Tewodros's journey from Debre Tabor to Meqdela, between October 1867 and March 1868, is described by Waldmeier *Autobiography* pp.97–102 and *Erlebnisse* pp.66–76, by Flad *Zwölf Jahre* II pp.43–63 (including the diary of his wife, Pauline). The 'idols of Tewodros . . .' comes from Stern *Captive Missionary* p.359. Waldmeier *Erlebnisse* pp.68–9 refers to Sevastopol as '*Ungeheuer*'. Markham's response to seeing the road is from his *History* pp.295–6; the description by Blanc is in his *Captivity* p.339. The quotation from Moorehead is from *The Blue Nile* p.205. For '*meqagna*' and Ethiopian literature about Tewodros see *Kasa and Kasa* ed. Beyene etc. p.3. Tewodros's statement 'Having heard reports from the time I was born . . .' is from a letter, Tewodros to Guillaume Lejean, March 1863 (Rubenson *Tewodros* Document no. 122). The scene of the Portuguese at Lebne Dengel's court is described first-hand in *The Prester John of the Indies: The Portuguese Embassy to Ethiopia, 1520* Beckingham and Huntingford pp.285–8. 'How long shall we thrust our swords . . .' from the Ethiopian Chronicles, quoted in Caraman *Lost Empire* p.154. 'At length the sheep of Ethiopia . . .' from the Ethiopian Chronicles, ibid. p.152; the treaty with the Muslims, ibid. p.156. For Tewodros's battle at Debarki see Rubenson *King of Kings* pp.39–40, Zeneb *Chronicle* and Dufton *Journey* pp.123–4.

Chapter 1

Walter Chichele Plowden's *Travels in Abyssinia* is the main source for Plowden. For his adventurous journey to England see *Travels* pp.315–53. He also wrote a great number of letters to the Foreign Office which can be seen at the Public Record Office, in *Confidential*

Print at FO 401/1, and in the original FO 1. His *Notes on Peculiar Customs* is in the Oriental and India Office Collections (OIOC), British Library, London EUR F127/99. A portion of Bell's notebook from the years 1840–42 (Bell 'Extract . . .') is the only direct record of his time in Ethiopia. For other accounts of military lore and Ethiopia at this time, I have used Walker *The Abyssinian at Home*, Parkyns *Life in Abyssinia*, Pearce *Life and Adventures*, and Bruce *Travels*.

Chapter 2

Plowden's proposal can be seen at FO 401/1 'Memorandum by Mr Plowden' 12 August 1847, and pp.11–13 'Memorandum on the Trade of Abyssinia'. William Coffin was originally the servant of Lord Valentia (Earl of Mountnorris), and together with Henry Salt they made up an exploratory expedition to the Red Sea in 1804–05. From the coast Coffin and Salt accepted an invitation to visit Ras Welde Selassie in Tigray. Five years later they went again and this time Coffin stayed behind. Seventeen years later Coffin emerged with his letter. See Annesley *Voyages and Travels*, Halls *Life and Correspondence*, Pearce *Life and Adventures*. For the death of Coffin's son, see Parkyns *Life in Abyssinia* p.221. The original letter in Ge'ez can be seen FO 1/1 fol. 73, with a translation in fols 155–6. For Plowden's return journey to Ethiopia, and the signing of the treaty, *Travels* pp.376–422. The treaty is Document no. 135 Rubenson *Treaties and Correspondence*.

Chapter 3

Ras Gugsa's measures come from Zeneb *Chronicle*. Abir *Ethiopia: The Era of the Princes* provides a very good overview of the *Zemene Mesafint*. Ethiopia's Judaic origins are told in the *Kebre Negest*, a collection of stories including that of Solomon's seduction of the Queen of Sheba and of their child, Menelik, who took from Jerusalem the Ark of the Covenant. The Ethiopian Chronicles (Weld Blundell's *Royal Chronicle* for an English translation) give a good deal of colour to the complexity and chaos of the *Mesafint*. See also

Shiferaw Bekele's revisionist essay in *Kasa and Kasa*, eds Beyene etc. pp.25–69. For the glut of fallen kings in Gondar, see a begging letter from Yohannis III ('the Fool') to Napoleon III, 1854 – 'After a king has been deposed, he does not go to other people's houses but lives in poverty at home. I am starving . . .' Document no.185, Rubenson *Treaties and Correspondence*.

I prefer 'time of the judges' to 'era/time/age of the princes' as a translation for *Zemene Mesafint*, not least because it resonates with the Old Testament Book of Judges. The *Mesafint* (1769–1854) is generally seen as a time of chaos, as in Judges 17:6 – 'there was no king in Israel: every man did that which was right in his own eyes'. The promise of Tewodros therefore was an end to this disorder. More convincing though is that, for Ethiopian Christians, it was a time of dynastic decline, national humiliation, even divine retribution, when the mainly Muslim Oromo people were in the ascendant and, under the family of Ras Gugsa, in a position to rule. Other passages from Judges, for example those quoted – 2:11 and 2:14 – support this wider perception of biblical precedent. The principal town of the period, Debre Tabor ('Mount Tabor') echoes the Israelites' parallel plight and hopes of escaping from it: from Mount Tabor, Deborah sent Barak and his 10,000 to slaughter the host of Sisera (Judges 4).

The Tewodros prophecy was for many years a central column of Ethiopian national belief. In the early fifteenth century, Tewodros I ruled for a couple of years. His life is briefly recorded in *Synaxarium* Vol. IV, p.1045 (trans. Budge); on the day of his death, Sene 29 – 'he used to give away all his possessions to the poor and the beggars'. James Bruce was involved in a battle against a Tewodros pretender and wrote that the prophecy involved the second coming of Tewodros I (Bruce *Travels* Vol. IV). That may have been part of the myth at the time, but in fact the myth predates the reign of Tewodros I. The prophecy is explained in the Ge'ez *Fekkare Iyesus* but in turn draws on one from much earlier, from the late Roman period. A Greek oracle told that a man with the letters THEOD in his name would rise in the east and spread peace through all nations. In due course a man named Theodosius appeared, but was killed by the Roman emperor. He was followed by another

Theodosius, and Theodotos and Theodolus, and they were all killed (see Weld Blundell *Royal Chronicle*, Appendix F). At the back of dozens of bound manuscripts, biblical books, hagiographies and synaxaria, the Ethiopian scribes wrote in hope the name 'Theodotus', or 'Tewodros'. See also letter from the King of Shoa, Sahle Selassie to Queen Victoria 1843 (Rubenson *Treaties and Correspondence* Document no. 64), decorated with some of Ethiopia's most cherished religious images (though lacking Maryam) – at the top the Trinity (*'selassie'*), with the two archangels, the symbols of the four evangelists, the chariot of Solomon, St George (Ethiopia's patron saint) with a dragon, an imperial lion – and among them all, the prophesied Tewodros.

Chapter 4

The ups and downs of Plowden's waiting come from his correspondence to the Foreign Office FO 401/1. An account of his quarters in Monculu appears in Rassam *British Mission* Vol. I, pp.19–20. The town of Massawa is located on an island a little way offshore. One theory of the origin of the name Massawa is from the Ge'ez verb *'tsaua'*, meaning 'to call', the distance between the island and mainland being a *'metsaua'* – the distance a man can call (Munzinger cited in Markham *History* pp.15ff).

Chapter 5

For Kasa's early life, see Rubenson *King of Kings* pp.15–17, Taddesse Tamrat in *Kasa and Kasa*, eds Beyene etc., pp.117–23. I am grateful too to a group of Tewodros's living descendants, in particular Colonel Damtew Kassa, who came to see me one evening in Addis. See also Welde Maryam *Chronique* pp.1–3. For Tewodros's interest in his forebear King David and the Psalms, see Dufton *Journey* pp.115–16, also William Simpson *Diary* p.122 and Plowden *Travels* pp.90–1 – 'they teach but one book to the children of the laity – the Psalms of David'. In Zeneb's *Chronicle* there is a quote from Psalms 37: 11 ('But the meek shall inherit the earth . . .') when young Kasa's life is spared during the attack on Mahbere Selassie.

Chapter 6

For Tewodros/Kasa's four early letters, see Document nos 93, 94, 96, 100, Rubenson *Correspondence*. The letters are all in Arabic. Tewodros/Kasa used different scribes and the quality of the orthography varies. Tewodros himself spoke a colloquial Arabic – later this was a common language between him and Hormuzd Rassam. He also had a command of the liturgical language, Ge'ez, which he struggled to replace in the Church with the vernacular Amharic, itself the main language of his court. He also spoke Oromigna (the language of his principal enemy, each of his two wives and his mistress, Yetemegnu). But it is probable that his first language was Agewigna, the language of the Agew people.

Tewodros/Kasa's path to the throne is told in Welde Maryam *Chronique* pp.2–10, in Zeneb, in Rubenson *King of Kings* pp.35–45. The verse about Gur Amba comes from Welde Maryam *Chronique* p.4 and makes use of the literary devices of Amharic, in particular word-play. A study of these traditions was made by Levine in *Wax and Gold*. The exchange between Kasa and Wube – 'great Goliath' – comes from Dufton *Journey through Abyssinia* p.130.

Chapter 7

Plowden's account of his visit to Tewodros and his report to the Foreign Office can be seen at FO 401/1 25 June 1855. The report is reproduced in part in Plowden's *Travels*. For Tewodros's campaign to Shoa, see Welde Maryam *Chronique* pp.9–17.

Chapter 8

First section of reforms from FO 401/1 Plowden, Report 25 June 1855. The plan for roads comes from Dufton *Journey* pp.137–8. See also Rassam *British Mission* I p.199 for dress reforms. For the praise of Tewodros by de Jacobis see *Lettres de Jacobis* February 1855 quoted in Crummey *Priests and Politicians* pp.97–8. See Crummey 'Tewodros' pp.457–69 for a view of Tewodros's importance as a moderniser. Dufton *Journey* pp.151–2 mentions 'Bell's Bible', saying of Tewodros, 'His knowledge of our [British] national history and customs is considerable, and he might put some of our countrymen to shame by his acquaintance with Shakespeare, which he used to get Mr Bell to translate to him, when on his campaigns the Englishman shared the royal tent.' Lejean spoke of the 'unparalleled influence which Mr Bell exercised over this extraordinary man', Lejean in Blanc *Story of the Captives* p.126.

Chapter 9

'Without Christ, I am nothing' comes from Plowden's Report FO 401/1 25 June 1855. The corruption of the priests is from Zeneb *Chronicle*. For the importance of Kasa's alliance with Abune Selama in 1854 see Crummey 'Tewodros' p.459. Their meeting in 1854 achieved a 'Concordat' in which 'secular and religious power would be used in mutual support for the restoration of national life'. In Weld Blundell *The Royal Chronicle* p.528, he cites the synod in 1855, shortly after the kingdom of Shoa fell to Tewodros. The newly crowned emperor called the monks of Debra Libanos – a centre of the 'Three-Birthers' – to Azazo. 'The theologians of Debra Libanos had all the logic, but Theodore like Henry VIII prided himself on his theology and had the unanswerable argument of despotic power.' He threatened them with the executioner and starved them until they agreed the 'Two-Birth' Christology of Abune Selama. Crummey also discusses the schisms in *Priests and Politicians* pp.14–29. The scene with the priests in Gondar comes from Zeneb *Tewodros*.

The robust prejudices of early European visitors and the complexity of Christological doctrine have combined to produce a number of misunderstandings about the Ethiopian Church. It is not Coptic ('Coptic', from the Arabic for 'Egyptian', is used for Egyptian Christians whose affiliation with the Ethiopian Church therefore led to the misapplication; the Ethiopian Church has been autocephalous since 1955); it is not 'Orthodox' – which is a term more generally applied to the Eastern Churches under Constantinople (Greek, Serbian, Romanian, Russian, Georgian etc.) and which have been distinct from the Armenian, Coptic, Syriac and

Ethiopian Churches since the Council of Chalcedon in 451 (the Ethiopian Church is known as the 'Ethiopian Orthodox Church', but the confusion arises if the 'Orthodox' is taken out of context – the Ethiopians themselves refer to their Church as '*Tewehado*', 'united'); nor is it 'monophysite' – Ethiopian clergy, as other non-Chalcedonians, resist this term for their view of Christ, preferring 'miaphysite'.

Chapter 10

HH Cyril IV, 'the reformer', needed the help of 'armed Abyssinians' to secure his election to the patriarchate in Alexandria, see Butcher *The Story* Vol. II p.398. For the visit of the patriarch see Zeneb *Chronicle* and Plowden's letters to Clarendon FO 401/1, in particular 15 January 1857, and Flad *Notes* p.51. Lejean gives a colourful account of Tewodros's opening meeting with the patriarch, of the emperor sitting before the patriarch with pistols in his belt and saying, 'My father, bless me.' But Lejean was in Ethiopia later and clearly picked up on some of the oral tradition around the visit: Lejean in Blanc *Story of the Captives* p.127.

Chapter 11

The letters can be seen in Documents nos 23, 24, Rubenson *Tewodros*. Plowden's letters to the Foreign Office FO 401/1 give an idea of his struggles of the time. Details of his request for guns can also be followed through 401/1 January 1858–October 1859.

Chapter 12

The account of Tewodros at this time comes from Zeneb *Chronicle* and Welde Maryam *Chronique* pp.24–7. During the eighteenth and nineteenth centuries, Meqdela became a fortress of the Oromo (see Zeneb); previously it was in Christian hands, and its toponymic origins lie in the city of Magdala on the shores of Galilee. Meqdela is an *amba*, one of many flat-topped mountains in the Ethiopian highlands which lend themselves equally well to natural forts and places of isolation for monastic communities. 'Believing I had power . . .' comes from one of the last letters Tewodros wrote, to Robert Napier on 11 April 1868 (Rubenson *Tewodros* Document no. 241). Theophilus Waldmeier (*Autobiography* pp.79–80) talked of Tewabach and John Bell as his 'two good guardian angels'. The verse from the Psalms is 3:1. Tewabach's death is described in Welde Maryam *Chronique* pp.26–7, and the verse laments for her come from him. The one by Ras Ali contains two double meanings – 'My thief' is a homophone of 'my heart', while 'coffin' could be heard as 'throne'. I am grateful to Dr Mandefro Belayneh for explaining something of the intricacies of Gondarene Amharic and making the meaning clearer. For the embalming of the body see d'Abbadie *Catholic World* VII, 1868.

Chapter 13

The decline of Plowden's later years as consul emerges clearly from his correspondence in FO 401/2 1857–60, as does the growing exasperation of the Foreign Office; see also Plowden *Travels* in which his brother, Trevor Chichele Plowden, inserts some pages from Walter's notebooks (pp.459–62) including the passage about Tewodros's son. Trevor Plowden adds too a section (pp.462–5) on his brother's final years and months in Ethiopia. For an overview of British policy towards Ethiopia during this period see Rodgers 'The Abyssinian Expedition' pp.129–34, as well as Rubenson *Survival* pp.180–9. 'Nothing but my death' comes from FO 401/2 Plowden to Malmesbury 1 February 1859. For Niguse and the French, see Rubenson *Survival* pp.189–207. On 19 October 1858, Niguse wrote to Pope Pius IX: 'Many are my enemies but by the power of your prayer I hope to destroy them. And if it is the will of God, I intend to be enthroned with the ointment of kingship according to the rules of the Catholics' Document no. 65, Rubenson *Tewodros*. For Tewodros's campaign against Niguse, and later with Garad, see Welde Maryam *Chronique* pp.28–30. See Dufton *Journey* pp.147–51 for the death of Plowden, Bell and the reaction of Tewodros. Plowden's tomb can be seen in Gondar, in the compound of the church of Gemjabet Maryam.

Chapter 14

Samuel Gobat was in Ethiopia from early 1830 until the end of 1832, and again for eighteen months a few years later, see Gobat *Journal*. As Anglican Bishop of Jerusalem from 1846 onwards, he kept abreast of Ethiopian news through the Ethiopian monks and pilgrims. He was asked on several occasions to protect their interests at the Holy Sites. He arranged with the St Chrischona Institute in Basel to provide missionaries for Ethiopia, and with the emergence of Tewodros and the promise of stability under him a provisional journey was made by Flad and Krapf. They reached Tewodros in April 1855, and John Bell advised them to play down their religious ambitions with Tewodros, in favour of sending men with more secular skills. In their meeting with the new emperor, the talk was of artisans. The confusion persisted throughout the mission's life (see Crummey *Priests* pp.115–20). Tewodros's letter to Gobat (Document no. 5, Rubenson *Tewodros*) was written in response to their visit. Gobat's address to the missionaries is quoted at length in Waldmeier *Autobiography* pp.46–58.

Chapter 15

For Waldmeier's early life, his journey, and his relationship with Tewodros, I have used Waldmeier *Autobiography* and *Erlebnisse*; his writing is remarkable for its biblical tone and its transparency, through which shines his remarkable holy innocence.

Chapter 16

The wooden cannon comes from Zeneb *Chronicle*. Pankhurst's two articles 'History of Firearms' and 'Firearms' provide a comprehensive study of the perennial problem for Ethiopian rulers of obtaining weapons. They prove how much the procurement of small arms and artillery characterised the early exchanges with Europeans. Artillery was particularly prized for its effectiveness against *ambas*, flat-topped mountains which could be defended against small arms indefinitely, as Biru Goshu managed to do against Ras Ali (see

Crummey's theory quoted in Caulk 'Firearms and Princely Power' p.3). In the mid-sixteenth century a force led by Christavao da Gama managed to take the unapproachable Amba Sanet in Tigray, using mortars (see Caraman *Lost Empire* p.8 and Beckingham and Huntingford *Some Records* XXXVI, Introduction).Tewodros's letter to the Europeans at Gefat does not survive in the original. Waldmeier published a version in *Erlebnisse*, and it is from this that Rubenson has translated it into English (Document no. 108, *Tewodros*). The letter is addressed to 'Messrs Kienzlen, Waldmeier, Saalmuller, Moritz, Bender and Bourgaud' – two of whom (Moritz Hall and Bourgaud) were not missionaries. For Moritz Hall, see Holtz and Holtz Berger 'The Adventuresome Life' and Bell *Sir Peter Ustinov* in which he corrects a family tradition of the actor and proves that he was descended not from Saalmuller but from Moritz Hall. M. Bourgaud, according to Dufton *Journey* p.83, was 'a French gunsmith'. The scene with the testing of the cannon is also recorded in Dufton *Journey* pp.103–4.

Chapter 17

Cameron gives an account of his own reception by Tewodros – 'the best His Majesty has yet accorded an envoy' – in a letter to Lord Russell, FO 401/1 31 October 1862. The letter provides the details for the first half of this chapter. The letter that Tewodros wrote to Queen Victoria was sent in Amharic with an English translation. The text with Rubenson's own better translation is Document no. 117 in Rubenson *Tewodros*. The original is FO 95/721 fol. 126. Tewodros also wrote to Napoleon III (Document no. 118, Rubenson *Tewodros*), probably on the same day. That version was sent only in French.

Chapter 18

The quotation from Cameron promising to 'give his head' if a reply did not soon come to Tewodros's letter to Queen Victoria is from Waldmeier *Autobiography* p.81. Waldmeier said he 'had often to translate' for Tewodros and Cameron. The scene in the palace at

Gondar was vividly recorded by several of those present. Lejean in Blanc *Story of the Captives* pp.140–51, Stern *Captive Missionary* pp.39–44. '... the Englishman an ass' is quoted by Lejean, see Rubenson *Survival* p.238 – the word used for the Frenchman Bardel is '*buda*', a still widespread Ethiopian breed of lycanthropic spirit.

Chapter 19

'Providence wills that some delay ...' is quoted by Plowden in a letter FO 401/1 Malmesbury 1 February 1859. 'This is a stiff-necked people ...' and '... a terrible brink' come from Lejean in Blanc *The Story of the Captives* p.139. Stern's quotation comes from Stern *Captive Missionary* pp.33–4. 'Since the death of my queen ...' Rassam *British Mission* I p.271. The physical description of Tewodros is by Henry Dufton (*Journey* pp.97–8), who travelled in Ethiopia in the years 1862–63. Tewodros's campaign to Gojjam against Tedla Gwalu is recorded in several accounts – but Lejean was actually there (Blanc *The Story of the Captives* pp.134–40). Dufton *Journey* pp.186–8 also gives a version of Lejean's eventful time with Tewodros in Gojjam. Rassam (*British Mission* I pp.238–40) tells the story of the massacre of the prisoners when he passed the site in 1865. For discussion of the Egyptian incursions of 1863 see Rubenson *Survival* p.228. The carving of the gun-carriages is recorded in Lejean (Blanc *Story of the Captives* p.139), and in the same passage can be found the 'Eat all!' command. 'The righteous shall rejoice ...' Psalms 58: 110–11. Rubenson (*Survival* p.241) identifies the period 1861–63 as being both the greatest extent of Tewodros's rule and the start of his decline – 'the increasing ruthlessness with which the King conducted his campaigns had led to dissaffection'.

Chapter 20

Stern's own acount of 13 October can be found in his *Captive Missionary* pp.44–58, and this account, though written some time later, provides most of the material for this chapter. Several others note the detail of the chewed finger. Lejean (Blanc *Story of the*

Captives p.143): 'this gesture has a particular meaning among the Abyssinians, denoting the menace of momentarily impotent anger'. The arrest of Henry Aaron Stern marked the turning point for Tewodros, so far as foreigners were concerned. Stern's own identification of his arrest as the turning point of Tewodros's entire reign: 'his power began to wane from the very hour that a scarred, lacerated, and bleeding missionary lay insensible at his feet', comes from *Captive Missionary* p.278.

Chapter 21

The early life of Stern comes from Isaacs's *Life*. After Stern's arrest, his possessions were searched and several offensive papers found. A copy of his *Wanderings among the Falashas* – the account of his first journey to Ethiopia – revealed him calling Tewodros's mother a *ḳoso*-vendor. In the coming years, Tewodros frequently repeated the various offences that individual foreigners had committed against him. Stern's *ḳoso*-vendor accusation – a widely-used insult of Tewodros's enemies (see Tamrat 'The *Koso*-vendor' in *Kasa and Kasa* eds Beyene etc. pp.117–27) – was cited a great deal. Other offensive material found among Stern's papers included an account by him of 'My first meeting with the wild beast'. He had also said that Tewodros had invited Plowden's acting successor Barroni up from Massawa so that they could get drunk. Rubenson, in *Survival* p.233, suggests that this is a confusion between *ḳar* ('commemoration of the dead') and *seḳḳere* ('to get drunk'); Tewodros was actually inviting Barroni to commemorate Plowden's death. Stern gives an account of his trial in *Captive Missionary* pp.76–103 and 146–8. For a list of Ethiopia's rulers from 800BC to the ousting of Colonel Mengistu by the EPRDF in 1991 see Munro-Hay *Ethiopia* pp.361–7.

Chapter 22

The letter from the Foreign Secretary to Cameron is FO 401/2 Russell to Cameron 22 April 1863. It was delivered by a young Irishman, Laurence Kerans. The account of the execution of the

Ethiopian peasants is from Stern *Captive Missionary* pp.109–12. Throughout the latter months of 1863, rumours of an Egyptian invasion were filtering down to Ethiopia (see Rubenson *Survival* p.236). Details of Cameron's arrest *Captive Missionary* pp.121–4. Tewodros explained his actions to Flad – Cameron was arrested because of the unanswered letter to Queen Victoria, Stern and Rosenthal because they had insulted him, and the others because he realised that all white people were wicked (from Flad *Zwölf Jahre* Vol. I pp.75–6, quoted in Rubenson *Survival* p.237). Cameron's note was signed 'C.D.C.' and sent to Captain Speedy who was acting as consul in Massawa FO 401/2 14 February 1863, enclosed in Merewether to Colquhoun 21 April 1863, and Colquhoun to Russell 28 April 1863.

Chapter 23

For the route of British mail, see Bates *The Abyssinian Difficulty* p.53, and for the Foreign Office at the time p.52. In FO 1/23, a memo December 1867 pp.523–37, a résumé is given of what happened to the letter. The minutes can be read in FO 401/2 during 1863–64 and FO 1/13–1/14 in the original. See also Rodgers 'The Abyssinian Expedition' pp.134–5. The saga was one not of incompetence at the Foreign Office but of 'reckless indifference' (Rubenson *Survival* p.235). The eventual response in 1864 to Tewodros's letter and Queen Victoria's reply can be followed through FO 401/2, including instructions to Hormuzd Rassam. One of the myths that grew up around the letter was that it contained a proposal of marriage from Tewodros to the bereaved Queen Victoria (*Sun* 6 August 1864, *The Times* 9 September 1864).

Chapter 24

Material for this chapter draws on Stern's account in *Captive Missionary* (pp.143–92), and a letter of Cameron's FO 401/2 Cameron to Shaw 28 May 1865.

Chapter 25

For Hormuzd Rassam see *The Times* 17 September 1910. The main source for his Ethiopian years is the two-volume account of the mission to Tewodros (*British Mission*). It is also one of the best sources for the remaining part of the story – clear, measured and detailed. The early chapters of Vol. I provide much of the material for the period in Massawa. See also FO 401/2 p.68 Rassam to Merewether 19 July (wrongly dated 19 April in the Confidential Print) 1864. Dr Henry Blanc published two books on his time with the British mission. One slim version (*Story of the Captives*) was based on an account sent from Ethiopia to Bombay in 1867, while he was still captive. The following year he published a fuller account (*Narrative of Captivity*) which incorporates much of *Story of the Captives* but continues to the resolution of the crisis. His 'Thermometrical Observations in Abyssinia', thrice-daily measurements of temperature taken for two and a half years, are published as Appendix C in Markham *History* pp.405–21. Lieutenant Prideaux published a much shorter account which appears as Chapter III in Markham *History*. For the death of Bishop Bianchari see Document no. 149 Zekkariyas Tesfa Mikhael to Guillaume Lejean 12 October 1864, Rubenson *Tewodros*. For the Naib of Arkiko see Rubenson *Survival* pp.228–9.

Chapter 26

The sources used for Theophilus Waldmeier are his two books, *Erlebnisse* and *Autobiography*. Stern *Captive Missionary* pp.169–212 provided much of the detail for the second half of the chapter. Rassam *British Mission* I p.206 mentions Tewodros moving many of his political prisoners from Zur Amba to Meqdela at this time.

Chapter 27

Most of the details for the mission's long wait in Massawa come from Rassam *British Mission* I Chapters II–IV, Blanc *Story of the Captives* pp.9–24, *Narrative* Chapters IV–V and Prideaux, in Markham *History* pp.90–2. Mention of cholera in Mecca and Massawa was the beginning of an epidemic that followed the British mission. It spread down the Red Sea, reaching Massawa in October 1865 and the camp of Tewodros in June 1866 – see subsequent chapters (Pankhurst 'History of Cholera' p.265).

Chapter 28

Tewodros's disastrous campaign in Shoa is mentioned in Welde Maryam *Chronique* p.36, in Stern *Captive Missionary* pp.201, 216 and in FO 401/2 Rassam to Badger 20 January 1865 and Rassam to Merewether 10 April and 12 May 1865. Bezzabih's claim to be king of Shoa is the subject of a letter from Bezzabih to Gebre Hiywet Welde Ab (Document no. 151, Rubenson *Tewodros*) 'Half the aristocracy . . .' FO 401/2 Cameron to Shaw 14 July 1865. Details of the escape of Menelik, the massacre of the prisoners and Tewodros's confrontation with Abune Selama come from several sources: FO 401/2 Cameron to Shaw 14 July 1865 (also includes details of Queen Wurqit's atrocities). The quotation 'Wurqit has found a son who is free . . .' comes from Stern *Captive Missionary* p.220. For further details of those days see Stern *Captive Missionary* pp.218–23, Blanc *Narrative of Captivity* pp.214–15, Welde Maryam *Chronique* p.39. For Tewodros's intentions – 'God willing, when [Rassam] comes all his requests will be granted to him'– see Rubenson *Tewodros* Document no. 153 – Tewodros to Muhammad 'Abd al-Rahim 5 July 1865. The Welde Selassie exchange is told in Rassam *British Mission* I p.296.

Chapter 29

Tewodros's letter to Rassam is reproduced in Rubenson *Tewodros* Document no. 152. Rassam also says in his Preface to Vol. I p.iv that Tewodros was concerned about the safety of the mission and the lesson of Plowden's death (many refer to his killing as an 'assassination', suggesting a deliberate blow against the British). Cameron's warning to Rassam not to come up to the highlands – 'For God's sake, don't think of coming up here, with or without safe conduct. You will only get chains for your pains' – is from FO 401/2 Cameron to Rassam 6 April 1865. The correspondence for this period in FO 401/2 provides details for the final weeks in Massawa, Rassam's trip to Cairo and the brief appointment of William Palgrave.

Chapter 30

The journey from Massawa round to Metemma, and then into the Ethiopian highlands is told in Rassam *British Mission* I pp.120–42, Blanc *Narrative* pp.85–116 (duplicated from *Story of the Captives* pp.24–46), and Prideaux in Markham *History* pp.91–4. The letter from Cameron to Rassam is dated 'Magdala Prison, October 10, 1865' – see Rassam *British Mission* I p.170 – and includes in it quotations from a letter he had received from the missionaries at Gefat. The letters from Tewodros to Rassam are in Rubenson *Tewodros* Documents nos 157 and 158.

Chapter 31

The late rains of 1865 were reported in a long letter, FO 401/2, Rosenthal to Eisener 1 July 1865. In this letter too is an account of Rosenthal's son Henry. Further details of Henry Rosenthal come from Stern *Captive Missionary* pp.232–9, in which is described the smallpox epidemic as well as the sufferings caused by the chains. Kerans's letter to his father is in FO 401/2 Kerans to Kerans 14 July 1865. The story of Laurence Kerans's unfortunate carpet is told in Stanley *Coomassie* p.279 and by Lejean in Blanc *Story of the Captives* p.147, while his medical skills, and those of the other prisoners, are mentioned in FO 401/2 Cameron to Shaw 28 May 1865 and in Stern *Captive Missionary* pp.243–4. News of Dr Blanc's arrival in Ethiopia reaching Meqdela is mentioned in his *Narrative* p.123.

Chapter 32

Details of Dr Blanc's medical adventures come from his *Narrative* pp.122–4 – 'I was at all hours of the day surrounded by an importuning crowd, of all ages and sexes, afflicted by the many ills that flesh is heir to.' The approach to Tewodros's camp comes from Rassam *British Mission* I pp.215–43, Prideaux in Markham's *History* pp.95–7 and Blanc *Narrative of Captivity* pp.124–5.

Chapter 33

Rassam wrote a very detailed account of his long-anticipated meeting with Tewodros, *British Mission* I pp.243–52; Blanc was briefer, *Narrative* pp.126–8, as was Prideaux in Markham *History* pp.97–100. The protracted greeting exchanges are still a feature of Ethiopian life. Tewodros's letter to Rassam was sent in both Arabic and Amharic though only the Arabic survives. 'Negashite' is simply the Arabic for the dynasty – *al Najashiyya* – and Negash is the site of the first Muslim settlement in Ethiopia where Muhammad's followers settled having been given asylum by the Christian King of Aksum.

Chapter 34

Tewodros being unable to sleep comes from Rassam *British Mission* I p.265. The letter he dictated is in Document no. 162, Rubenson *Tewodros*. Samuel Giorgis, who had been appointed Rassam's *baldereba*, translated it from Amharic into Arabic, and Rassam translated it into English. In FO 1/26 Tewodros to Victoria 29 January 1866 is the Amharic original and Rassam's translation. The interview between Rassam and Tewodros is described in detail in Rassam's *British Mission* I pp.265–71, and in less detail in Blanc *Narrative* pp.129–30 and by Prideaux in Markham *History* pp.99–100. The reception of Queen Victoria's letter to Tewodros, his reply to it and the conditions understood by him became matters of contention following events in April 1866. Rassam, writing this account in the light of accusations about his own conduct, dwells in some detail on his first days with Tewodros. Tewodros later claimed that he had been given the right to claim something in return for the prisoners' release. Cameron records giving Tewodros a 'barrel organ' (FO 401/2 Cameron to Russell Gojjam 31 October 1862). For Tewodros's dismissive reaction see Dufton *Journey* p.108.

Chapter 35

The quotation 'All his soldiers have deserted. The king has grown weak' is from Asseggahen to d'Abbadie 14 January 1866 Document no.160, Rubenson *Tewodros*. Debtera Asseggahen was from Wadla, north of Meqdela. He had converted to Catholicism and maintained contact with Antoine d'Abbadie. Travelling with Tewodros and his army is described by Rassam in *British Mission* 1 Chapter X and in Blanc *Narrative of Captivity* pp.131–3, and by Prideaux in Markham *History* p.100.

Chapter 36

Both Rassam (*British Mission* I pp.294–6) and Blanc (*Narrative* p.133) give an account of this conversation on world affairs. Blanc records Tewodros's questions thus: 'Is the American war over? How many were killed? How many soldiers had they? Did the English fight with the Ashantis? Did they conquer them? Is their country unhealthy? Is it like this? Why did the King of Dahomey kill so many of his subjects? What is his religion?' Dahomey's King Gezo – whose bloody forty-year rule had ended eight years earlier – remained a benchmark of regal brutality. A couple of years later, Henry Dufton, having met and been fascinated by Tewodros, answered the unequivocal criticisms of the emperor in England: 'There are those who think they have described the man when they have stigmatised him as an inhuman despot, a bloodthirsty tyrant, a Nero, worse than the King of Dahomey ... Others, like myself, have been well treated by him . . .' Dufton *Journey* p.105. The rest of the chapter draws on Rassam *British Mission* I pp.296–307 and Blanc *Narrative* pp.134–5.

Chapter 37

Details for this chapter come from Rassam *British Mission* II pp.1–15, Blanc *Narrative* pp.136–42, and Prideaux in Markham *History* pp.101–3. The British mission were disdainful of the *tankwa*, the papyrus rafts which they travelled by during their time on Lake Tana. Blanc *Narrative* pp.137–8 was particularly scathing: 'To say that these boats leak is a mistake; they are full of water, or rather, like a piece of cork, always half submerged: their floating is simply a question of specific gravity.' Tewodros was keen to improve the lake's transport, and asked the mission if they knew anything about boat-building: 'We replied,' wrote Blanc, 'in the negative.' Only in recent years has the *tankwa* begun to be replaced on Lake Tana by displacement craft and outboards. The letters sent by Tewodros to Rassam between the beginning of February and 12 April 1866 are kept at the Oriental and India Office Collections, the British Library (Eur F 103). They are reproduced in Rassam *British Mission* II pp.1–78, and more fully in Documents nos 167–189, Rubenson *Tewodros*.

Chapter 38

For Aggafari Golem see Stern *Captive Missionary* p.265: 'Agha Faree Gholam, our uncouth, semi-negro friend, did not share in the satisfaction which prevailed in our small camp. There was a forbidding leer in that one glittering eye, which the small-pox had most ungenerously left him.' The *aggafari* travelled with the British mission as far as Qorata, then carried on to Meqdela. Prideaux described him as 'truculent in disposition and ill-favoured in person' (Markham *History* pp.100–1). Details of the release come in the main from Stern *Captive Missionary* pp.249–50. For letters from Tewodros to Rassam see Rubenson *Tewodros* Documents nos 167–89, and also quoted in Rassam *British Mission* II Chapter XIV. Details of the trial and of the medals planned for the British mission come from this chapter and from Stern *Captive Missionary* pp.255–61. In Ethiopia the symbol for Solomon's Seal is the double triangle of the Star of David – Tewodros had three carved on his throne; the medals were discovered on Meqdela after its capture in 1868, see Simpson *Diary* p.90. Blanc *Narrative* pp.142–4 and Prideaux cover the same period more briefly.

Chapter 39

The Ethiopians observe a strict fifty-six-day fast – *hudaddie* – before Easter ('fast generally implies one meal a day to be taken either in the evening or after 2.45 p.m. with total abstinence from meat, fats, eggs, butter, milk, cheese' Wondmagegnehu *Ethiopian Orthodox Church* p.63 – enemies of the country like the Muslim Ahmed Gragn in the sixteenth century found this a good period in which to launch an offensive). Ethiopian Easter in 1866 was a week later than the Easter of the Western Churches. The collection of the horses and the women is mentioned by Rassam *British Mission* II p.53. Tewodros wrote to Rassam on consecutive days – 20 and 21 March – referring to the business he had to attend to (Documents nos 180–1, Rubenson *Tewodros*). The visit to Zeghie on 25 March and the hearing are recounted by Rassam *British Mission* II pp.56–65 and Blanc *Narrative* pp.149–51. Prideaux did not refer to it. Rassam's quoting of Tewodros's desire to have his sons taken to England is coloured by the fate of Alemayehu (see Epilogue) – Speedy adopted the boy for a while, and it is clear that Rassam felt himself slightly usurped in this. For references to Speedy, his background and earlier trip to Ethiopia, see Chapter 72.

Chapter 40

Stern *Captive Missionary* pp.265–7 has 12 April for the arrest while Rassam, Blanc and Prideaux have 13 April. (Waldmeier in his *Autobiography* oddly cites the date 13 April 1866 for his own arrest, which actually came a year later on 17 April 1867.) Stern's high spirits he describes in *Captive Missionary* pp.267–8. Details of the arrest of the British mission come from all three: Rassam *British Mission* II pp.82–3, Blanc *Narrative of Captivity* pp.153–4 and FO 401/2 Blanc to Merewether 26 May 1866, and Prideaux in Markham *History* pp.105–6. Flad (FO 401/2 Flad to Clarendon received 10 July 1866) also provides material for the account of the arrest.

Chapter 41

Several of the Europeans wrote reports of the trial: Rassam *British Mission* II pp.92–103, Blanc *Story of the Captives* pp.62–3 and *Narrative* pp.159–62, Prideaux in Markham *History* pp.107–8. In FO 401/2 Flad to Clarendon received 10 July 1866, Flad quotes the 'syphilis' comment. Cameron himself wrote of the trial in FO 401/2 Cameron to Seymour 25 May 1866. The quotations from Stern are from *Captive Missionary* pp.278–81. FO 401/2 Flad to Clarendon received 10 July 1866 says of the citing of Tewodros's lineage, 'about fifteen witnesses he called out of his Court, who witnessed that his mother was from the line of the ancient Kings, and that he, the King, had from his mother's side, in more than ten different provinces of his Empire "galt", that is territory, granted by Government for continual possession'. 'A fence around Senaar' – Tewodros's words to Rassam *British Mission* II p.96, also quoted in Stern *Captive Missionary* p.281. The scene of Tewodros's asking for forgiveness draws on Rassam *British Mission* II pp.98–9.

Chapter 42

Rassam's optimistic expectation of this meeting, the dictation of the letter and Rassam's realisation of their detention are described in his own account *British Mission* II pp.99–101. A translation of this letter is quoted in these pages, but I have used the translation from the original in Document no. 191 Rubenson *Tewodros*. The reasons behind Tewodros's detention of the prisoners and envoys on 13 April 1866 have been the subject of much debate over the years. For a discussion of the various parties' involvement and all the sources see Rubenson *Survival* pp.244–8, in which he is perhaps a little harsh on Rassam. Quotations from Tewodros regarding the artisans come from FO 401/2 King Theodore to Flad, enclosed in no. 403. The 'shopping-list' is enclosed in the same package. Flad's departure from the camp is told in his letter FO 401/2 Flad to Clarendon received 10 July 1866 (in the original he had written more fully of Tewodros, 'cruel, inhuman, tyrannical, barborous, cunning, crafty and sly despot', but in the 'Confidential Print' it was edited – see Rubenson *Survival* pp.248ff). The assessment of the detainees' mood comes respectively from Stern *Captive Missionary* p.283, Blanc *Narrative* p.164, Prideaux in Markham *History* p.108, and Rassam *British Mission* II p.106.

Chapter 43

Rassam *British Mission* II pp.107–22 is the main source for this chapter. Blanc *Narrative* pp.163–4 tells more briefly of 'duck shooting on the lake' with Tewodros, his obsession with boat-building ('strange to say that he spent his time in that frivolous way and never took notice of a large rebel force not four miles from his camp'), and the appearance of the 'true character of the tyrant': 'we felt that our position was most dangerous and critical'. Prideaux is more brisk: 'Our five weeks' stay at Zeghie may be dismissed in a very few words,' Markham *History* p.108.

Chapter 44

Cholera as 'the rider on the pale horse' is cited in Stern *Captive Missionary* p.288. The previous epidemic is mentioned in Zeneb *Chronicle* and Welde Maryam *Chronique* pp.21–2. Tewodros reading the Psalms is mentioned in Stern *Captive Missionary* p.288. Pankhurst's 'History of Cholera' article provides background to the cholera epidemic, as well as the Amharic term for it. Blanc's assessment of the unhealthy camp comes from FO 401/2 Blanc to Merewether 26 May 1866. In FO 401/2 Mrs Flad to Flad 7 July 1866, Mrs Flad also gives an account of the epidemic to her husband in London. Waldmeier's description of the journey to Debre Tabor is in his *Autobiography* pp.89–91, while Stern's, including the death of Aggafari Golem, is in *Captive Missionary* pp.287–90. For the early days at Gefat see Rassam *British Mission* II pp.130–7, Waldmeier *Autobiography* pp.90–1.

The meeting with Tewodros and the discussion of Alexander the Great took place on 21 June 1866 and are told in Rassam *British Mission* II pp.137–8. The popular Ethiopian 'History of Alexander', *Zena Eskander*, is a remarkable document, stitched together from Pseudo-Callisthenes's legends of Alexander with some colourful elaborations of its own. The copy in the British Museum, translated by Budge, was the one looted from the church of Medhane Alem on Meqdela. The section cited here is a visit to Queen Candace, who is of great significance in Ethiopia. It was a eunuch from her court who was converted to Christianity by St Philip, Acts 8:27, which is seen by many Ethiopians as marking the real beginning of Christianity in Ethiopia, linking the Church with the Apostles and predating the historically accepted arrival of the faith by nearly two hundred years.

Chapter 45

For Flad, see his own *Zwölf Jahre* and *Notes from the Journal of F.M.* [sic] *Flad*. After leaving Ethiopia in May 1866 he wrote two long and undated letters to Clarendon (FO 401/2 Flad to Clarendon received 10 July 1866). The first he ended by begging Clarendon to excuse his English. The quotations come from the second. Merewether's costings come from a long memo he wrote in August 1866 in FO 401/2 ('Suggestions by Lieutenant-Colonel Merewether CB, Political Resident at Aden').

Chapter 46

For Egyptian advances and their take-over of Massawa on 30 April 1866 see Rubenson *Survival* p.250. For Tewodros's waning influence in the north see Document no. 197 Asseggahen to Antoine d'Abbadie (Rubenson *Tewodros*): 'Tigray and Lasta seem to be controlled by the hand of Dejazmach [or Wagshum] Gobaze. Hamasen and Serawe are Habal Haylu's. Shire is under Tewodros.' The railway is mentioned by Flad (FO 401/2 Flad to Murray 21 September

1866). For Tewodros's gratitude for the Bibles and for suspicions of British involvement in Egyptian advances and the hearing on 25 June see Rassam *British Mission* II pp.139–45, Blanc *Narrative* pp.170–1. In a letter to Rassam some time later, Tewodros cites his suspicions: 'I heard rumours that the English and Turks [Egyptians] had become allies and were hostile to me,' Document no. 207 Tewodros to Rassam 5 January 1867, Rubenson *Tewodros*. The mention of the *Fetha Negest* and the quotation of Tewodros about Rassam's mouth being sweet come from FO 401/2 Mrs Flad to Martin Flad 7 July 1866. For Rassam's 'moping' see Rassam *British Mission* II p.147.

Wagshum means literally 'chief of Wag', the continuation of a dynasty of the Agew people who as the Zagwe ruled Ethiopia in the twelfth and thirteenth centuries, and remained as hereditary rulers of Wag and Lasta. According to the *Kebre Negest*, this dynasty originated from King Solomon and Sheba's servant-girl – the 'true' Ethiopian dynasty came from him and Sheba herself. The *Kebre Negest* was written after the fall of the Zagwe. Wagshum Gobeze's father Wagshum Gabre-Medhin was hanged by Tewodros for rebelling against his rule (Blanc *Narrative* pp.263–4). The message from Tewodros to Rassam is quoted in Stern *Captive Missionary* p.293.

Chapter 47

Henry Dufton's portrait of Tewodros is in Dufton *Journey* pp.100–6. It was Dufton too who described Waldmeier's house as '*à l'allemand*'. The drama at Gefat on 3 July is taken mainly from Blanc, who witnessed it (*Narrative* pp.174–5). For its continuation back in Debre Tabor I have used the witnesses too: Rassam *British Mission* II pp.151–3, Blanc *Narrative* pp.175–7, Stern *Captive Missionary* pp.294–5, Prideaux in Markham *History* pp.112–13. Likewise the scene with Tewodros that evening was witnessed by Rassam (*British Mission* II pp.153–6), Blanc – 'He was calm, and rather serious though he made efforts to appear gay. He must have remained at least an hour' – *Narrative* pp.177–9, Prideaux in Markham *History* pp.113–14, and Stern *Captive Missionary* p.296.

Chapter 48

Martin Flad's English translation of his wife's letter is in FO 401/2 Mrs Flad to Flad 7 July 1866. Reaction to the unfolding crisis in the London press is explored in Pankhurst's exhaustive article 'Popular Opposition'. Flad refers to the 'Jerusalem Convent affair' in his letter FO 401/2 Flad to Murray 21 September 1866. The Coptic–Ethiopian conflict over the Convent of Deir es-Sultan is one of the more complicated and ancient in a place famous for complicated and ancient disputes. In 1862 persecutions of the Ethiopians had increased. The Copts took to beating the Ethiopians and broke the locks of their church. They denied them access to Deir es-Sultan. The British consul in Jerusalem had previously supported the Ethiopians, but had now left. News of the plight of Ethiopians in Jerusalem reached Tewodros throughout this period and helped confirm his view that the British, the Turks and the Egyptians were all working against Ethiopian interests. (Even today, the Ethiopian monks live in makeshift shelters on the roof of the Holy Sepulchre.) Pederson *History of the Ethiopian Community* pp.17–38, and HH Abune Philippos *Know Jerusalem* pp.11–76, also Rubenson *Survival* pp.220–1, 236. See also Documents nos 109–12, Rubenson *Treaties and Correspondence* for the same dispute in 1848.

In London, the struggle over the Reform Bill came to a head in the summer of 1866. The Liberal government was replaced by a Conservative one under Lord Derby who appointed his own son, Lord Stanley, as Foreign Secretary. 'Cautious, thoughtful and addicted to compromise' (Rodgers 'The Abyssinian Expedition' p.139), Stanley put his hopes in the unpromising chances of Flad's mission, simply delaying the military option by twelve months. Arnold *Prelude to Magdala* pp.270–98 gives a good account of the unfolding crisis in London during this period. The Armenian intervention in the dispute with Tewodros is documented in FO 401/2, and the story is told in Saprichean *Deux ans de séjour* Book II.

Chapter 49

Details of the journey to Meqdela and the early days on the mountain come from the vivid accounts of Rassam *British Mission* II pp.159–214, Blanc *Narrative* pp.179–224, Prideaux in Markham *History* pp.115–124, Stern *Captive Missionary* pp.301–4. Tewodros appears to have kept at Gefat those earlier prisoners like Staiger and Brandeis who had experience as artisans.

Chapter 50

The eccentric movement of the stars is mentioned in two sources, Welde Maryam *Tewodros* (p.22 Weld Blundell's translation), and a letter from Asseggahen to Antoine d'Abbadie 15 April 1867 in Document no. 213, Rubenson *Tewodros* – 'On the 6th day of Hidar it appeared as if all the stars were falling. Then Tewodros set fire to Gondar . . .' Details of the sack of Gondar come from the same letter, and more are added in another, also to d'Abbadie, eighteen months later (Document no. 248 26 November 1868, Rubenson *Tewodros*). In the first letter is mentioned the proclamation of Debre Tabor as the new Gondar (which is corroborated in Welde Maryam *Chronique* p.49, Mondon-Vidailhet translation). Mrs Flad in her diary (Flad, *Zwölf Jahre* 11 December 1868) records the sacking of Gondar, saying that Tewodros returned laden with looted gold, and gave much to the Gefat community, including 50 thalers to her 'which saddened me deeply, the money burned me and I secretly sighed every time I thought of the poor unfortunates he had robbed it from'. For the grief and punishment of Kentiba Hailu see Rassam *British Mission* II pp.16–20. FO 1/18 Mrs Flad to Flad 28 August 1866 suggests Tewodros's plan to provoke an invasion. 'Call me a woman . . .' is quoted in Markham *History* p.291. The letter quoted from Tewodros to Rassam 5 January 1867 is Document no. 207 in Rubenson *Tewodros*, and appears in a slightly different translation in Rassam *British Mission* II pp.234–5. Waldmeier's warning about the ruler he once admired is from his *Erlebnisse* p.59.

Chapter 51

Details of the arrest of the missionaries come from Waldmeier *Autobiography* pp.91–2 and Blanc *Narrative* p.321. Flad *Zwölf Jahre* II pp.39–40 for his arrival in Tewodros's camp and in Debre Tabor. Blanc *Narrative of Captivity* pp.321–5 for Tewodros's reception of the telescope. In a letter from Flad to Rassam 16 May 1867, Flad says that Tewodros had come to Debre Tabor and 'inquired about the telescope. Mr Waldmeier said that he and Mr Zander had tried it, and found it to be a good and excellent telescope' (Holland and Hozier *Record* I p.20).

Chapter 52

Blanc's urge to send messages comes from *Narrative* p.199, and 199–202 for the means; details of messengers also come from Rassam *British Mission* II pp.245–7 and Stern *Captive Missionary* pp.303–6. Blanc's despondency is detailed in *Narrative* p.230. Blanc wrote several long letters to Colonel Merewether (FO 401/2 30 April, 10 and 18 June 1867) in which he made the case for their rescue: 'Nero, Attila, Tamerlane, were sheep when compared to Theodorus' (18 June). These letters were also republished in Holland and Hozier *Record* I pp.21–30. Details of everyday life for the European prisoners come from Rassam *British Mission* II pp.187–214, Stern *Captive Missionary* pp.306–9 and Blanc *Narrative* pp.205–47. Blanc's disdain for the Ethiopians is in *Story of the Captives* p.107, and the elephantiasis on p.97. For the final collapse of Tewodros's reign and his brutality at Debre Tabor, see notes for Chapter 51. Stern's letter to his wife was forwarded to the FO. 'Return and thank,' wrote Stanley (FO 401/2 June 1867).

Chapter 53

The deterioration of Tewodros during the summer of 1867 (the Ethiopian 'winter', when the *keremt* rains fall) is recorded by many of those caught up in it. The first quotation comes from the chronicler Welde Maryam *Chronique* p.44. Waldmeier in *Erlebnisse* pp.63–7 does not spare the details: 'Everything was suddenly upside down and death was everywhere – in the house, under the door, in the neighbourhood, left and right, near and far.' Welde Maryam *Tewodros* pp.33–42 (Weld Blundell translation) is equally graphic, as is Debtara Asseggahen in his letter to Antoine d'Abbadie (Rubenson *Tewodros* Document no. 248, 26 November 1868). Further material and corroboration come from Rassam *British Mission* II pp.168, 238–41, 250, Flad *Zwölf Jahre* II pp.39–41, and Stern *Captive Missionary* pp.312–15: 'according to the statement of eye-witnesses, upwards of three thousand persons perished by the sword, the rope, whip, stick, and mutilating knife. This homicidal mania became more ungovernable as the victims multiplied. No one was safe. The executioner of to-day bled on the morrow.' The 'God and the emperor' rhyme is quoted in Welde Maryam *Tewodros* (Weld Blundell p.20). See also Stern's letter to *The Times* 15 August 1867, and one from Blanc, *The Times* 22 August 1867, also Blanc to Merewether FO 401/2 10 and 18 June.

Chapter 54

Waldmeier in his *Autobiography* pp.93–4 gives an emotional first-hand account of the building of Sevastopol; Tewodros's quotations come from this account. Flad *Zwölf Jahre* II pp.39–40 gives the missionaries' tally of recent weapons made for Tewodros. The thalers from Gondar come from Welde Maryam *Tewodros* p.58 (Weld Blundell translation). A number of the Europeans had tried to escape and been betrayed by Bardel. They were chained (as was Bardel). Tewodros called one to him – Makerer – and cocked his pistol to shoot him, but with 'soft answers' Makerer managed to dissuade him. Tewodros put aside the pistol, saying, 'Another day I will kill you' (FO 401/2 Blanc to Merewether 18 June 1867). Blanc said that Tewodros 'had done every kind of injury to the white men except spilling their blood', but believed that once he 'gives full licence to his passions, and knows that he is done for – that blood calls for blood, and that he has not even pity to expect; he will therefore, before seeking for safety in flight, murder every white man in his power' (ibid.).

Chapter 55

Although the decision to send troops to Ethiopia was taken in August 1867, a combination of constitutional chicanery and Parliament's long recess meant that it was not debated until November, by which time the expedition was well under way. The Liberal opposition was in no position to object anyway, as the Tories were able to say that the crisis had its roots in their own bunglings in the years 1863–66. After the expedition a vast 953-page, two-volume quarto-size report (plus another volume of maps) was published by order of the Secretary of State for War, and compiled by Major Trevenen J. Holland and Captain Henry Hozier (Holland and Hozier *Record*). The report was not intended to address faults but to record the crisis's build-up and, for future expeditions, its astonishing logistics. 'The din of preparation in Bombay' from Holland and Hozier *Record* I p.155, the 'flutter of delight' from *The Times*, quoted in Pankhurst 'Popular Opposition' p.155. 'Harriers, ensigns . . .' comes from *Friend of India* 19 September and the realisation about 'monetary matters' 25 November 1867. 'Any unnecessary expense' is from Holland and Hozier *Record* I p.154. Hozier, in his own account, wrote: 'The disasters of the Crimea still hung heavy on men's minds.' He also explained how much the enthusiasm in India for a military solution had swayed doubters in England: 'Men in India, confident in the power shown in the suppression of the great mutiny . . . [were] accustomed to treat with a high hand restive princes . . . who so much as lifted a voice against the English name, [and] writhed beneath the insult which a British envoy had received at the hands of an African savage.' These opinions 'were carried home', and helped change the less bellicose climate in England (Hozier *British Expedition* pp.46–7). David Urquhart's article appeared in *Diplomatic Review* 6 November 1867, which also used the Crimean war as a warning: 'It is announced that the Abyssinian Expedition is to be composed of 10,000 men. The Crimean Expedition was announced at the outset to be composed of the same force . . . Yet three years were expended, the 50,000 men sent in the first period all perished except those invalided home. A hundred millions [of pounds] . . . was swallowed up.' The 'gorilla king' comes from the *Examiner* 21 September 1867. Details of the preparations for the expedition come from Holland and Hozier *Record* I–II. For the military 'asses' see *Punch* 5 October 1867. For the use of thalers on the expedition see *Illustrated London News* 18 July 1868 and Semple *A Silver Legend* p.37. For the 'expense' ditty, *Punch* 7 December 1867. The first use of RE Flag Signallers comes from *Engineers History* Part 7, Royal Engineers Museum (www.remuseum.org.uk). The figures regarding increases in income tax are detailed in Bates *Abyssinian Difficulty* p.212.

Chapter 56

For Blanc on Cameron see *Narrative* p.241, Stern *Captive Missionary* pp.281–2. For Cameron's gloom, FO 401/2 Cameron to Merewether 16 April 1867. Waldmeier's warning to Tewodros regarding the firing of Sevastopol comes from Welde Maryam *Chronique* pp.71–2. The killing of the lions 'with arsenic' comes from Mrs Flad's diary 25 August 1867, in Flad *Zwölf Jahre* II p.40. During these dangerous months, Mrs Flad kept her diary hidden in her corset. The capture and killing of the cattle are mentioned in Rassam *British Mission* II p.241, Flad *Zwölf Jahre* II p.41, Blanc *Narrative* p.336, where the prophecy also appears. Blanc also tells a story of a man who was found with a cow the day after the slaughter. The man's wife had just died in childbirth and he defended himself by saying he had kept the cow to give milk to the baby. 'Why did you not know that I would be a father to your child?' asked Tewodros. He then ordered the man to be killed, and the baby brought to him. The letter to Yetemegnu is in Rubenson *Tewodros* Document no. 219.

Chapter 57

An account of the reconnaissance is in Hozier *British Expedition* pp.70–5, also Holland and Hozier *Record* II pp.278–306. 'An irregular amphitheatre . . .' is in Markham *History* pp.156–8 where he continues to give a detailed and lyrical description of the Devil's Staircase: 'The scenery is magnificent; the beetling cliffs leaving but a narrow strip of sky dotted with vultures and eagles, and the mighty precipices, with huge masses of rock hurled down at their feet . . .'

Chapter 58

The early part of Tewodros's journey is described in a number of sources: Waldmeier *Autobiography* pp.97–8 and *Erlebnisse* pp.68–79, Mrs Flad's diary 13 October–15 December 1867, Flad *Zwölf Jahre* II. In Welde Maryam *Tewodros* (Weld Blundell translation pp.27–8) are details of the transportation of the 'bomba' and mention of 'English powder'. The quotation from Blanc comes from *Narrative* p.337, and in pp.337–41 he gives details of the early section of the journey, and of Tewodros facing its dangers: 'he seemed, for a time, to have regained much of his former self, and behaved with more consideration towards his followers'. 'He never shuts his eyes . . .' comes from a conversation between Sir Robert Napier and Welde Yesus and his brother, chiefs of Amba Alagi, quoted in Stanley *Coomassie and Magdala* p.371. A description of the climb up to Zebit and the quotation 'Why does God not kill me . . .' can be found in Stern *Captive Missionary* p.356. Tewodros's hearing of the news of the landing of British troops is told in Waldmeier *Erlebnisse* p.70 and Rassam *British Mission* II pp.254–5; 'I hear that some donkeys . . .' comes from Blanc *Narrative* pp.341–2. Napier's proclamation is reproduced in Rassam *British Mission* II p.255.

Chapter 59

The approach to Meqdela of King Menelik and Wagshum Gobeze is told in Rassam *British Mission* II pp.250–4. Blanc also records in detail the same period of tense expectation in *Narrative* pp.263–72, as does Stern *Captive Missionary* pp.345–8 (the *wagshum*'s 'My soldiers will frown at me . . .' is quoted on p.346). 'There was no one who did not love Menelik . . .' Welde Maryam *Tewodros* (Weld Blundell translation p.24). For the physical decline of Abune Selama see Blanc *Narrative* p.286: 'Almost without society, leading a dull misanthropic life, he did not remember that sobriety in all respects was essential to his health ...' Cameron had earlier written to Rassam in 1865 (FO 401/2 Cameron to Rassam undated, but with other enclosures September 1865): 'the bishop is exceedingly anxious to have some French brandy ... please send me plenty if you can'. Stern's pills were very popular on Meqdela: 'My own laboratory contained paste of colocynth, opium, and tartar emetic. The selection, if not very choice, was, at least, very potent. Not accustomed to dabble in the healing art, I made experiments on myself ere I tried to tamper with the health of others. My colocynth pills obtained a fame at Magdala that Morison and Holloway might have envied. In-door and out-door patients applied for that wonderful specific against all diseases ...' *Captive Missionary* p.242.

For the *abun*'s self-inflicted decline – 'several times a day he sent to inquire if he could drink some arak, take a little opium, or indulge in some of his more favourite dishes. It is not astonishing that relapse quickly followed ...' Blanc *Narrative* p.287. For his death, see also Prideaux in Markham *History* pp.125–6, Stern *Captive Missionary* p.328, Rassam *British Mission* II pp.195–6, and Welde Maryam *Chronique* p.53. Debtara Asseggahen (Document no. 248 in Rubenson *Tewodros*) wrote a more colourful account of the prelate's death which tells more perhaps about his unpopularity in certain quarters – the *debtera* was a Catholic – than the actual facts: 'News about Abune Selama. Abune Selama collected much gold, gave it to a goldsmith, and had a monk's belt and a habit made. But then since he had contracted syphilis, his genitals swelled and became like a log. They seared it with fire. Neither pus nor blood came out ... On the third day after searing, he died.' Rassam vindicated the *abun* with his own observations: 'His character has been shamefully maligned by individuals who really knew nothing about him' *British Mission* II pp.194–5.

Stern *Captive Missionary* pp.348–53 gives an account of the days that Menelik camped at the foot of the mountain with his army, then disappointed them all with his retreat. Blanc *Narrative* pp.300–7 also expresses the disappointment: 'The "fat boy", as we also now called him, we hated and despised.' He said that Menelik's tactics 'did us a great deal of harm'. Had Menelik not brought his army, he believed, the powerful Oromo Queen Mestawat and her '20,000 horsemen' would have liberated the mountain.

Chapter 60

Accounts of the happy day of Friday, 13 December 1867 were written by some of those who experienced it: Prideaux in Markham *History* pp.126–7, Blanc *Narrative* pp.307–8 and Stern *Captive Missionary* pp.355–6.

Chapter 61

For activity at Zula from October until the end of December 1867, see Holland and Hozier *Record* I pp.301–43. 'The English army . . .' Stanley *Coomassie and Magdala* p.290. 'The worst saddle . . .' from Markham *History* p.213. For the gathering of mules Holland and Hozier *Record* II pp.199, 202–19. For problems of the transport train see Holland and Hozier *Record* II pp.84–5, 302, 308, 313, 317, 334, 339, 346, 353, 380, 412, Markham *History* pp.210–18, *London Gazette* 7 August 1868, Report on the Transport Train by Lt-Col. R. Warden (who was in charge of the transport train, as he had been in the Crimea); see also *Hindoo Patriot* 23 March 1868. For the 'mutiny' of muleteers see *Pall Mall Gazette* 4 March 1868. For the problems of water see Holland and Hozier *Record* I p.389, II p.343; the £4,000 daily cost comes from Captain Frank James *Extract*.

Chapter 62

Tewodros's progress from Zebit is recorded in Flad *Zwölf Jahre* II pp.40–1, Waldmeier *Autobiography* pp.97–102 ('the King accomplished this great task which often reminded me of Napoleon's road across the Simplon from Switzerland to Italy'), *Erlebnisse* pp.68–9, Blanc *Narrative* pp.343–4.

Chapter 63

For the arrival of Napier at Zula and his early work there see Hozier *The British Expedition* pp.80–7 and Holland and Hozier *Record* I pp.344–6, 384–5. Napier defended his strategy against those advocating a swift advance to cut off Tewodros in a memo dated 20 January 1868, despatched to the Secretary of State for India, quoted in Markham *History* p.208.

Chapter 64

'Those marvellous engines . . .' comes from Stern *Captive Missionary* p.359. Rassam's letter from Tewodros and their friendly correspondence, Rassam *British Mission* II pp.256–60. For Blanc's reaction, *Narrative* p.347, and for Stern's discussion of the relationship between Rassam and Tewodros *Captive Missionary* pp.359–60. Rassam mentions Tewodros's ordering of food from Yetemegnu *British Mission* II pp.256–7. The letters to her are Documents nos 228–32 in Rubenson *Tewodros*. Document no. 228f says that they were written between September 1867 and March 1868, and probably at this period when the road opens. It is possible too that they were written earlier, even from Debre Tabor before it was burnt in October.

Chapter 65

Information about the railway comes from Holland and Hozier *Record* I pp.289, 299, 359, 376, 412, 431; II pp.19, 87, 108, 336. For the telegraph Holland and Hozier *Record* II 5, 137–47, 149, 344, 352. Also Markham *History* p.219, Hozier *British Expedition* p.94..

Chapter 66

Tewodros's information was wrong: they were not coming 'by the salt plain'. Merewether and the reconnaissance team had pressed on towards those plains, but rightly deemed them a strength-sapping obstacle for an invasion force. They had landed to the east of

Massawa, but would cut into the highlands before the plains. The salt plain – home of the Danakil – is one of the hottest, and lowest, points on earth. The quotations of Tewodros to Flad and Waldmeier are all quoted in a letter from Flad to Rassam, Royal Camp, Delanta, 11 February 1868 (published in Rassam *British Mission* II pp.266–70). The 'make a great bloodbath' quotation is repeated also in a slightly different form in Blanc *Narrative* p.358 and Rassam *British Mission* II p.272. The alliances open to Tewodros are from Rassam *British Mission* II p.270. For Tewodros's 'evil spirit' see Blanc *Narrative* p.309. For Waldmeier and Tewodros see Waldmeier *Erlebnisse* p.74, Waldmeier *Autobiography* pp.100–1, and Blanc *Narrative* pp.355–6.

Chapter 67

An account of the meeting between Napier and Kasa appears in Holland and Hozier *Record* I pp.413–18. The account is also published in Hozier *British Expedition* pp.125–35. 'Kassai was a young man of about thirty-five years of age. His face, of a dark olive colour, was intellectual, but bore a careworn and wearied expression which justified the statement that he did not desire power, but that it was thrust upon him by the people of Tigray.' Nevertheless, Kasa later became King of Kings of Ethiopia himself. See also Document no. 235 Kasa Mircha to Napier and Document no. 236 Kasa to Merewether: 'You know I have waited till now, many days for you. Now do not begrudge me two weeks,' Rubenson *Tewodros*. The meeting is also described in Markham *History* pp.261–4. For scorn of the British guns compared to Tewodros's, see Stanley *Coomassie and Magdala* p.331.

Chapter 68

Tewodros's and Rassam's reopened correspondence in mid-March comes from Rassam *British Mission* II pp.272–5. The letter Rassam received on 18 March, freeing him from his chains, is published in the Amharic original in Rubenson *Tewodros* Document no. 238. The arrival of Tewodros at Selamge, and his summoning of his people, comes from Rassam *British Mission* II p.277, Blanc *Narrative* pp.360–1, Stern *Captive Missionary* pp.368–70. 'The spiritual class . . .' Saalmuller, Gefat, 13 January 1861, from *Staatsarchiv des Kanton Basel Stadt, CF Spittler Privat-Archiv* quoted in *Kasa and Kasa* ed. Beyene etc. p.343. The hearing of the priests is told in Welde Maryam *Chronique* pp.59–61. The story of Saul, David and Ahimelech is in I Samuel 21:2. Rassam *British Mission* II p.280 mentions the trial of two priests at this time 'who had publicly called the King a "Frank" to his face for having failed to keep the Lenten fast'. The grabbing of the priest the following day is told in Blanc *Narrative* p.366.

Chapter 69

Blanc *Narrative* pp.347–8 for the 'great mental excitement'. Tewodros sent a message to Rassam on the night of 27 March: 'I hope you will excuse me for not having come to see you, as I intended. I have had some disputes among my Magdala people to settle, and am now rather excited,' Rassam *British Mission* II p.282. The trial of the commandant is recounted in ibid. pp.280–1. 'We slept but little . . .' Blanc *Narrative* p.366. Hiding the letters comes from Rassam *British Mission* II p.286. Tewodros being a *'little* drunk', Blanc *Narrative* p.366. Rassam's first meeting with Tewodros is recounted in *British Mission* II pp.287–91. Waldmeier, who also attended, gave a brief account, *Autobiography* p.103. Blanc and Prideaux came to the meeting once their chains had been removed. Blanc p.369: 'At first we could hardly walk. Our legs seemed to us as light as feathers; we could not guide them, and we staggered very much like drunken men; if we met with a small stone in our way, we involuntarily lifted up the foot to a ridiculous height.' Blanc also quotes Tewodros's comparison with a pregnant woman (*Narrative* p.370), and the exchange regarding the 'nice home' is from him. Tewodros's comments later that day, and the next, come from Rassam *British Mission* II pp.293–4, 302.

Chapter 70

The final hauling of the guns up the cliff to Selamge is told in detail in Rassam *British Mission* II pp.303–6, and Blanc *Narrative* pp.373–9. Waldmeier *Autobiography* p.102 says of the hauling: 'For the large gun Sevastopol it took in some places 800 men to move it forward.'

Chapter 71

For encountering Tewodros's abandoned camps see Hozier *British Expedition* p.177. Stanley *Coomassie* pp.306–7 describes the camp at Bet Hor. Stanley, when checked against other sources, is often revealed to exaggerate, but his discovery of human remains at Bet Hor is made more credible by Captain James, who a few days later records the finding in Tewodros's Delanta camp of 'the skulls of wretches he has beheaded' (James *Extract* p.26). For elephants see Holland and Hozier *Record* I pp.148, 173, 199, 214, 226, 234, 346, 360. For their health and treatment, II pp.226–30. For the elephants' climb up to Delanta see II p.40. The destruction apparent on Delanta is in II p.29. The problem of supply for the force when it reached Delanta is mentioned by Hozier *British Expedition* p.179 and Stanley *Coomassie and Magdala* p.398, and Southon *Rise and Fall* p.86.

Chapter 72

For the story of Speedy, I am grateful to Jean Southon (his great-niece), and Sandy Holt-Wilson, who has gathered an archive of material which includes many of his papers. Jean Southon and Robert Harper have published an account of his life, *The Rise and Fall of Basha Felika*, and most of the details come from this and from private papers. Henty's response to seeing Meqdela for the first time is from Henty *March to Magdala* pp.367–8. For the surveying of the Beshilo see Napier's Despatch no. 3, 12 May 1868 in Holland and Hozier *Record* II pp.453–5.

Chapter 73

For Tewodros's activity with the telescope see Rassam *British Mission* II pp.309–10, 6 April 1868: 'For the last three days, Theodore has done scarcely anything but ascend the heights of Selassie, scanning with a telescope the country towards Delanta.' 'There go the donkeys . . .' was quoted by his valet, Welde Gabre in a statement made some time later, translated by Captain Speedy and published in Holland and Hozier *Record* II pp.56ff. For Tewodros's statement to Waldmeier regarding the approach of the British force see *Autobiography* p.102. The address made by Tewodros to his forces on the morning of 8 April is told in Rassam *British Mission* II pp.311–13. Blanc *Narrative* pp.384–6 also reports the address, and Tewodros's own costume: 'When in January 1866, he received us at Zeghie, we were struck by the simplicity of his dress, in every respect the same as his common soldiers; of late, however, he had adopted a more gaudy attire, but nothing compared to the harlequin coat he wore that day.' The coming of the prisoners is told in Blanc *Narrative* p.386. The sheep: Blanc *Narrative* p.388 says 'probably Berbera sheep', Rassam *British Mission* II p.314 says 'they might be Somali sheep'. In fact these are two names for the same breed (also known as Berbera Blackhead, Blackheaded Somali, Ogaden), reared primarily for meat production, and this was their use to the British forces.

'Il se leva comme un lion en fureur,' Welde Maryam *Chronique* p.65. The killing of the prisoners is also recounted in Blanc *Narrative* pp.388–90, Rassam *British Mission* II pp.314–16: 'On that dreadful afternoon the King, in my opinion, must have been quite insane,' Stern *Captive Missionary* pp.380–3, Waldmeier *Autobiography* p.107: 'the Abyssinians said that the King had become insane'. Welde Gabre, in Holland and Hozier *Record* II pp.57ff, says that he had been drinking, and later that night heard the emperor in his prayers 'confess that he was drunk when he ordered the massacre'. 'The perfect fiend . . .' Stern *Captive Missionary* p.383.

Chapter 74

For the advance across the Beshilo river see Markham *History* pp.316–20, Hozier *British Expedition* pp.186–95. Operations from 7–10 April are described in Holland and Hozier *Record* II pp.32–5. The General Order can be found pp.32–3. For Napier's account see Despatch no. 6, 1 June 1868, in Holland and Hozier *Record* II p.482. Stanley gives his account of the operation in *Coomassie and Magdala* pp.402–10. He describes in typically colourful prose the landscape on the approach to Meqdela, which 'must be seen to be realised. Away to the right and left horizons of the sky trend indistinct and interminable groups of peaks, which have their numerous points buried in the blue firmament. Mountains crossing mountains, hills set upon hills, shoot upwards as if purposely placed one upon another by a race of Titans in a vain endeavour to pierce the boundless bulwark of ether which God erected between the immortal realms and the globe.'

Chapter 75

Waldmeier in his *Autobiography* pp.107–8 gives an account of the morning of 10 April. Stern's quotation is from *Captive Missionary* p.383. The quotation about Napier being 'sent by a woman' and the letter from Napier come from Rassam *British Mission* II p.317. Waldmeier's experience with Tewodros for the rest of the day comes from *Autobiography* pp.108–10, and *Erlebnisse* pp.93–6. See also Welde Gabre in Holland and Hozier *Record* II pp.57ff. Tewodros's speech is quoted in Waldmeier *Autobiography* pp.108–9. Markham *History* p.324 tells of Tewodros's hesitation.

Chapter 76

The Battle of Aroge is described in several first-hand accounts. Waldmeier recounts his view of it in *Autobiography* pp.109–10 and *Erlebnisse* pp.94–6 (viewing the battle from the heights of Fala, helping with the artillery, Waldmeier said: 'after a two-hour bombardment not a single English soldier had been killed' *Erlebnisse* p.95), Hozier *British Expedition* pp.190–8 (duplicated in Holland and Hozier *Record* II pp.35–8), Stanley *Coomassie and Magdala* pp.409–24, Welde Gabre in Holland and Hozier *Record* II pp.57ff, Markham *History* pp.319–25, Sir Robert Napier's Despatch no. 3, Antalo, 12 May 1868, in Holland and Hozier *Record* II pp.455–8, Sir Charles Stavely Enclosure in Despatch no. 6 in Holland and Hozier *Record* II pp.482–3.

Chapter 77

Waldmeier was with Tewodros for much of this time, and his accounts in Waldmeier *Autobiography* p.110 and *Erlebnisse* pp.96–8 provide the details. Welde Gabre was also present and his verbal statement (Holland and Hozier *Record* II p.57) also includes an account of Tewodros receiving news of the battle dead; this is the basis for the equivalent section in Hozier *British Expedition* p.198. The 'execution' quotation comes from Waldmeier *Autobiography* p.110. Tewodros's message for Rassam is quoted in both Waldmeier *Autobiography* p.111 and Rassam *British Mission* II pp.318–19. The text, and the times, are slightly different. I have taken Rassam's version: on matters of detail, Rassam tended to be more reliable. Waldmeier said Tewodros called him at about midnight, and it could not have been much less than an hour before he reached Rassam on Maqdela. Yet Rassam said they arrived at 10.30 p.m. A third version is recorded in Holland and Hozier *Record* II p.39. The rest of the chapter draws on the accounts of Waldmeier and Rassam, on the same pages.

Chapter 78

For the morning after the battle, Stanley *Coomassie and Magdala* pp.426–7. Reaction to the arrival of the delegation is described in Hozier *British Expedition* p.205: 'the news burst through the ranks like wildfire', and Markham *History* p.326. Napier's reply to Tewodros's verbal message is published in Holland and Hozier *Record* II p.40. Flad himself described the reaction of Dejazmach Alemi to the British weapons and the elephants in a statement published in Holland and Hozier *Record* II pp.45ff. Waldmeier said later that when asked to explain what the words 'honourable treatment' meant, he 'was afraid to do so, but Theodore understood them to mean imprisonment' (from a letter from Geneva reporting on a public lecture given by Waldmeier, *Diplomatic Review* 7 October 1868, quoted in Pankhurst 'Popular Opposition' p.203); in *Erlebnisse* p.98 he claims he 'mistranslated' the letter. The quotation regarding the number of Tewodros's wives and children comes from Flad's statement, published in Holland and Hozier *Record* II pp.45ff.

The 'letter' (it was unaddressed, undated, unsigned and unsealed), and that dictated by Tewodros the following day, were for some time lost in their original. 'The two letters were not, however, destroyed as some suspected but passed (how it is not established) into the possession of Holland House Library, a private library in Holland Park, West London ... The library was badly damaged by enemy bombing during World War II, but Tewodros's letters survived' (Pankhurst 'The Last Two Letters' p.1). They were later discovered by Richard Pankhurst who 'arranged for their private purchase by the Ethiopian Ministry of Culture', and now form part of Ethiopia's national archives. I have used David Appleyard's translation, as being more literal than Rubenson (*Tewodros* Document no. 241). The sentences regarding the women without men, and the people without children, do not follow on from the statement regarding the Christians in heathen land. Also, the letter written the next day on 12 April claims Tewodros was afraid of 'leaving the army without a provider' – so it is possible that when he began to redirect the letter to Napier, it was provision for his followers that was one of his main concerns; perhaps he planned to ask Napier to protect them after his death, surrounded as they were by Oromo keen to avenge themselves on his followers.

Chapter 79

As a witness, Waldmeier gives an account of the suicide attempt (*Autobiography* p.113 and *Erlebnisse* pp.104–7). Writing an Appendix to his travels back in England (Dufton *Journey* p.297), Henry Dufton had recently speculated that should Tewodros 'be hard pressed by us, rather than fall into our hands, he would certainly put an end to his life'. The reassembling of his forces and 'The English are fond of sleeping . . .' quotation come from Flad's statement, published in Holland and Hozier *Record* II pp.45ff. Rassam picks up the account as he hears the news of their 'release' Rassam *British Mission* II pp.321–2. Blanc *Narrative* p.400. Stern describes the moment: 'As we emerged out of our prison we encountered many faces bathed in tears. It was touching to see that even at Magdala there were hearts not indifferent to the foreigners, or unconcerned about our freedom and release. The kind and sympathetic groups, like ourselves, imagined that the march into the royal camp was a short funeral procession to execution and the grave.' *Captive Missionary* pp.388–9.

Chapter 80

Rassam is the source for his farewell scene with Tewodros, *British Mission* II pp.322–4. The departure of the others is recounted in Blanc *Narrative* pp.400–4. Blanc says that as they left Tewodros's camp, some soldiers called for them to stop. 'Had Theodore again changed his mind? So near liberty, were we again doomed to captivity or death?' But it was one of Tewodros's servants running towards them, carrying the swords of Blanc and Prideaux that had been taken from them on their arrest in Debre Tabor. Stern *Captive Missionary* pp.388–93 also describes their release. He relished his freedom, and the next day found himself 'in a state of delicious ecstasy and dreamy raptures'. But he was quick to give his solipsism a more transcendant context: 'It was indeed a resurrection festival – a foretaste of that glorious resurrection, when the grave will be deprived of its precious treasures, death of its ghastly trophies, and the lap of decay and mortality become the abode of life and everlasting beauty,' *Captive Missionary* pp.393–4. The champagne is mentioned in Markham *History* p.336.

Chapter 81

The letter Tewodros dictated early on Easter morning is translated as Document no. 242 in Rubenson *Tewodros*, and in Pankhurst 'Two Letters' pp.32–4. The two sides now had different perceptions: Tewodros clearly thought negotiations were possible, while Napier would accept only total submission. The problem for Napier was that Tewodros still held a number of Europeans. The matter of Tewodros's Easter gift of cattle and sheep has been much discussed, and accusations of dishonour followed Napier back to England. Did he deliberately deceive Tewodros, telling him the gift was accepted in order to secure the release of the remaining Europeans? Blanc *Narrative* p.406 reports that Ato Samuel, who had long been an interpreter for Rassam, told Tewodros that the cattle had been accepted. Among those in the tent at the time were Napier, Aleqa Ingida, Ato Samuel, Rassam, Merewether and a Lieutenant Tweedie – Amharic, Arabic and English were being read, spoken and translated. Rassam claimed that Napier had accepted the gift, and it was he who confirmed it to Ato Samuel in Arabic. Merewether claimed that Napier simply bowed his head, thinking that the gift was just 'a few cows' and was therefore not significant. When Napier realised the scale of Tewodros's gift, he gave orders for the cattle to be refused entry to the camp. But by that time the message of their acceptance was already on its way up the mountain. Whether Napier was aware of the deception is still open to question – the ambiguity certainly solved a very great dilemma for him: had the gift not been offered, how would he have persuaded Tewodros to give up the remaining hostages? Markham *History* pp.339–40 (in which he claims the gift made up the total stock remaining to Tewodros), Rassam *British Mission* II pp.325–30, Waldmeier *Autobiography* pp.115–16 and *Erlebnisse* pp.108–10. Flad's statement in Holland and Hozier *Record* II pp.46–7ff, Napier's Despatch no. 1 in Holland and Hozier *Record* II p.443, FO 1/27a Rassam's report 1 September 1868, FO 1/29 Rassam to Argyll 27 March 1869, FO 1/29 Napier to Argyll 11 February 1869, referred to in Rubenson *Survival* pp.266ff. Tewodros's farewell to Waldmeier *Autobiography* p.116 (Psalms 126:1–3) and *Erlebnisse* p.109. For Tewodros after the artisans had left, Welde Gabre's statement in Holland and Hozier *Record* II p.58. Blanc gathered various accounts of Tewodros on the night of 12 April: 'All night he walked up and down Selassie anxious and cast down,' as did Markham *History* p.342.

Chapter 82

Napier's assessment of Meqdela is in Despatch no. 3, 12 May 1868, in Holland and Hozier *Record* II pp.453–5. Stanley, who was in the camp, reported the surprise on seeing the health of the released prisoners and their entourage, *Coomassie* pp.434–6.

Chapter 83

Blood-red moon, Welde Maryam *Chronique* p.70. Captain Frank James *Extract* p.30 speaks of the sun the next day: 'a peculiar fact that as the storming party advanced the sun was surrounded by the most extraordinary halo, as bright as a rainbow'. Markham *History* p.342 provides the detail of his short sleep under a spear-propped *shamma*, and also the quotation 'Warriors who love me . . .'; Blanc *Narrative* p.407 'towards early morn called upon his people to follow him'. An extensive account of operations on 13 April from the British point of view is in Holland and Hozier *Record* II pp.50–9 (duplicated in Hozier *British Expedition* pp.221–43). Napier's account is in his Despatch no. 1 Napier to the Secretary of State for India in Holland and Hozier *Record* II pp.444–6. Other details from Welde Gabre in Holland and Hozier *Record* II p.58, Captain Frank James *Extract* pp.30–2. Details of horse and rifle during challenge for champion from Markham *History* p.348. Flad in his statement, Holland and Hozier *Record* II p.48 quotes 'Waldmeier and others' claiming the pistol was the one presented to Tewodros by Cameron in 1862.

Epilogue

Waldmeier's account of seeing Tewodros's body is in his *Autobiography* p.118, Rassam's in *British Mission* II pp.338–9. The post-mortem probe is mentioned in Markham *History* p.362. Blanc's version of the examination is from *Narrative* p.408. Stanley gives his own account in *Coomassie* pp.451–2. For the forces arriving on Meqdela and the plundering see Markham *History* pp.356–60, Myatt *March* (Myatt identified the plunder of treasures as 'in the best tradition of the British army at the time' p.165), Captain Frank James *Extract* p.33 (for raw eggs), Captain Adrian Jones *Evening Standard* 11 February 1936 p.13 (for exploding guns), Stanley *Coomassie* pp.458–9. For the auction see Markham *History* pp.372–3, and the *Kwer'ata Re'usu* Bailey, *The Art Newspaper* no. 80, April 1998. Napier's General Order is in Holland and Hozier *Record* II pp.78–9. Other quotations are from *Reynolds'*, quoted in Pankhurst 'Popular Opposition' p.187, editorial *Jewish Chronicle* 1 May 1868, editorial *Christian World* p.187. For figures on the campaign see Pankhurst 'Popular Opposition' p.184 and *Report from the Select Committee on the Abyssinian War 1868–69*, quoted and discussed in Bates *The Abyssinian Difficulty* pp.215–16. Rassam's libel case and later life are from *The Times* obituary 17 September 1910. Flad's quotation is from FO 401/2 Flad to Clarendon received 10 July 1866. The 'mean station' quotation is from editorial *Diplomatic Review* 2 September 1868. Layard's description of Rassam is from Waterfield *Layard of Nineveh* p.478. Waldmeier tells of his own homecoming in *Autobiography* p.148; for his mission work on Mount Lebanon see the second half of *Autobiography*. His final judgement on the campaign is on pp.119–20.

For the burning of Meqdela, the 'two queens', travelling with Tirunesh and her death see Rassam *British Mission* II pp.345–8. On several recorded occasions, Tewodros said he wanted to send his son/sons to England. To Plowden, in *Travels* pp.480–1, he mentioned the idea with regard to Meshesha (Meshesha remained in Ethiopia; he took his father's body from Meqdela and buried it at Mahbere Selassie monastery, private interview with Colonel Damtew Kassa, Tewodros's great-grandson). To Rassam Tewodros said in

March 1866: 'Mr Rassam, I wish this son of mine and another at Magdala [Alemayehu] to be adopted children of the English; and when you go back to your country, I want you to recommend them to your Queen, in order that when I die, they may be looked after by the English.' Rassam *British Mission* II p.58 (this quotation may have been moulded a little by events, Rassam's account being written after his return to England). Alemayehu's arrival in England, his time with the Speedys, his journey with them is from Southon and Harper *Rise and Fall* pp.118–42, also Bates 'The Abyssinian Boy', *History Today* December 1979. Details of his death, his 'foolish act', also come from Ransome *Autobiography* (unpublished, Brotherton Collection, Leeds); Cyril Ransome was the father of Arthur Ransome.

The arrival of Yohannis the Fool comes from Markham *History* p.364. The two Oromo queens are described in ibid. pp.368–70 and Stanley *Coomassie* pp.464–5 (description of Mestawat eating). For Menelik grieving for Tewodros see Prouty *Empress Taytu* p.11.

Some ten years after the death of Tewodros, another Tewodros rose. In Shoa, people began to gather around a man who claimed he was the great conqueror. He had long fair hair, a great blond beard and spoke, as well as Amharic and Oromigna, French, Italian, English and German. It was believed he was Russian. Menelik came to hear of him, gave him food and mules, and sent him away from Ethiopia. Weld Blundell *Royal Chronicle* Appendix F. The story of Lt-Col. Wurqneh in 1960 is from Greenfield *Ethiopia* pp.82–3, of General Teshome Tesema at Massawa from *Ay Mitsiwa!* by Taddesse Telie Salvano.

BIBLIOGRAPHY

Abbadie, Antoine d', 'Abyssinia and King Theodore', *The Catholic World*, VII, 1868

Abbadie, Arnauld d', *Douze ans dans la Haute-Ethiopie*, Paris 1868

Abir, Mordechai, *Ethiopia: The Era of the Princes* London 1968

Acton, R., *The Abyssinian Campaign and the Reign of King Theodore* London 1868

Annesley, G. (Viscount Valentia, Earl of Mountnorris), *Voyages and Travels to India, Ceylon, the Red Sea, Abyssinia and Egypt, in the years 1802, 1803, 1804, 1805 and 1806* London 1809

Armbruster, Stephana, *Life and History of John Bell and his Descendants* Palma de Mallorca 1966 (in IES, Addis Ababa)

Arnold, Percy, *Prelude to Magdala: Emperor Theodore of Ethiopia and British Diplomacy* London 1991

Bailey, Martin, 'The *Kwer'ata Re'usu* brought to light', *The Art Newspaper* April 1998

Bates, Darrell, *The Abyssinian Difficulty* Oxford 1979

Bates, Darrell, 'The Abyssinian Boy', *History Today*, 29, December 1979

Beckingham, C.F., and Huntingford, G.W.B., *The Prester John of the Indies: The Portuguese Embassy to Ethiopia* Cambridge 1961

Beckingham, C.F., and Huntingford, G.W.B. (translators), *Some Records of Ethiopia 1593–1646* London 1954

Bekele, Shiferaw, 'The State in the *Zemana Mesafint* (1786–1853)', *Kasa and Kasa* (ed. Tadesse Beyene, etc.) Addis Ababa 1990

Bell, John G., 'Extract from a Journal of Travels in Abyssinia, in the years 1840–41–42', *Miscellanea Aegyptiaca*, 1842 (in Bodleian Library)

Bell, Stephen, *Sir Peter Ustinov's Ethiopian Ancestry* www.anglo-ethiopian.org 2004

Beyene, Tadesse (ed. with Richard Pankhurst and Shiferaw

Bekele), *Kasa and Kasa: Papers on the Lives, Times and Images of Tewodros II and Yohannes IV (1855–1889)* Addis Ababa 1990

Blanc, Henry, *A Narrative of Captivity in Abyssinia*, London 1868

Blanc, Henry, *Story of the Captives (Including A Translation of M Le Jean's Articles on Abyssinia and its Monarch)* London 1868

Bruce, James, *Travels to Discover the Source of the Nile* London 1790

Budge, E.A. Wallis, *A History of Ethiopia* London 1928

Budge, E.A. Wallis, *The Life and Exploits of Alexander the Great* London 1896

Budge, E.A. Wallis, *Synaxarium: Book of the Saints of the Ethiopian Church*, 4 volumes, Cambridge 1928

Butcher, E.L., *The Story of the Church in Egypt* London 1897

Caraman, Philip, *The Lost Empire; The Story of the Jesuits in Ethiopia 1555–1634* London 1985

Caulk, Richard, 'Firearms and Princely Power in Ethiopia in the Nineteenth Century', *Journal of African History*, XII, 4, 1972

Cheesman, R.E., *Lake Tana and the Blue Nile* London 1936

Crummey, Donald, 'Initiatives and Objectives in Ethio–European Relations, 1827–1862', *Journal of African History*, XV, 3, 1974

Crummey, Donald, 'Missionary Sources and their Contribution to our Understanding of Ethiopian History 1830–1868', *Rural Africana*, 11, 1970

Crummey, Donald, *Priests and Politicians: Protestant and Catholic Missions in Orthodox Ethiopia (1830–1868)* Los Angeles 2007

Crummey, Donald, 'Tewodros as Reformer and Modernizer', *Journal of African History*, X, 3, 1969

Crummey, Donald, 'The Violence of Tewodros', *Journal of Ethiopian Studies*, IX, 2, 1971

Darkwah, R.H. Kofi, 'Emperor Theodore II and the Kingdom of Shoa, 1855–1865', *Journal of African History*, X, 1, 1969

Dimotheos (Timoteos Saprichean), *Deux ans de séjour en Abyssinie ou Vie morale, politique et religieuse des Abyssiniens par le R.P. Dimotheos* Jerusalem 1871

Dufton, Henry, *Narrative of a Journey through Abyssinia in 1862–3* London 1867

Flad, J.M., *Notes from the Journal of F.M. [sic] Flad, one of Bishop Gobat's Missionaries* London 1860

Flad, J.M., *Zwölf Jahre in Abessinien, oder Geschichte des Konigs Theodorus II und der Mission unter seiner Regierung* Leipzig 1887

Fusella, Luigi (ed.), *Yate Tewodros Tarik* Rome 1959

Gobat, Samuel, *Journal of a Three Years' Residence in Abyssinia in Furtherance of the Objects of the Church Missionary Society* London 1834

Greenfield, Richard, *Ethiopia: A New Political History* New York 1965

Hable Selassie, Sergew, 'Review of *Die Kirche in Debra Tabor'*, *Journal of Semitic Studies*, XXVIII, 2, 1983

Halls, J.J., *The Life and Correspondence of Henry Salt* London 1834

Harris, W. Cornwallis, *The Highlands of Aethiopia* London 1844

Henty, G.A., *The March to Magdala* London 1868

Holland, Trevenen J., and Hozier, Henry M., *Record of the Expedition to Abyssinia* London 1870

Holtz, Avram, and Holtz Berger, Toby, 'The Adventuresome Life of Moritz Hall', *Orbis Aethiopicus* (ed. Piotr O. Schulz) Albstadt 1992

Hozier, Henry M., *The British Expedition to Abyssinia* London 1869

Isaacs, A.A., *Life of H.A. Stern* London 1886

Isenburg, C.W., and Krapf, J.L., *The Journals of C.W. Isenburg and J.L. Krapf* London 1843

James, Captain Frank, 'The Abyssinian Campaign under Sir Robert Napier 1867–1868', *An Extract from my Father's Diary* Mrs E.P. Edwards (in National Army Museum, London)

James, Captain Frank, 'Letter to his Mother 15 April 1868' (in National Army Museum, London)

Jones, Captain Adrian, 'The Abyssinian Campaign', *Evening Standard* London 11 February 1936

Levine, Donald N., *Wax and Gold: Tradition and Innovation in Ethiopian Culture* Chicago 1974

McCann Smith, Mason, *When the Emperor Dies* London 1982

Mantel-Niecko, Joanna, 'Tewodros II: The Hero of Past and Present', *Kasa and Kasa* (ed. Tadesse Beyene, etc.) Addis Ababa 1990

Markham, Clements R., *A History of the Abyssinian Expedition* London 1869

Matthew, David, *Ethiopia: The Study of a Polity, 1540–1935* London 1947

Moorehead, Alan, *The Blue Nile* London 1962

Munro-Hay, Stuart, *Ethiopia: The Unknown Land* London 2002

Munro-Hay, Stuart, *The Quest for the Ark of the Covenant* London 2005

Myatt, Frederick, *The March to Magdala* London 1970

Napier, R., *Letters of Field-Marshal Lord Napier of Magdala* (ed. H.D. Napier) London 1936

Nöldeke, Theodor, 'King Theodore of Abyssinia', *Sketches from Eastern History* Beirut 1892

Pankhurst, Richard, *Economic History of Ethiopia 1800–1935* Addis Ababa 1968

Pankhurst, Richard, 'Firearms in Ethiopian History, 1800–1935', *Ethiopia Observer*, VI, 2, 1962

Pankhurst, Richard, 'History of Cholera in Ethiopia' *Medical History*, XII, 1968

Pankhurst, Richard, 'Indian Reactions to Anglo-Indian Intervention against Emperor Tewodros of Ethiopia 1867–8' Addis Ababa 1974

Pankhurst, Richard, '*Kwer'ata Re'usu*: The History of an Ethiopian Icon', *Abba Salama*, X, 1979

Pankhurst, Richard, 'The Last Two Letters of Emperor Tewodros II of Ethiopia (11 and 12 April 1868)', *Journal of the Royal Asiatic Society*, 1, 1987

Pankhurst, Richard, 'Misoneism and Innovation in Ethiopian History', *Ethiopia Observer*, VII, 4, 1964

Pankhurst, Richard, 'A "Missing" Letter from Emperor Tewodros II to Queen Victoria's Special Envoy Hormuzd Rassam', *Akten der Ersten Internationalem Littmann-Konferenz* Munich May 2002

Pankhurst, Richard, 'Popular Opposition in Britain to British Intervention against Emperor Tewodros of Ethiopia (1867–1868)', *Ethiopia Observer*, XVI, 3, 1973

Pankhurst, Rita, 'The Meqdela Library of Tewodros', *Kasa and Kasa* (ed. Tadesse Beyene, etc.) Addis Ababa 1990

Parkyns, Mansfield, *Life in Abyssinia* London 1853

Pearce, Nathaniel, *The Life and Adventures of Nathaniel Pearce, written by himself during a residence in Abyssinia from 1810 to 1819* (ed. J.J. Halls) London 1831

Pederson, Kirsten, *The History of the Ethiopian Community in the Holy Land from the Time of Emperor Tewodros II till 1974* Jerusalem 1983

Philippos, HH Abune, *Know Jerusalem* Addis Ababa 1972

Plowden, Walter Chichele, *Travels in Abyssinia and the Galla Country* London 1868

Plowden, Walter Chichele, *Notes on Peculiar Customs* MSS EUR F127/99 (Oriental and India Office Collections, British Library)

Prouty, Chris, *Empress Taytu and Menelik II: Ethiopia 1883–1910* London 1986

Ransome, Cyril, *Autobiography* (unpublished, Brotherton Collection, Leeds University Library)

Rassam, Hormuzd, *Narrative of the British Mission to Theodore, King of Abyssinia* London 1869

Rodgers, Nini, 'The Abyssinian Expedition of 1867–1868: Disraeli's Imperialism or James Murray's War', *The Historical Journal*, 27, I, March 1984

Rubenson, Sven, *Correspondence and Treaties 1800–1854* Addis Ababa 1987

Rubenson, Sven, *King of Kings: Tewodros of Ethiopia*, Addis Ababa 1966

Rubenson, Sven, *Tewodros and his Contemporaries 1855–1868* Addis Ababa 1994

Rubenson, Sven, *The Survival of Ethiopian Independence* London 1976

Salt, Henry, *A Voyage to Abyssinia* London 1814

Scholler, Heinrich, 'The Ethiopian Community in Jerusalem from 1850 to the Conference of Dar es-Sultan', *VI Conference of Ethiopian Studies* Tel Aviv 1980

Semple, Clara, *A Silver Legend: The Story of the Maria Theresa Thaler* London 2005

Shepherd, A.F., *The Campaign in Abyssinia* Bombay 1868

Simpson, William, *Diary of a Journey to Abyssinia, 1868* (ed. Richard Pankhurst) Addis Ababa 2002

Southon, Jean, and Harper, Robert, *The Rise and Fall of Basha Felika: Captain Speedy, his Life and Times* 2003

Stanley, Henry M., *Coomassie and Magdala: The Story of two British campaigns in Africa* London 1874

Stern, Henry A., *The Captive Missionary: Being an Account of the Country and People of Abyssinia* London 1862

Stern, Henry A., *Wanderings among the Falashas in Abyssinia together with a description of the country and its various inhabitants* London 1862

Tafla, Bairu, 'Four Ethiopian Biographies', *Journal of Ethiopian Studies*, VII, 2, Addis Ababa 1969

Tafla, Bairu, 'Tewodros's arrival in Shoa' *Journal of Ethiopian Studies*, XIII, 2, Addis Ababa 1975

Tamrat, Taddesse, 'The *Koso*-vendor Mother: A New Tradition of Origin', *Kasa and Kasa* (ed. Beyene, etc.) Addis Ababa 1990

Telie Salvano, Taddesse, *Ay Mitsiwa!* Addis Ababa 2005

Trimingham, J. Spencer, *Islam in Ethiopia* Oxford 1952

Ullendorff, Edward, *The Ethiopians: An Introduction to Country and People* third edition Oxford 1973

Ullendorff, Edward, *Ethiopia and the Bible* London 1968

Waldmeier, Theophilus, *The Autobiography of Theophilus Waldmeier, Missionary* London 1886

Waldmeier, Theophilus, *Erlebnisse in Abessinien in den Jahren 1858 bis 1868* Basel 1869

Waterfield, G., *Layard of Nineveh* London 1963

Weld Blundell, H., *The Royal Chronicle of Abyssinia 1769–1840* Cambridge 1922

Weld Blundell, H., 'History of King Theodore', *Journal of the Royal African Society*, 6, 21, October 1906

Welde Maryam (trans. C. Mondon-Vidailhet), *Chronique de Théodros II, roi des rois d'Ethiopie* Paris (no date)

Wondmagegnehu, Aymro, and Motuvu, Joachim (eds), *The Ethiopian Orthodox Church* Addis Ababa 1970

Zeneb, *Ye-Tewodros Tariḳ* (edited and published in Amharic by E. Littmann) Princeton 1902